# Plan Your
# Wedding
## ...In No Time

Leah Ingram

# Plan Your Wedding In No Time

International Standard Book Number: 0-7897-3222-X

Library of Congress Catalog Card Number: 2004107603

Printed in the United States of America

07   06   05   04          3   2

## Trademarks

All terms mentioned in this book that are known to be trademarks or service marks have been appropriately capitalized. Que Publishing cannot attest to the accuracy of this information. Use of a term in this book should not be regarded as affecting the validity of any trademark or service mark.

## Warning and Disclaimer

Every effort has been made to make this book as complete and as accurate as possible, but no warranty or fitness is implied. The information provided is on an "as is" basis. The author and the publisher shall have neither liability nor responsibility to any person or entity with respect to any loss or damages arising from the information contained in this book.

## Bulk Sales

Que Publishing offers excellent discounts on this book when ordered in quantity for bulk purchases or special sales. For more information, please contact

**U.S. Corporate and Government Sales**

**1-800-382-3419**

**corpsales@pearsontechgroup.com**

For sales outside of the U.S., please contact

**International Sales**

**international@pearsoned.com**

**Executive Editor**
Candace Hall

**Development Editor**
Lorna Gentry

**Managing Editor**
Charlotte Clapp

**Project Editor**
Matthew Purcell

**Copy Editor**
Kate Givens

**Indexer**
Mandie Frank

**Proofreader**
Wendy Ott

**Technical Editor**
Dorothy Morgan-Quelch

**Publishing Coordinator**
Cindy Teeters

**Designer**
Anne Jones

**Cover Illustrator**
Nathan Clement
Stickman Studio

**Page Layout**
Susan Geiselman

# Plan Your Wedding ...In No Time

# Contents at a Glance

# Table of Contents

## I  Now That You're Engaged

# II  Wedding Planning Nuts and Bolts

# IV Appendices

# About the Author

Leah Ingram is the author of seven books: *Plan Your Wedding In No Time* (Que Publishing, 2004); *The Complete Guide for the Anxious Bride* (Career Press, 2004); *The Balanced Bride: Preparing Your Mind, Body, and Spirit for Your Wedding and Beyond* (Contemporary Books/McGraw-Hill, 2002); *You Shouldn't Have! How to Give Gifts They'll Never Forget* (Contemporary Books/ McGraw-Hill, 2001); *Your Wedding Your Way* (Contemporary Books, 2000); *The Portable Wedding Consultant* (Contemporary Books, 1997); and *The Bridal Registry Book* (Contemporary Books, 1995).

As a wedding, gift-giving, and etiquette expert, she is a frequent guest on many television shows. She has offered on-camera advice or done in-studio demonstrations for Woman's Day TV, News 12 New Jersey, News 12 Long Island, "It's Your Call with Lynn Doyle" (on the Comcast Network), CNN, along with the FOX affiliate in Detroit and the NBC and ABC affiliates in Philadelphia.

In addition to her guest appearances, Ingram is a sought-after spokesperson and has completed national media tours for many companies and well-known brands.

Ingram is also an accomplished journalist. Her byline has appeared in such well-known publications as *Parade*, *Reader's Digest*, *Family Circle*, *Bridal Guide*, and *Self*.

In 2003 Ingram launched The Manners Mom, an eponymous website (www.mannersmom.com) through which she offers advice to parents who want to raise polite children.

Ingram, who lives in Bucks County, Pennsylvania, is married and has two daughters. Check out her website at www.weddingink.com.

# Dedication

*To my husband and daughters, whose help and support allowed me to write this book in no time.*

# Acknowledgments

Years before I knew I would write a book called *Plan Your Wedding In No Time*, I was one of those lucky brides who had less than a year to plan a wedding. Thanks to the help of family and friends, I was able to pull together my own wedding in no time and have it turn out to be a great success.

I wouldn't have been able to succeed in writing this book if it weren't for the help, assistance, and support of a number of folks. First and foremost, thanks to Candace Hall, for tracking me down for this project and believing that I was the right person to bring this book to life. Next, thanks to Lorna Gentry, for being available, pretty much 24/7 on email, to answer all of my insipid questions about formatting and whatnot.

Thanks also to my family and friends for providing real-life timesaving tips from their weddings, many of which were the inspiration for the advice I offer in this book. I also need to give a shout out to a couple of professional organizations and writers' groups that helped me tremendously in writing this book by providing ongoing, online moral support. These include Profnet, Freelance Success, and the American Society of Journalists and Authors.

I hope that every bride-to-be who reads this book and follows my advice is able to plan a fabulous wedding in no time.

Leah Ingram

September 2004

# Tell Us What You Think!

As the reader of this book, *you* are the most important critic and commentator. We value your opinion and want to know what we're doing right, what we could do better, what areas you'd like to see us publish in, and any other words of wisdom you're willing to pass our way.

You can email or write me directly to let me know what you did or didn't like about this book, as well as what we can do to make our books stronger.

*Please note that I cannot help you with technical problems related to the topic of this book, and due to the high volume of mail I receive, I might not be able to reply to every message.*

When you write, please be sure to include this book's title and author as well as your name, email address, and phone number. I will carefully review your comments and share them with the author and editors who worked on the book.

**Email:** feedback@quepublishing.com

**Mail:** Candace Hall
Executive Editor
Que Publishing
800 East 96th Street
Indianapolis, IN 46240 USA

For more information about this book or another Que Publishing title, visit our website at www.quepublishing.com. Type the ISBN (excluding hyphens) or the title of a book in the Search field to find the page you're looking for.

# Introduction

My husband proposed to me at the end of May, and by mid-November we were husband and wife. Had I wanted to find a book that would help me go from engaged to married in less than a year, I would have been out of luck. There were books that laid out specific timelines for planning a wedding in six months, or even four months. But those timelines didn't match my schedule. What I needed at that point in my life was a soup-to-nuts book that would help me plan a wedding in no time, period. That book didn't exist then, but it does now.

The idea behind *Plan Your Wedding In No Time* is simple: With organized, easy-to-follow to-do lists, this book will teach anyone how to pull together a fabulous wedding affair quickly and efficiently. While a wedding can absolutely be a dreamy affair, I don't want either of you to end up daydreaming when you should be calling caterers or considering your honeymoon plans. You've got a wedding to plan, and I know how easy it can be to waste time when you're facing a humongous task. Don't worry—I've written this book in a way that will keep you on track, help you have fun as you make your plans, and provide you with everything you need to know to make decisions fast. Unlike other wedding books, *Plan Your Wedding In No Time* approaches every element of your wedding with a timesaving frame of mind.

For example, if you're not sure what kind of flowers you should have at your reception, I've outlined how you can choose your flowers fast based on your favorite colors and the season of your wedding. So by the time you're finished with Chapter 5, "The Words, Music, and Flowers That Bring Your Ceremony to Life," not only will you have found fabulous flowers for your ceremony but also you'll have done so with time to spare.

Can't figure out what kind of wedding gown you want to wear? No problem. Turn to Chapter 8, "Taking Care of the Bride," and I'll help you find the perfect dress to fit your wedding, based on simple facts, like body type and time of day of your affair. Whether you're planning a wedding for 40 or 400, or whether you have a few weeks or a few months to plan your wedding, this book is for you.

# Who Should Read This Book

The expert advice and timesaving techniques in *Plan Your Wedding In No Time* help every couple get ready for their big day. If you answer "yes" to any of these questions, this book is for you:

- Will you two be planning your wedding while holding down  time-consuming jobs?
- Do you have limited funds and limited time to plan your upcoming wedding?
- Are you both just starting out in your career and unsure what kind of wedding you can afford?
- Are you planning a destination wedding from afar?
- Would you like to have an intimate wedding for just family and a few friends?
- Are you planning to have a big bash with hundreds of guests?
- Do you want your wedding to reflect who you two are in both your professional and personal lives?

*Plan Your Wedding In No Time* will help you make the most of your time and energy for planning a wedding to remember, and it won't leave you feeling frustrated or as if you're spinning your wheels.

# How This Book Is Organized

It's your wedding and you'll cry if you want to, but with *Plan Your Wedding In No Time*, you won't need to shed tears over the planning process. This book approaches wedding planning ingeniously and explains the process quickly in simple-to-follow text and illustrations that let you use the book any way that works best for you. You can read the book cover to cover, or you can pick and choose chapters in whichever order you please and read sections a la carte. However, I must admit that if you're really in a time crunch, you would be wise to read the book in sequential order. That's because if you really want to save time, you should complete certain tasks before others or you could end up wasting time. For example, I wouldn't advise booking your band (discussed in Chapter 7, "Entertainment and Extras for Your Reception") before deciding on your wedding budget (discussed in Chapter 2, "Money Matters and Essential First Steps"). If you discover after the fact that you can't afford a certain vendor, you'll have to start all over again in the search and selection process for that vendor.

The reason this book works, regardless of how you read it, is because of its organization. Let me explain.

Every chapter has a concise introduction and conclusion that help place that chapter's information in context with the entire planning process.

Also, the text throughout the book appears in bite-sized portions. This means that if you only have a few minutes during your commute or while waiting for a conference call to begin, you can pick up some valuable wedding-planning information that will help you complete another item on your to-do list.

My goal with this book is not to waste your time talking about ideas that "might" work for your wedding. Instead, everything I present in this book is designed to help you make decisions quickly and thoughtfully so your wedding plans can come together in no time at all.

## The Book's Parts

*Plan Your Wedding In No Time* is organized in three parts:

- Part I, "Now that You're Engaged," describes decisions you'll have to make together, now that you've decided to get married. These include sharing the good news of your engagement with the important people in your lives and figuring out how much money you can afford to spend on your wedding.

- Part II, "Wedding Planning Nuts and Bolts," describes all of the elements of your wedding you'll need to deal with now. These include planning your ceremony, choosing your attendants, finding your invitations, and deciding on everything you'll need for your reception. This section is chock-full of suggestions for rapid ways to find your wedding gown and how to plan a happy honeymoon.

- Part III, "After the Big Day," focuses on post-wedding plans that you'll likely face after you've returned from your honeymoon, such as writing your thank-you notes, getting your wedding photographs back from the photographer, and taking care of your wedding gown.

- Part IV, "Appendices," gives you a list of resources, references, and some valuable planning aids.

## Special Elements Used in the Book

I've used a number of special elements throughout the book that give you valuable extra information about relevant topics in a quick, visual format. At the start of major sections in every chapter you will find "To do" list, which spell out exactly what you'll accomplish in the section that follows. If you're like me, you live and breathe by such lists. If not, trust me—they're a great tool to use when you've got a big project to complete. As you go through the book and find your ceremony site or decide on the attendants you'll have in the wedding, you'll feel a tremendous sense of satisfaction when you can cross something off your "list." To make accomplishing those tasks even easier, each section's "You'll need list" helps you plan for any specific materials or supplies you'll need while completing the tasks in that section.

In addition to these lists, the book contains a wide variety of general notes, tips, and cautions, with advice that will help you plan your wedding quickly and simply while avoiding common pitfalls. You'll also see the following special icons and elements in the book:

Text marked with the Using Your Lunch Hour Wisely icon offers quick, topic-specific ideas for wedding-planning activities you can accomplish by changing your lunch hour downtime into your wedding planning "up-time."

The Being a Weekend Warrior icon marks suggestions for ways to use your days off efficiently to get items on your "To do list" completed.

Websites Worth Surfing icons flag tips about places on the Internet you should visit for comprehensive information related to that chapter's task.

## AND THE BRIDE SAID...

These sidebars provide quotes from real-life brides on tips they used or slip-ups they faced when planning their wedding. Hopefully, you can use these anecdotes to share the successes and avoid the problems that these brides experienced while planning their weddings.

Periodically, you'll also find planning flow charts. These charts explain when you should complete each task mentioned in that chapter and in what order you should tackle those tasks.

Congratulations on your engagement! I'm sure you're both excited to begin planning your wedding, and I'm excited to help you do so. I'm confident this book is going to make your wedding preparations easy and, dare I say, fun, so turn the page and let's get started.

# Part 1

## Now That You're Engaged

# First Things First

**Y**ou're engaged! Congratulations. The goal of this first chapter is to help you make the most of your engagement period—an admittedly whirlwind time, and a veritable calm before the wedding storm—without becoming overwhelmed with all that lies ahead.

I'll help you stay organized as you write your engagement announcement, find someone to take your engagement picture, and do everything else that goes hand in hand with getting engaged, including putting together your guest list—a document that, once completed, will dictate everything else you do when it comes to planning your wedding.

In addition, you'll learn how to become a weekend warrior and get your engagement announcements out in one fell swoop. You'll also learn what it takes to prepare for registering (yes, it's harder than it looks) and how to get it done pronto. And if your family is insisting on throwing you an engagement party, I'll help you get prepared for that, too.

## In this chapter:

- ✳ Everything you need to know about engagement announcements
- ✳ Fast track to your engagement photo
- ✳ Putting together your guest list
- ✳ Announcing your engagement
- ✳ Deciding on an engagement party
- ✳ Organizing your gift registry

## To do list

- ☐ Write your engagement announcement
- ☐ Find a photographer for your engagement photo
- ☐ Get your engagement photo taken
- ☐ Organize your guest list
- ☐ Send out your engagement announcements
- ☐ Prepare for any engagement parties people will be giving
- ☐ Insure your engagement ring
- ☐ Discuss where you're going to register for gifts
- ☐ Go and register

# The Who, What, Where, When, Why, and How of Engagement Announcements

When I was a journalism major in college, one of the first things I learned was the five W's (Who, What, Where, When, Why) and the one H (How) that would constitute anything and everything I wrote. As you write your engagement announcement, you need to think about these elements, too.

## You'll need list

- ☐ Pad of paper
- ☐ Pen or pencil

### Telling the Full Story

Not sure what I mean? Let me use my own engagement story as an example:

Who:      Leah Ingram and Bill Behre

What:     Became engaged to be married

| Where: | At their favorite French restaurant in their hometown on Long Island |
|---|---|
| When: | Mother's Day weekend |
| Why: | Because they knew they wanted to spend the rest of their lives together |
| How: | Bill presented Leah with his grandmother's vintage diamond ring and asked if she would be his wife. |

Okay, so you've got the basics of the five W's and the one H. Now I'd like to apologize in advance to the fourth estate (journalism) because we're going to finagle the five W's and the one H a bit when writing your engagement announcement. If you take the basics as I've spelled out above, you're going to end up with a pretty odd sounding engagement announcement. I mean, don't most people get married because they want to spend the rest of their lives together?

So, if I were to use this information, less the extraneous stuff, my engagement announcement might look like this:

> Leah Ingram and Bill Behre became engaged to be married on Mother's Day weekend. Bill popped the question at their favorite French restaurant in their hometown on Long Island when he presented Leah with his grandmother's vintage diamond ring and asked if she would be his wife.

## Adding the Details

Now, once you've got the basics covered, you're almost finished with your engagement announcement. (See, that was easy.)

All you have left to do is add in some family details, such as your parents' names and where they currently live, and any other details about your work or educational background.

So, if I were adding those kinds of details to my engagement announcement, next I would write:

> Leah is the daughter of Judy Ingram, formerly of Smithtown, New York, and Michael Ingram, of Yonkers, New York. Bill is the son of Rita Behre, formerly of Smithtown, New York, and John Behre, of Stuart, Florida. They both graduated from Smithtown High School West in Smithtown, New York. Leah holds a bachelor's degree in journalism from New York University and is currently a freelance writer. Bill holds a bachelor's degree in economics from Vassar College; a master's degree in education from Hunter College; and a doctorate of philosophy in special education from the University of Michigan. He is currently a college professor.

The icing on the engagement announcement cake would be to finish with your wedding date (if you've already set it) or a generic statement such as "The couple plans to marry next year."

Again, if I were to finish my engagement announcement with my wedding date, here's what it would read:

> Leah and Bill have planned a November 16th wedding in New York City.

## Or, Go Shorter and Simpler

Now, I understand that you may not want to get so cutesy with your engagement announcement by adding in such things as "how" your fiancé proposed. So, with that in mind, here's how to do a down and dirty, "just the facts, ma'am" engagement announcement. And keep in mind, when in doubt, shorter and simpler is probably the better (and safer) route to take:

> Leah Ingram, daughter of Judy Ingram, formerly of Smithtown, New York, and Michael Ingram, of Yonkers, New York, and Bill Behre, son of Rita Behre, formerly of Smithtown, New York, and John Behre, of Stuart, Florida, became engaged to be married on Mother's Day weekend. They are planning a November 16th wedding in New York City.
>
> They both graduated from Smithtown High School West in Smithtown, New York. Leah holds a bachelor's degree in journalism from New York University and is currently a freelance writer. Bill holds a bachelor's degree in economics from Vassar College; a master's degree in education from Hunter College; and a doctorate of philosophy in special education from the University of Michigan. He is currently a college professor.

## A Traditional Announcement

Some traditionalists believe that it should be the bride's parents who announce the engagement of their daughter. Given that today's bride is in her late 20s, on average, if not older, it may seem a bit arcane to have her parents "announce" her engagement when she's been out of their home and living on her own for years. However, many people do like that tradition, so this is how a traditional version of my engagement announcement would have read:

> Judy Ingram, formerly of Smithtown, New York, and Michael Ingram, of Yonkers, New York, announce the engagement of their daughter, Leah, to Bill Behre, son of Rita Behre, formerly of Smithtown, New York, and John Behre of

Stuart, Florida. The couple is planning a November 16th wedding in New York City.

The couple graduated from Smithtown High School West in Smithtown, New York. The bride-to-be holds a bachelor's degree in journalism from New York University and is currently a freelance writer. The groom-to-be holds a bachelor's degree in economics from Vassar College; a master's degree in education from Hunter College; and a doctorate of philosophy in special education from the University of Michigan. He is currently a college professor.

## Finding Announcement Ideas Fast

Still on the fence about how your engagement announcement should sound? You can use your computer to scan online newspapers speedily and get a sense of what sounds good—and what sounds awful—when writing an engagement announcement.

Start with the online site of your hometown newspaper—or any other paper you might consider sending your announcement to. Click on the "weddings" or "engagements" sections, and spend a few minutes of your lunch hour reading other people's engagement announcements. Jot down any phrases or word arrangements that you like—or print out certain announcements you find and like how they read—and then keep those in your wedding organizer so you can refer to them when writing your own announcement.

# Prepare for Your Engagement Photo Pronto

Engagement photos come in handy for a number of reasons. First, most newspapers like to run a picture of the engaged couple with the engagement announcement. Second, if you're hoping to have your wedding announcement run in the newspaper on the very day of your wedding (as papers like the *New York Times* do), obviously you won't have a wedding picture to send in (because none of them will have been taken, developed, and printed yet). However, if you have an engagement photo on hand, you'll be set. And third, I think it's a lovely idea to treat yourself to a portrait of the two of you, outside of all the photos you'll have taken together on the big day.

## Fast Ways to Find a Photographer

So you've decided to hire a professional to take your engagement picture. Where are you going to find the perfect photographer for your needs? There are a couple of places to look:

- **Word of mouth**. Been to a friend's home lately? Noticed any professional-looking pictures of your friend that were sitting on a mantelpiece or hanging on a wall? Did you like how the photographer captured your friend in this picture? If so, don't be shy—ask your friend who took her picture, and get that photographer's contact information. Friends and family are two of the best resources to turn to when you need to hire someone for a job. They've had firsthand experience with the photographer and can give you an honest view of how easy (or hard) the photographer was to work with, how fair they felt the photographer's fees were, and, most importantly, whether they were pleased with the final result.

- **The newspaper**. Take a look through a couple of back issues of your local paper and see if there are any engagement photos or other kinds of family portraits printed in the paper that look great to you. Then look at the photo credit either underneath or beside the picture. This credit tells you which photographer did this work and gives you a clue as to whom you might want to call about your own engagement picture.

- **Search engines**. One of the best ways to research anything for your wedding is to do it online. To become efficient at using search engines (my favorite is Google), you've got to get as specific as you can when plugging words into the search box. So in order to find an engagement photographer in your area by looking online, I'd suggest typing in "portrait photographer" (since most portrait photographers are the ones who take engagement pictures) and "your hometown." (Obviously, fill in the city and state of your hometown here.)

- **The Yellow Pages**. And, of course, don't forget to check the Yellow Pages (look in the "photographer" section for someone who does "portraits"). You'll probably find a lot of photographers listed that also do weddings but that's not a must-have when it comes to your engagement photograph. However, on the flip side, you can look at your engagement photograph as a trial run for any potential wedding photographer, and if you like the photographer well enough during this trial period, you might want to hire him or her for your wedding.

## Planning a Great Engagement Photo

When it comes to your engagement photo, I want you to have some fun. Did the two of you meet on a park bench? Consider having your engagement photograph taken on the very bench where you exchanged your first hellos. Do you spend all of your free winter weekends together hitting the slopes? Perhaps you should don your ski garb or your snowboarding gear for your engagement picture. Better yet, if you live near a ski area, have the picture taken there. Is your shared love of animals what brought you together? Then gather all of your furry and feathered friends around you when the photographer snaps your engagement picture. By doing so you'll allow a little bit of your personality to shine through in your photo.

**FIGURE 1.1**

Add some personality to your engagement photo by choosing a creative location, such as the park bench where you first met.

www.mccory.com

There's another reason to think about doing something a bit offbeat with your engagement photo.

"Because wedding photos are so formal, you end up with a very different portrait of the two of you if you try to do something different with an engagement photo," says McCory James, a photographer in Denver, Colorado. "For example, if a couple is going to have a wedding in the middle of a city, I might go for more of a mountain or park setting for their engagement photo." McCory likes to see his couples dressed in comfortable, relaxed clothing so that they look true to themselves.

Besides the formality (or informality, as the case may be) of your clothing, another consideration to keep in mind is what your clothing looks like, including any patterns or colors that might appear on them. "I usually shoot engagement photos in both black and white and color," says McCory. If your photographer will be doing the same, it's important that you choose clothing that will look good with your skin tone, both in color and in black and white. The following table offers some basic advice for matching colors to skin tones.

## Complimentary Colors

| If your skin is… | You should wear… |
|---|---|
| On the light side | Darker colors, like blue or black |
| Darker or olive in complexion | Red, green, pink, or purple |
| On the ruddy side | Anything *but* red |
| Medium | Blue or gray |

Here is some more advice for choosing clothing that will look its best in your engagement photo:

- Avoid patterns at all costs. No plaids, no polka dots, no stripes. Solid colors work best.

- Stay away from yellow. It will make even the healthiest person look sickly.

- Bring a couple of different tops with you in the suggested color schemes for your skin type and make sure the photographer takes your picture while you're wearing different outfits. (Both of you should do this.) That way you'll have more "looks" to choose from when you get the photos back.

**tip** There's no rule that says you have to hire a professional to take your engagement photo. If someone you know is good with a camera—and you'll be seeing him or her soon at an event—ask that person to bring along a camera and take a picture of you and your fiancé together. Why at an event? Because when you go to an event (whether it's a backyard barbecue, a day at the races, or a friend's house for dinner), you're likely to be dressed nicely and looking spiffy enough to have your picture taken.

**FIGURE 1.2**
Solid colors work best in portraits, including engagement photos.

www.mccory.com

# You'll need list

- ☐ Your address book
- ☐ Your Rolodex
- ☐ Your PDA
- ☐ Pad of paper
- ☐ Pens and pencils

# Creating a Guest List

It's important to organize your guest list *before* you do anything else for your wedding. The number of guests you invite will affect every other decision you make about your wedding, including where you'll get married, on what date you'll get married, how much of a budget you'll have for your wedding, and where you can have your reception.

Think about it this way: until you know how many people you plan to invite to your wedding, you can't look at a house of worship (what if your first-choice church can't handle the number of people on your guest list?), you can't consider reception spaces (again, because of capacity), and you won't be able to decide on what day you'll become husband and wife because you can't choose a day until you've found a ceremony and reception site, and checked on their availability.

With that in mind you'll need to figure out your guest list *first* before you dial the phone, write an email, or lick a stamp to announce your engagement. The people you announce your engagement to are likely to be the people you're going to invite to your wedding. You don't want to waste time shot gunning your way through your address book and calling or emailing tons of people who you have no intention of inviting to your wedding. That's why you need to formulate your guest list now.

If you thought you could put off compiling your guest list until later on in your wedding plans, guess again. By getting it out of the way sooner rather than later, you'll become organized quicker and be able to make all of your wedding decisions faster.

## Setting Up the List

I still have the spiral-bound notebook that became my de facto wedding planner when I was getting married and in which I wrote all of my guests' names, addresses, and other contact information. Not only did I use this list when I was sending out announcements and invitations, but I also used it when I was writing down who gave me what gifts for my engagement, my bridal shower, and my wedding—and to whom I'd sent thank-you notes after receiving gifts.

## Gathering Names and Contact Information

As you undertake the task of putting together your guest list, first, you've got to figure out which of your family and friends you strongly believe you're going to invite to the wedding. Here's what I suggest you do to get your guest list underway:

1. Go through your address book (either online, in your PDA, or wherever else you keep people's contact information) and make a rough list of people you want to invite.

2. Suggest your fiancé and each of your parents do the same thing—go through their respective address books and write down people's names that they'd like to see invited to your wedding.

3. Don't forget to include people whose contact information you may have memorized and don't keep in an address book, such as your parents or siblings.

4. Once you've got lists compiled, compare them.

5. Create a master list, onto which you'll write all the suggested names from all of the lists.

6. Cross off names that appear multiple times on peoples' lists and add them to your master list.

> **tip**
> While asking your respective parents for their guest list suggestions, also ask them to recommend the names of newspapers to which they would like you to send your engagement announcement. Later on you can research each of these newspapers online and find out their specific submission criteria for engagement announcements.

## The Master List

When you've got your master list, your fiancé and you need to rank people on it. Put an A next to those you definitely want at your wedding, such as immediate family. Next, rank people for the B list. Put a B next to any person that you would like to have celebrate with you but it wouldn't crush you if they didn't end up invited. Finally, rank any remaining names in the C list, which would fall into the category of "would be nice to invite if many people RSVP no." (Of course, you don't share any of these rankings with the guests themselves—you could hurt people's feelings.)

Take your master list back to your parents and ask them to review your rankings. See if they'd like you to change any of your A, B, or C rankings. (Remember: It's considered good taste to ask your respective parents for input on the guest list, even if you end up paying for the wedding yourselves. Also, it helps to prevent family feuds.)

After you've received your parents' input, revise the master list and finalize it. Add in addresses, phone numbers, and email addresses, which you'll eventually need when sending out your invitations and following up with guests who don't RSVP in a timely manner. Again, you may be tempted to wait until later to compile this kind of information, but I strongly suggest you do it now and get it out of the way.

## Creating Your Notification Checklist

After you have your guest list and everyone's contact information, you can create your notification checklist and get busy.

By the way, I'm not wedded to any one kind of checklist, whether it's an Excel spreadsheet, an alphabetical listing created in a word processing program, or a handwritten list in a spiral notebook. All I want you to do is to make sure that you

- Write down everyone's name and contact information
- Use this information when notifying people of your engagement and any other wedding-related celebrations to come.

However, after you've determined your A, B, and C lists, here's what I would suggest you do:

1. Organize each of the A, B, and C lists separately and alphabetically.
2. Set up a page (either electronically or on paper) for each list. (You may want to go with a horizontal format because you'll have a lot of columns to deal with.) In Appendix B, "Planning Charts and Aids," Table B.1 is a sample of a guest list database.
3. Create columns on the page so you can include
   - Contact information
   - Date engagement announcement sent (if you decide to send them out)

- Engagement gift received (if any)/Date thank-you note sent
- Shower gift received (if any)/Date thank-you note sent
- Date wedding invitation sent
- Number of people you've invited with this person
- Date RSVP received and answer (yes or no)
- Number RSVPing yes
- Date called to follow up, if no RSVP received
- Gift received/Date thank-you note sent

4. When you've got the lists separated, you can create rows where you begin to list names alphabetically.

   With each entry include
   - Names
   - Address
   - Phone number
   - Email address

> **tip** An organized bride is a happy bride. That said, one of your first shopping trips should be to buy an organizer for anything and everything wedding-related. That way you can keep all of the items you need for your wedding plans in one place. It doesn't matter what kind of organizer you get—just get one that you'll use that fits with your personality. Your organizer could be a three-ringed binder with section dividers; an accordion file; a box with a handle that holds hanging files; a spiral notebook with built-in folders; or anything else that strikes your fancy and will keep you organized.

# Getting the Word Out on Your Engagement

You have three options for letting people know that you're engaged to be married. You can

- Call or email everyone to let them know the good news.
- Put an announcement in your local newspaper.
- Send out formal engagement announcements.

You can do all or you can do none; the choice is yours. This table lists some pros and cons of each.

> **tip** When sending engagement announcements to your target newspapers, check each paper's website to see if they take submissions electronically. If so, you can cut and paste your announcement into an email and attach a digital image of your engagement photo, if you're sending a photo. (Be sure to speak with your photographer ahead of time about supplying you with a digital picture.) This will save you time and postage on getting the word out about your engagement.

## Engagement Announcement Methods' Pros and Cons

| Announcement Method | Pros | Cons |
| --- | --- | --- |
| Calling/emailing everyone | You're still so excited about the new prospect of getting married that you'll have a tremendous amount of energy when you're sharing the good news with everyone. | In all of your excitement, you may end up calling or emailing people whom you do not intend to invite to your wedding. If so, you'll need to backpedal once you're ready to send out invitations. |
| Putting an announcement in the newspaper | You can send your engagement announcement to the newspaper immediately after getting engaged or you can wait until you're closer to your wedding date. This option gives you the most flexibility. | Newspapers will often hold engagement announcements until just before a wedding date. If you were hoping to use the newspaper announcement to notify people of your engagement—but not your actual wedding date—you may be out of luck. |
| Mailing out formal engagement announcements | You can wait to send out a formal announcement until you know exactly when you'll be married and who you'll invite. | Because you can wait awhile to send out a formal engagement announcement, you'll need to make sure that you only send them to those you'll definitely include on your wedding guest list. Also, sending out a formal engagement announcement will require you to spend time and money on printing and postage. |

With your notification checklist in hand, you're ready to start, well, notifying people. Read on to find out how I suggest you approach each of the three announcement methods in a swift fashion, so that you can set aside one weekend day and get it all done.

## Calling and Emailing

To get the job done faster, you two should split the list. Let's say you've put together a notification list of 250. You take 125 and he takes 125. Start with those who have email and you know that they check it regularly. Write a quick announcement in an email and then send it out to everyone. (This method should probably take care of 75 percent of your list.)

I would suggest you bcc (blind carbon copy) everyone in one email message, rather than sending out individual emails to everyone, which would require a lot of cutting and pasting. By doing one email, you won't spend hours notifying your family and friends.

Now you're ready to call the people on your list who don't have email. If one of you ends up with more folks to call, you can split the list again so that the majority of calls don't end up falling on one person.

To save even more time, you can split the original list with each of your parents and have them call or email their own friends or family members (or those they would add to your guest list) and tell them of your engagement.

**tip** You can order formal announcements from a stationer, which may take a few weeks. Or if you want to get it done fast, you can buy specialty papers for the computer from a local stationer or office supply store and make the announcements on your home computer.

## Putting an Announcement in the Newspaper

Remember when you were putting together your guest list, I suggested that you also get the names of newspapers from your parents? Now you'll need that list of names so you'll know exactly which of these papers you'll be sending your engagement announcement to. These papers might include each of your hometown local newspapers and a newspaper where each of you lives now.

Most newspapers today take submissions electronically, which saves you time on mailing and saves you money on postage.

# You'll need list

- ❏ Copies of your engagement announcement
- ❏ Copies of your engagement photo
- ❏ Envelopes
- ❏ Snail mail addresses of each newspaper
- ❏ Return address labels
- ❏ Postage stamps

## Mailing Out Formal Engagement Announcements

Whether you mail out formal engagement announcements is entirely up to you and how your family expects you to handle your announcements. If everyone in your family has always mailed out formal engagement announcements, you should do so, too—even if you're having a small, casual wedding. If none of your siblings ever did engagement announcements, you can buck the trend and send them out or you can skip them all together.

If you do decide to send announcements, you can use your notification checklist to get started. It tells you exactly how many engagement announcements you'll need to make or order (see the previous Tip about ordering engagement announcements) along with how many photos you'll need to order to include with the announcement. (Including a photo is optional but it adds a nice touch.)

I would then recommend creating a mailing label file on your computer of everyone on your notification list and then generating labels. (You'll use this mailing label file again when sending out other wedding-related invitations.) Finally, don't forget to buy stamps at the post office.

Then, like the calling and emailing notification process, you and your fiancé should split the list when mailing out your announcements. Set aside one afternoon to assemble them all—postage stamps included—and in a few hours you'll have all of your engagement announcements ready for mailing.

> **tip** To cleverly combine your engagement announcement and your engagement photo, why not have your announcement printed on a folding card? Then you can have your engagement photo printed on the front of the card.

# Deciding on an Engagement Party

There are a couple of elements of your wedding plans that you will not have complete control over. One of them is your bridal shower (which is usually planned as a surprise by your maid of honor). The other is an engagement party, which your parents, family members, or friends may decide to throw in your honor.

If the people who care about you do want to celebrate your engagement with a party, I would suggest that you delicately ask or politely suggest that they make the engagement party as simple as possible. Here's why.

I was once invited to colleague's engagement party, and that party turned into a mini-version of her eventual wedding. It was held in a catering facility, we had assigned seating, we brought a wrapped gift, and there was even a chicken-dance-playing deejay to entertain the guests. The only thing that kept reminding me that this wasn't a wedding reception was the fact that the bride and groom weren't dressed in wedding garb.

Now I understand that their parents (who threw this engagement party for them) had the best intentions in mind, but after going to this engagement party, and then a bridal shower, and then the bachelorette party, and eventually the wedding, I was sick and tired of fêting this couple. Don't get me wrong—I love weddings, which is why I write about them—but the old adage "everything in moderation" applies to wedding celebrations as well. And this family had done every element of her wedding in an over-the-top way that left me feeling worn out instead of happy for the happy couple.

So why am I telling you this? Because if your parents or his parents insist on throwing a celebration to commemorate your engagement (and family is likely the proper people to be putting together such a celebration), please make sure that the party looks nothing like a wedding. Maybe you can have it be a wine tasting dinner at a winery. Maybe your fiancé's sister could decide to host a brunch in your honor. Maybe you'll have a clambake on the beach. Whatever you do, understand that you don't have to have an engagement party—it's not a must—but ask that the hosts make it an intimate get together of important people to you who want to celebrate your special time. That will make it the most meaningful for all involved.

**tip** If you're going to have multiple pre-wedding celebrations (engagement party, a few bridal showers, and so on), you might ask the host to let your guests off the gift-giving hook. You don't want your family and friends to feel as if the only reason you're having these celebrations is to get as many gifts as possible. Specifically ask that guests do not bring gifts to one of these parties or, if you think they won't respect that wish, designate a charity as the beneficiary of your celebration.

# DON'T PUT OFF INSURING YOUR ENGAGEMENT RING

An engagement ring is undoubtedly an expensive piece of jewelry, and you should treat it as such by insuring it properly. Think your homeowner's insurance will cover it? Think again. (You do have homeowner's insurance, right?)

"While homeowner's insurance covers a lot of things, it doesn't provide adequate coverage for jewelry," says Kevin Craiglow, a spokesperson for Nationwide Insurance, who explains that most insurance policies cover all jewelry worth up to $1,000. Unless you've got a teeny tiny rock on your left hand, you're going to need extra coverage.

Craiglow recommends getting a separate jewelry policy, which some companies call an endorsement and others call an insurance rider. Both provide additional coverage for your engagement ring.

Before you can get an endorsement or a rider, you need to know exactly how much your ring is worth so should it be lost or damaged, the insurance company will know its replacement value. "Most reputable jewelers offer appraisals for a small fee," says Craiglow. In many cases, the jeweler who originally sold your fiancé the ring will have offered to appraise it before it left the shop. In addition to providing a "current and accurate appraisal of the engagement ring," says Craiglow, insurance companies will also want a description of the ring—carat weight, metal used, and so on—and a photo of it for their files.

Riders or endorsements add only a nominal amount to a current insurance policy and are well worth the expense because they offer both protection and peace of mind.

# Getting Your Gift Registry Organized on the Double

Many couples look at registering for their wedding as a free-for-all to get stuff, stuff, and more stuff. Others don't take registering nearly seriously enough—they show up at a store during a lunch hour and think they can register in less than an hour. Neither approach works in my book.

Handle registering as you might prepare for any trip to the grocery store. Before you grocery shop, you probably take inventory of what you already have in your kitchen. Then, you plan for what you're going to need in the coming weeks for specific menus or just staples that you've run low on.

## Deciding What You Really Want and Need

Before you register,  you need to take inventory of what you already have in your home—or homes, if you haven't lived together and will be combining two households' worth of stuff into one. Go from room to room and note all the things that you own just as you might when making an insurance claim after a home disaster. Yes, this preparation might be a bit time-consuming now, but it will be well worth the effort down the road.

Next, sit down together and discuss what you want based on what you don't already have. Are you using hand-me-down dishes and towels from your college dormitory days? If so, you might want to add a new set of everyday dishes and some matching towels to your wish list. Do your drinking cups consist of a mish-mosh of free plastic cups that come with take-out drinks? Consider requesting a set of non-plastic drinking glasses.

Finally, you need to consider what you *don't* want. Why? Because when you get to the place you're going to register in, you're bound to fall into what I call a shopping nirvana. That is, most stores these days make registering as easy as using a hand-held scanner gun and zapping the UPC code on a product. (These scanner guns are just like the kind you see at the checkout counter.)

With scanner gun in hand, you may consider the entire store your shopping oyster and, what the heck, just add everything and anything that tickles your fancy to the registry. And then off you go, scanning item and after item. You really don't want to do this. When your guests start buying you these things that you really don't want or need, you're either going to have to rent a storage facility to keep all those unopened gifts, or you're going to be schlepping stuff to return to the store weekend after weekend for weeks to come.

So that's why I want you to take some extra time when considering your registry and write down what you really don't want or really don't need— either because it doesn't fit your lifestyle or because you owned something similar once and never used it.

Case in point: my husband and I succumbed to shopping nirvana way back when and asked for an indoor grill. Now, we live in a house with a great backyard and a great grill but for a second we thought, oh, wouldn't it be great just to grill inside? Well, guess what? We grill 365 days a year outside and never once took that indoor grill out of the box. I think we recently donated it to charity.

**tip** While avoiding shopping nirvana, make sure instead that you register for enough items for the size of your wedding. For example, if you're inviting 150 people to celebrate with you, having a registry list of only 15 items isn't enough. Ideally, your total registry should include half the number of items as people on your guest list, if not a bit more. So for a wedding of 150 guests, register for at least 75 necessary items.

## Organizing Your Registry List

You can use the following chart—or a reasonable facsimile of it—to organize your registry haves, wants, and don't needs before you actually hit the store. Then when you go to register, you'll get it all done in no time because you'll have planned ahead and approached registering in an organized fashion. In addition, by organizing your registry haves, wants, and don't needs this way, you'll be able to figure out where to register in a snap.

## Gift Registry Haves, Wants, and Don't Needs

| What We Have | What We Want | What We Don't Need |
|---|---|---|
|  |  |  |
|  |  |  |
|  |  |  |
|  |  |  |

# DECIDING WHERE TO REGISTER

Trying to decide where to register? Consider these points:

- Are Mother Hubbard's cupboards completely bare—or at least stacked with mismatched plates, dishes, silverware, plus towels, throw rugs, and other housewares? Then consider registering at a one-stop super housewares store, such as Bed Bath & Beyond, Target, Linens 'n Things, Crate and Barrel, or another comparable store with a registry. These kinds of stores usually have very competitive prices.

- Do you have all the basics but want to treat yourself to fine china, crystal, and silver? Register with a department store that allows all of your guests nationwide to access its registry, such as the Federated Department Stores (these include Macy's and Bloomingdale's) or The May Company (which owns Strawbridge's, Hecht's, and Filene's). These stores also stock everyday housewares as well.

- Are you looking for an offbeat online place to register? While many of the stores named above have registries with an online presence, e-tailers like Amazon.com let you register for more across-the-board items, such as books, DVDs, CDs, and more.

Can't imagine stuffing more stuff into your already over-crowded home? Then consider registering your wishes with a good cause and have your guests make donations to charity instead. These websites are a good place to start:

www.benevolink.com

www.idofoundation.org

www.marriedforgood.com

For more ideas on registering, check out my website www.weddingink.com.

## Summary

By the time you've reached this point in the book, I'm sure that reality has sunk in—you're getting married! That's wonderful news, but beyond the initial excitement, there's a lot to be done. Hopefully this chapter has helped you to accomplish some of your primary engagement tasks without breaking a sweat.

In this chapter, you've learned the basics of writing an engagement announcement, finding an engagement photographer (and planning what to wear in your photo), and announcing your engagement. Hand in hand with that, you've also learned the basics of putting together your guest list and registering for gifts—that latter task in preparation for any engagement parties your family or friends may choose to hold in your honor.

In Chapter 2, "Money Matters and Essential First Steps," we move on to a topic that not everyone likes discussing—but one you can't avoid when planning a wedding— money. Get ready by getting out the bank statements, paycheck stubs, and other financial data you have lying around so you're ready to talk about how much you and your fiancé are prepared to contribute to your wedding.

# Money Matters and Essential First Steps

Weddings are not immune to inflation, and like other things in life, the cost of throwing a wedding has gone up over time.

## Coming to Terms with What Weddings Cost

According to most experts, the average wedding in the United States will set a couple back about $22,000. That's the average.

While that figure might make you choke a bit, keep this in mind: If you're getting married in a major metropolitan area, you should double that average wedding cost—I kid you not. In fact, most brides who have a traditional Saturday night ceremony and sit-down wedding reception in places like Philadelphia, New York, Chicago, Dallas, or Los Angeles will tell you that for them, the average cost of a wedding is closer to $50,000.

On the flipside, "average" weddings in less-expensive American areas come in at around $20,000, which is still a significant sum of money. So as you start to consider your wedding budget, keep these figures in mind.

If you're looking to throw a big-city bash on a Saturday night, your wedding is likely going to cost on the upper end of the "average" scale. If your idea of the ideal wedding is a Sunday brunch in the country, you might not spend as much as the urban bride, but you should still budget liberally.

# THE COST OF SAYING "I DO" AROUND AMERICA

According to 2004 data from the Conde Nast Bridal Group, the average wedding in the United States costs about $22,300. Here's how the numbers break down according to region:

- Northeast: $37,650
- Southeast: $20,310
- Midwest: $22,900
- West: $20,800

Here is a quick look at eight weddings, all with approximately 200 guests, held in different areas of the country. This should give you a sense of how much wedding budgets can range:

Couple Number One
Location: Denver, Colorado
Number of Guests: 200
Total Budget: $10,000

Couple Number Two
Location: Charleston, South Carolina
Number of Guests: 200
Total Budget: $19,300

Couple Number Three
Location: Los Angeles suburbs
Number of Guests: 200
Total Budget: $30,000

Couple Number Four
Location: Chicago, Illinois
Number of Guests: 200
Total Budget: $36,325

Couple Number Five
Location: Atlanta, Georgia
Number of Guests: 200
Total Budget: $55,000

Couple Number Six
Location: Philadelphia, Pennsylvania
Number of Guests: 195
Total Budget: $58,235

Couple Number Seven
Location: New York City suburbs
Number of Guests: 196
Total Budget: $65,000

Couple Number Eight
Location: New York, New York
Number of Guests: 205
Total Budget: $350,000

# To do list

- ☐ Get your finances in order
- ☐ Make a date to talk money with your fiancé and your respective parents
- ☐ Figure out who is going to pay for what
- ☐ Order your credit reports
- ☐ Figure out ways to cut your spending and increase your savings
- ☐ Open a separate "wedding savings" account
- ☐ Weigh pros and cons of hiring a consultant
- ☐ Organize your wedding-planning priorities

# A Fast (and Realistic) Look at Finances

Remember in the last chapter how I said that before you can do anything for your wedding, you need to have your guest list in place? Well, before you can set your budget for your wedding, you need to have a strong sense of what your finances look like—and who will be contributing to your wedding and how much. Then you have to determine, based on those contributions, just how much money you can spend on your wedding.

# You'll need list

- ☐ Paper and pencil
- ☐ Past year's bank statements
- ☐ Past year's credit card statements
- ☐ Paycheck stubs or past year's W-2
- ☐ Complete list of all monthly expenses

## Be Frank About Funds

First, you need to plan ahead to talk about money with all the major players in your life—your fiancé, your parents, and your fiancé's parents—who might be paying for a portion of your wedding. Why plan ahead? Money can be a contentious topic for many to discuss. "Next to sex, money is the biggest generator of problems, arguments, and resentment in long-term relationships," warns Tina Tessina, Ph.D., a psychotherapist and author of *How to Be a Couple and Still Be Free* (New Pages Books, 2002). "People attach a lot of emotional and symbolic significance to money, so it's easy to become stressed and argue about it."

To avoid arguments, give the involved parties fair warning that you want to talk money in the very near future. Call to let them know that you're trying to get a sense of your wedding budget, and you can't do that without knowing upfront what their financial contributions to your wedding might be—if any. Then set a date to have that discussion, even if it has to be a long-distance conversation done over the phone.

## Agreeing About Who Pays for What

Traditionally,  it used to be that the bride's parents paid for everything except the rehearsal dinner and the tuxedo rentals, the latter two falling to the groom's parents. While many families still follow these traditions, some do not.

Instead, here's what today's modern bride needs to keep in mind. You need to figure out an equitable distribution of wedding costs, based on the financial discussions you've had with your respective parents, and who can afford what. Have your parents offered to pay for the entertainment as their gift to you? Great, go for it. Would your fiancé's parents like to stick with tradition and pick up the tab for the rehearsal dinner? That would be wonderful.

On the other hand, while it would be great if everyone's parents could help pay for a wedding, that isn't always a reality. Today's brides and grooms marry later in life, and because they are more self-supportive in other areas of their life, their parents may just assume that they'll be so with their wedding as well. Also, I've heard of families who'd originally set aside money to pay for a son or daughter's wedding but when that didn't happen as soon as the parents expected, they used that money to buy a vacation home or to funnel into their retirement savings. Sure, that's not an ideal situation but it may be your reality. So don't just assume that you can hand your parents a bill at the end of your wedding plans and expect them to pony up thousands of dollars.

It's worth repeating that you've got to talk to your families first and find out what kind of financial contributions they can afford to make towards your wedding. Don't go into your wedding plans assuming or expecting anything you haven't talked about with your parents already. You'll only end up disappointed and potentially in greater debt than you anticipated.

## Solutions with Divorced Parents

If either of your parents is divorced, that will add a level of complication to your wedding finances because parents who are no longer married likely do not want to share the same costs of the wedding. If you're looking for financial assistance from your divorced parents, you need to think seriously about the best way to approach this topic so that you do not cause any conflicts—and decide whether it makes sense to try to pay for your wedding without parental help. Remember, relationships in every divorced situation are different.

Here's how my husband Bill and I worked things out with our divorced parents. We decided that the easiest way to pay for our wedding was to pay for everything ourselves. We didn't want things to get too sticky when it came to money (money+parents=potential fights; money+divorced parents=potential world wars) and we were lucky enough to be able to work that out financially.

However, we also wanted to allow our parents the freedom to add their friends to our guest list, but we didn't want the burden of paying for these extra guests who weren't meaningful to us. So we came to a happy medium: we asked each of our parents to pick up the tab for the guests they'd invited. This decision permitted our parents to invite their friends without adding a financial burden to our wedding. Most importantly, this decision allowed us to keep the peace among all the involved individuals during a time when things could have easily become ugly.

## Fitting Your Event to Your Finances

At the same time that you're discussing finances with your respective families, you and your fiancé need to have a heart-to-heart talk about your money situation. Why? So you can figure out how much you can afford to spend on your wedding. Take an honest look at your spending patterns, debt, and expenses, and see how much money you can realistically set aside in time for your wedding.

If you come up with a small number—and no help from your respective parents—you'll have a few options. One, you can look at that guest list you put together in Chapter 1, "First Things First," and cut it down to a more manageable size. Two, you can figure out a way to have everyone at your wedding but to cut your overall wedding costs. Three, you can consider alternative funding options, such as taking out a home equity loan to pay for your wedding (see "Using Loans to Help Pay for the Wedding," later in this chapter). Or, four, you could reshuffle your expectations of a wedding during a popular month (anytime between May and October) and plan to get married during the more affordable off-season (see "Choosing a Time, Day, and Month That Can Save You Money," later in this chapter).

If you come up with a sizeable amount of money, you know that you'll have the freedom to be a bit more extravagant with your planning, such as arranging for more food, extra flowers, or a bigger band. Or with more money to work with, you can become that June bride that you've always dreamed of being.

# Using Loans to Help Pay for the Wedding

When interest rates are low, savvy homeowners understand how smart it can be to tap into their existing equity in their home to pay for purchases. If either of you own a home and aren't currently saddled with a lot of consumer debt, a home equity loan may be an option for you to consider to pay for your wedding.

Before you can consider borrowing money to pay for your wedding, you need to know how financial institutions see you. That is, do you have impeccable credit (you pay all of your bills on time, for starters) so you're the kind of customer that banks want to do business with? Or is your credit on the shaky side (you've fallen behind in paying back loans, for example) so banks might see you as a credit risk? The only way to get a sense of how credit-worthy you are is to get a copy of your credit report.

### Checking Your Financial Report Card

 You'll need list

- ❏ Computer
- ❏ Internet access

There are three major companies that issue credit reports, and these credit reports are what banks, credit card companies, and other financial institutions refer to when considering a loan application from someone.

Devote one weekend day to requesting each of your credit reports at each of these company's websites:

Experian.com

Equifax.com

Transunion.com

You'll have to pay a nominal fee for each credit report request. Then you can expect a hard copy of your report in the mail a few days later.

Keep in mind that the reason that you want to get credit reports from each of these companies is this: You want to ensure that your credit is squeaky clean at each of these three companies because you can never be sure which one a financial institution might call when checking on your credit. Also, credit bureaus have different ways of collecting credit information—and different criteria for grading your credit—so you should be on the safe side and see all of your credit reports. Yes, I know this seems a bit absurd—that you can't even control your own credit—but that's just the way it is.

## Using Your Home Equity

Do either of you own a home? Do you own a home together? Did you know that the equity in your home may be the solution to any of your financial shortcomings?

"Your wedding will be something that occurs only once, and that experience will be with you for a lifetime," says John Barton, a spokesperson for the Wells Fargo Consumer Credit Group. "As a lifetime investment, equity is a very appropriate way to fund an investment like a wedding."

## Pros and Cons of Using Equity to Pay for a Wedding

Like I said earlier, using a home equity loan or line of credit to pay for a wedding might make sense for you. However, it doesn't always. Here are some pros and cons to consider as you make your decisions:

Financing your wedding with home equity makes sense if

- Interest rates are currently low.
- You can confirm with your accountant that you'll receive a tax benefit from having a home equity loan or line of credit.
- Home prices in your area continue to escalate, meaning that your home is worth more over time. Higher value means more equity you can tap into.
- You like the idea of having a home equity line of credit available for you to use for your wedding and other expenditures down the road.
- You get a loan that has a set percentage rate, not a variable rate. These can go up over time and increase your payments.

Using home equity to pay for your wedding doesn't make sense if

- Interest rates are at an all-time high.
- There's the potential for one of you to lose your job in the near future, such as if you're employed in an unstable occupation. You don't want to take on a huge debt if you can't make payments down the road.
- Home values are decreasing where you live.
- When you do the math, getting a home equity loan or line of credit means you'll have larger mortgage payments going forward and you can't afford those larger monthly payments.
- You get a loan or line of credit with a variable interest rate.

Before you consider tapping into equity in your home to pay for a wedding, get a good sense of what interest rates look like. If rates are low, it might make sense to take out a home equity loan or start a home equity line of credit to pay for a wedding. However, should rates shoot up to 1980s levels, when people were paying double-digit rates on their mortgages, equity probably shouldn't be a consideration.

One of the best and fastest ways to get a quick read on interest rates is via the Internet. One site in particular, www.bankrate.com, is a soup-to-nuts financial website that not only chronicles current interest rates but also offers excellent lifestyle editorial on how to use your finances smartly. (Bankrate.com is the website that financial institutions turn to in a pinch as well, so you know it must be a great source.)

# Saving Money and Cutting Costs

Because it's rare these days for the bride's parents to pick up the entire tab for a wedding (regardless of how much the wedding costs), you and your fiancé are likely going to have to cut some

**tip** There's no reason for you and your fiancé to schlep from bank to bank, applying for home equity loans. You really can make banks come to you by applying for your home equity loan through a website like LendingTree.com.

What makes this website such a great find is this: It compiles all your financial information (which you have to enter only once on its secure site), and then submits it to as many as four different financial institutions around the country. Shortly thereafter, you'll get emails directly from those financial institutions with details on their home equity loan offers.

Each financial institution understands that you're likely to be getting offers from three other financial institutions as well, which is why you usually get competitive offers in return. My husband and I have used LendingTree.com multiple times when looking to pull equity out of our home, and I can tell you that the banks that LendingTree.com works with really do offer rates worth taking a second look at.

of your spending in the weeks and months before your wedding so you can sock away some savings.

In addition, every bride (regardless of her wedding budget) wants to make sure that she stretches her wedding dollar as far as she can. Read on to uncover some creative ways to put away money for your wedding and to get more bang for your wedding buck.

## Ten Swift Ways to Save for Your Wedding

When my husband and I were planning our wedding, we figured out that we needed to put away $12,000—and fast—if we wanted to have the wedding of our dreams on our desired date.

One of the ways we met this savings goal was to set up a separate savings account where we could deposit all the money we were saving for our wedding. Some couples open an old-fashioned passbook savings accounts that isn't hooked into an ATM or an electronic checking account, and this makes sense for a simple reason: if it isn't easy to access the money, you're less likely to cheat and dip into your wedding savings.

The other important thing you should do is determine a real figure that you need to save, and then you can strive to reach that goal. It's easier to stick with a plan that says "We are going to save $10,000 by next June" than to say something vague like "We're going to put away 10 percent of our salary."

Here are some other savings' tips I've picked up over the years. Together, they will help you cut your spending and put away the money you need to pay for your wedding:

1. Does your employer offer an automatic savings option with your paycheck each week? If so, choose an amount that your payroll department will deduct with each paycheck and direct deposit it into your savings account.

2. Become disciplined about spending cash and using your credit cards. If you agree to each take out, say, $100 from the ATM on Monday—and that's your only trip to the ATM that week—you'll learn to make that $100 last. (And no cheating by using your debit or credit cards.)

3. Cut back on extraneous expenses. These might include:
   - **Morning cup of coffee**. At $2.50 each morning, for example, a cup of coffee on the way to work or the gym on the weekend doesn't seem like such an extravagant expenditure. But factor that out over a year's worth of mornings, and you're looking at $912.50. Instead, invest in a good coffee maker, coffee beans, and a travel mug (cost: less than $100) and make your coffee each morning.

- **Lunch or other food on the run**. Like the cup of coffee, a meal eaten on the run adds up to a lot of cash going out of your wallet each week. If a year's worth of coffee adds up to more than $900, imagine what drive-through food twice a week or a turkey sandwich from the deli three times a week must add up to—a lot of dough.

- **Frivolous reading material**. Are you a newspaper or magazine junkie? If so, do your savings account a favor and subscribe to your favorite publications. A magazine that costs $3 on the newsstand might only cost $12 to subscribe to. That means that instead of paying $36 a year for the honor of reading that publication, you'll save $24 annually by subscribing instead. If you read many magazines, these savings will add up.

4.  Hoard your change. Instead of just letting loose change float around your home, start collecting it. Once a month, roll it and deposit it in your bank account. One bride I know spent an afternoon doing a clean sweep of her apartment for loose change and came up with $53.

5.  Deposit bonuses, tax refunds, or any "unexpected" income right into your wedding savings account. Given your financial austerity before the wedding, you might be tempted to "treat" yourself when you get a windfall, like an income tax return. Don't. Use this windfall to bolster your savings account and remind yourself that the more money you put into that account, the sooner you can end your self-imposed spending hiatus.

6.  Reduce commuting costs. Do you and your fiancé live together and do you each drive a separate car to work? If so, could you carpool and save money on gas and tolls that way? Or, if one of you has a longer commute—and a gas-guzzling car—could you switch cars? The person with the longer commute could take the most fuel-efficient car so that you spend less on gas in the long run. What about public transportation? Might it help you save spending money by switching to this commuting mode for the short term?

7.  Become a library patron.  In the time before your wedding, try to curtail your purchases of extraneous books and movies and take advantage of your public library instead. If you're a member of a book club, you could save money by borrowing the book-of-the-month instead of buying it new—especially if it's in hardcover, which is very expensive.

8. Cut back on entertaining costs. Do you favor going to the movies every Friday night? What about going Saturday afternoon instead? Matinee movie prices are nearly half of what prime-time movies cost, and if you and your fiancé have a regular date to see movies, you could save big bucks by moving your movie date night to a movie date afternoon. Or start seeing second-run movies at a "value" cinema, where ticket prices are significantly cheaper. Or wait a few months until the movie is on DVD and rent it instead.

9. Forgo a vacation this year. Soon enough you'll be taking your honeymoon, and you should be saving up for that trip instead of other vacations. So instead of going on your annual ski trip to the mountains or week in the Caribbean, avoid spending thousands on those trips by not going at all.

10. Be smarter about food shopping. Instead of stopping into the grocery store when you're rushed or hungry—and therefore likely to overspend—follow mom's advice and plan ahead. Make a grocery list each week, plan meals, use coupons, and you'll end up saving hundreds of dollars on food shopping in the process.

## Choosing a Time, Day, and Month That Can Save You Money

When you think about weddings, you probably think of the proverbial June bride. You're not alone in thinking June, which is why it continues to be one of the most popular months for weddings. (See the sidebar, "Weddings Through the Year" for an exact breakdown of the popularity of certain months for weddings.)

June also continues to be one of the most expensive months for weddings because of simple supply and demand. There are usually only four weekends in the month of June (supply) but thousands of brides who want to be a June bride (demand). Based on simple economics, vendors and venues know that they can charge more for a June wedding—and they surely do.

For couples with a bit of flexibility about when they get married, it's good to know that by changing the month, day, or time of day that you get married, you can save big bucks. Here are some examples of how that can work for you and your wedding budget:

- Weddings are at a premium Saturday evenings, and if you'd like to pay anything but a premium for your celebration, you can still have a Saturday wedding reception. That is, you can have your wedding ceremony in the morning and then serve lunch for your reception. One bride did just this and was able to cut her reception costs in half.

- Have your wedding on any day other than Saturday. Again, everyone wants to have a Saturday evening wedding and reception, which means that option is the most expensive one. By having your wedding and reception on either Friday night or Sunday afternoon, you won't spend as much money.
- As you'll see in the sidebar, May through October is when most weddings occur. By moving your wedding to April or November (or one of the other less-popular months) you'll have more vendors and venues available—and better negotiating power with prices.

**tip** When choosing a time of year for your wedding, be sure to keep in mind where you think you're going to want to honeymoon. If you've always wanted to honeymoon in Paris and you're planning an August wedding, the two notions might not work together. Most of Europe goes on "holiday" in August, leaving tourists with fewer places to go and things to do. So if you've got your heart set on a Paris honeymoon, you may want to alter the date of your wedding so you can make that honeymoon dream come true. For more on coordinating your wedding date with your honeymoon, turn to Chapter 9, "Planning a Happy Honeymoon."

# WEDDINGS THROUGH THE YEAR

For years June has been the most popular month to tie the knot. Although it no longer is number one (by just a small margin), it's still up there in popularity. Following is a look at the percentages of marriages that occur each month: (Source: Hallmark.com)

| Month | Percentage of Marriages |
| --- | --- |
| January | 5.13 |
| February | 6.45 |
| March | 6.85 |
| April | 7.49 |
| May | 9.34 |
| June | 10.37 |
| July | 9.92 |
| August | 10.43 |
| September | 9.63 |

| Month | Percentage of Marriages |
|---|---|
| October | 9.6 |
| November | 7.43 |
| December | 7.37 |

Keep in mind that many brides try to plan their celebration for a holiday weekend, when guests are likely to have time off from work and will be freer to travel to a wedding. The following are some of the most popular holiday weekends for weddings, and if you want to have yours then, you're going to have to plan far in advance to do so:

* Memorial Day (May)
* Fourth of July (July)
* Labor Day (September)
* Columbus Day  (October)

## Deciding Whether a Wedding Consultant Can Save You Time and Money

Given that nearly all of today's modern brides are employed full time, they don't have a lot of free time to devote to their wedding plans. That's why if you're a busy, working bride, a wedding consultant may be your best investment in your wedding.

By budgeting a couple thousand dollars to pay for her services, you will save time on your plans and you may end up saving money in the long run. Consultants have established relationships with vendors, and can often get you better deals than you could get on your own.

I recently spoke with Joyce Scardina Becker, a certified meeting professional and experienced wedding planner who owns Events of Distinction in San Francisco. Although she has a vested interest in promoting her profession, I thought she had some very valid suggestions for why a wedding consultant may make sense for today's busy bride:

- If you're planning a long-distance wedding, you need someone nearby who can help you with the details. Unless you can travel to your location every weekend to tie up loose ends, a wedding consultant who knows venues and vendors in the area can do all of your legwork for you. "If you have 150 people on your guest list, I won't waste your time showing you places that can only handle 100," says Scardina Becker.

- The consultant will know the right vendor for your needs. Most reputable wedding consultants do not take kickbacks from their vendors, but you should always ask. Instead, they develop relationships with these caterers and florists and other vendors over years of working together, and know the best in the business—or the best for your budget. One kind of vendor that Scardina Becker likes working with is a vendor who does both corporate and social events like she does. "Vendors doing both markets are more experienced," she says. "The corporate market has a quick turnaround time, and a company that can do a conference in three weeks will do a fabulous job with a wedding [that takes longer to plan]."

- With a consultant you won't have to deal with impersonal "packages." The easy way out for many wedding vendors is to create a limited number of packages (whether they're menus, song play lists, or photography offerings) and not to stray too much from the tried and true. If you're looking for unique elements in your wedding that reflect your personality, you likely won't find that in packages— and consultants know that. A consultant custom designs every wedding to reflect the couple. Also, because "we're asking [vendors] only for what they want," says Scardina Becker, "the couples end up getting more value for their money," because they're not paying for extraneous package elements that they're not interested in using.

Many wedding planners or wedding consultants (the titles are synonymous) also plan corporate events. Those who do both are usually the most experienced in the business.

There are two organizations that these kinds of professionals belong to—the International Special Events Society and Meeting Planners International. Both have websites worth checking out. They are:

www.ises.com

www.mpiweb.org

**tip** When asking about a wedding consultant's fee structure, look for someone who charges by the hour or charges a flat fee. You do not want to hire a consultant whose fee is based upon a percentage of your total wedding budget. Why? When you think about it, this consultant would have an incentive to make your wedding cost as much as possible. The more your wedding total is, the higher her fee.

**tip** Want to feel confident that your wedding consultant or wedding planner really knows how to work with vendors? Ask about his or her four-year degree, and make sure that it's in hospitality management. (One of the best universities for this kind of degree is Cornell University.)

If the person doesn't have a four-year degree, look for a degree or certificate of completion in meeting planning, special events, or wedding management—and ideally, from an accredited institution.

# USE YOUR CONSULTANT WISELY

Throw away the notion that you can hire a wedding consultant for just the "day of." "No one can just show up on the day of the wedding, wave their hands like a conductor, and make everything happen," says Joyce Scardina Becker, owner of Events of Distinction in San Francisco.

If you need help on the day of your wedding, understand that you need to bring your consultant into the loop weeks beforehand. "In order to do what the bride thinks she needs done on the day of her wedding, you're really talking about a consultant working for her for at least 30 hours," says Scardina Becker. In this capacity the consultant can review contracts, introduce herself to vendors, and make sure that all the loose ends of your wedding fall into place on time. "What you're really hiring is a project manager—not a real warm and fuzzy term, I realize," adds Scardina Becker, but that's really what someone coming at the end of your wedding plans is—a project manager.

# Getting a Broad Overview of the Planning Process

When planning a wedding, you may be tempted to start your planning before you're ready. Don't. Believe it or not, there is a certain order to wedding planning that shouldn't be messed with, and it's the thinking behind the very order of this book. Appendix B, "Planning Charts and Aids," offers a simplified look at the entire wedding planning process and where each task falls within it. Here, though, we offer a brief overview of the major phases of the process. You learn more about each of these phases in the remaining chapters of this book.

The things you should do first come first in this book. Things that can wait for later appear later in this book. That's why in the first chapter I encouraged you to get your guest list done, and in the second chapter I suggest you work on setting a budget. Now, it's time for you to start putting your planning process in order, by considering the essential elements of your wedding. Once these essentials are out of the way, you can wrap up the loose ends, such as favors for your guests and gifts for your attendants. In later chapters of this book, you accomplish all of the tasks outlined in the following sections. But for now, you should just give some consideration to the planning process you'll be undertaking, so you have a clear idea of the path that lies ahead.

## Considering Locations and Vendors

After you have a sense of your budget, you'll know whether you can have a high-season wedding (when things cost more) or if you need to be more cost conscientious about when you time your wedding. However, the best way to approach your wedding plans is with a few dates in mind. That way you can compare availability of vendors and the prices they charge with the various dates you're considering and which make the most sense for your budget. Armed with this information, you can begin looking at ceremony and reception locations.

After that you can begin considering caterers and cake bakers (if they don't come hand in hand with the reception location). Next, you should find your photographer or entertainment depending on what's most important to you. That is, if you place a higher priority on great music at your ceremony and reception than the person who will be taking the pictures, you want to book your musicians next. However, if you want to make sure that you get the best photographer possible but couldn't care less about the music (heck, you're even considering bringing your CD player to the reception), book your photographer next. Before you hire any person or company for your wedding, you want to check on his or her background. Make sure that this person or business has a good reputation for treating its customers well.

The best way to do this is to call your Better Business Bureau, State Attorney General's Office, or your local Office of Consumer Protection. All three are where everyday people report business violations, such as a vendor who took a bride's money but then didn't show up at the wedding or a photographer who kept a couple's photographs hostage while he demanded more money than agreed upon for his services.

When checking on the reputation of vendors, you don't want them to show up in any of these databases. If there's no record of the vendors, they haven't treated anyone poorly enough to have a complaint filed against them, and that's a good thing. However, that doesn't mean that you're off the hook. You should always check references, even with a vendor with a squeaky-clean reputation.

**caution** Remember: before you sign on the dotted line of any vendor's contract, make sure you check him or her out first. You should only do business with someone you know has treated other customers well. And speaking of contracts, only work with a vendor who is willing to put his or her terms in writing. A written contract is always a must.

## Starting to Shop for a Gown

At about the same time that you're considering vendors beyond the caterer, you can start thinking about shopping for your gown. You really need to wait until you know your wedding date and time to buy your gown because you don't want to buy something that's inappropriate. The biggest mistake a bride could make would be to buy, say, a casual wedding dress and afterwards decide that she wants a fancy, black-tie, sit-down wedding reception. The two wouldn't go together.

## Thinking About Printed Materials

Hand in hand with setting your date, you can begin thinking about your save-the-date cards, invitations, place cards, and programs. Again, you won't know what kind of theme or message you want your printed materials to send until you know what kind of wedding you're having.

# PAYING VENDORS WITH CREDIT CARDS

You may think that the best way to pay for everything wedding-related is to do so with cash. That way, you won't have any debt hanging over your head after the festivities are over. There's one reason that you shouldn't use this logic for paying wedding vendors directly.

If you pay for services in cash and then something goes wrong you're out that money, and there's nothing you can do short of legal action to get it back. However, if you pay for everything with your credit card, you at least have the law on your side should something go wrong.

The law of which I speak is the Fair Credit Billing Act, which protects consumers against charges on a credit card "for goods and services [that] weren't delivered as agreed," according to the Federal Trade Commission (FTC) website at www.ftc.gov. (The FTC enforces the Fair Credit Billing Act.)

These goods or services might include the bridal salon that doesn't deliver your wedding gown by the date it promises or a stationer who messes up your invitation order—and doesn't do anything to fix it.

In addition to the law, if you want to dispute services or goods you paid for with your credit card, you have companies like American Express, MasterCard, Visa, and Discover to back you up. Most credit card companies offer these kinds of customer protections but check with your credit card issuer first before deciding which credit card to use when paying for your wedding-related goods and services. I would recommend going with the "plastic" that offers the most protection for your needs.

# Summary

We got down to some nitty-gritty stuff in this chapter—namely, talking about money: how much money you need for your wedding, how much you think you can save for it, how much your parents will contribute, if any, and how much you can cut your costs without sacrificing quality. I also brought up the idea of how much wedding budgets can vary from person to person, and region to region, and why hiring a wedding consultant or wedding planner might make the most sense for a busy bride.

In this chapter, we also talked about priorities and why you need to plan certain elements of your wedding in a certain order. In the next chapter—and the next part of the book—we will talk about wedding-planning nuts and bolts, starting with your ceremony.

To prepare for your ceremony plans, you'll need to settle any unresolved issues of religion you two may have, including where you'll have your wedding and who will marry you. We'll also broach the subject of destination weddings—do you want to go away somewhere to get married?—and what your wedding rings should look like. So let's move closer to your saying "I do."

# Part II

## Wedding Planning Nuts and Bolts

# Planning for "I Do" Expediently

**3**

I'm sure that once you started looking at how much weddings cost, you came to realize that the actual "I do" part of the wedding isn't where the big bucks are spent. It's usually in the celebration afterwards that you'll spend a large percentage of your money.

But even if the ceremony portion of your wedding doesn't have a big price tag, it remains the centerpiece of your wedding plans, because it is the moment when you become a married couple.

One of the first decisions you're going to have to make after figuring out your budget and choosing the right time, day, and month for your wedding, is deciding where you're going to get married. This is especially important if one of you has your heart set on getting married in a specific house of worship; churches and synagogues tend to book up relatively far in advance.

When planning your ceremony, the first thing you need to do is check with your preferred house of worship before booking anything else for your wedding. Not only do you want to make sure that it is available, but you will avoid any potential timing conflicts by booking your ceremony site before you book any other venues or vendors for your wedding.

In addition, you'll also need to make sure that you and your future spouse are eligible to be married in your house of worship. Some houses of worship have rules or policies that prohibit them from marrying two people of differing religions. If you fall into this category, you should be prepared for this possibility. If you're not eligible, you'll need to come up with a Plan B for where you're going to get married.

> **And the Bride Said...**
>
> "We fell in love with our reception site and couldn't imagine having our celebration anywhere else. So we booked it, even before we'd booked the church. Big mistake. Turns out that our church wasn't available on the same day as the reception site, and then we had to switch everything around to fit in the church. In retrospect we should have booked the church first."
>
> Karen, New Jersey

## To do list

- ☐ Talk about where you want to get married
- ☐ Decide whether you'll have a religious or secular ceremony
- ☐ Figure out how your religion will play into your ceremony, if at all
- ☐ Start checking out officiants and choose one to marry you
- ☐ Organize your ceremony from start to finish
- ☐ Shop for wedding rings

## Streamlined Solutions for Figuring Out the Perfect Ceremony Site

Before you can decide where you're going to get married, you need to talk about what each of you envisions for your wedding day. Has your deeply religious fiancé always dreamed of being married in his boyhood church? Do you have visions of walking down a flower-filled path to your outdoor ceremony in the local botanical garden?

If you have divergent ideas on where your ceremony is going to take place, you need to talk things out. You're going to have to figure out a way to compromise on your ceremony ideas or you have to come up with a totally new concept for your ceremony—one that you both can live with.

## Deciding on a Religious or Secular Ceremony and Site

One of the ways to speed up any potential conflicts on your ceremony and to make a first step in choosing a site is to break down your discussions into two possibilities—the religious ceremony and the secular ceremony. Then you can discuss the pros and cons of each. Ideally, after you've laid out reasons for and against each scenario, you'll have your perfect solution.

Here are some sample questions you can ask yourself and each other to get your dialog going:

- How do I feel about my religion?
- Do I want to be married in a ceremony that is reflective of my religious upbringing?
- How much does it matter to us to have a religious aspect to our wedding?
- What role will religion play in our married life?
- How will I feel after I'm married if I didn't include my religion in my wedding ceremony?

Here are some reasons why a religious ceremony might work for you:

- You are religious people who share the same faith
- You are both currently active in the house of worship where you want to have your wedding ceremony
- Your parents expect that you'll have a religious wedding—and doing so will make things easier all around, even if it really doesn't matter either way to the two of you
- It's important to you to have your religion be incorporated into your wedding

**note** You learn more about incorporating religious elements into your ceremony in "Blending Religious and Cultural Elements in Your Ceremony," later in this chapter.

A couple having a secular ceremony usually hires a justice of the peace or someone else who is qualified to marry people to perform their ceremony. Here are some reasons a secular ceremony might be right for the two of you:

- Neither of you is overtly religious or committed to your childhood faith
- You are of differing religions and can't be married in a house of worship due to certain restrictions
- You no longer live near the house of worship in which you were raised and were once active

○ • It's more important for you to find someone to pronounce you "husband and wife" than it is for you to have a religious aspect to your wedding

- You're planning to be married in a secular space (at your reception site, in a garden, on the beach, in your backyard, and so on) and having a religious figure present might not seem appropriate

## Inventive Ideas for Finding a Site

Figuring out where you're going to get married is a snap if you've got a connection to a house of worship. Whether the two of you are members of a church or synagogue or your parents are, usually it's a no-brainer to have the wedding take place where you have some affiliation.

But let's say that you don't belong to a house of worship but want to be married in one. You have a couple of options that will allow you to find the right religious setting for your ceremony, including:

- **Joining a new house of worship.** If the two of you are the same religion, you just have to find a house of worship to join. If you are of a different religion, you may find a house of worship that offers a happy medium between your two religions. Or if you are of differing religious backgrounds, you may decide to "join" a third party, neutral religion, such as the Unitarian Universalist church, which is welcoming of all faiths. Joining a new house of worship is also a great way to find an officiant for your wedding (the subject of the next section of this chapter).

- **Considering a college chapel.** Unless you go to the campus of a school affiliated with one religion, such as Notre Dame and Roman Catholicism, you're likely to find an ecumenical college chapel on campus. This is a house of worship that is welcoming to students and others of all religions. If you're planning on marrying someone of a different faith, a college chapel may be your best bet.

> **And the Bride Said...**
>
> "When you ask 175 people to get in their cars and drive somewhere, no one will be on time. So we decided to have our ceremony right at our reception location. That way no one would have to drive from the ceremony to the reception, and no one would get lost or delayed."
>
> Karsha, California

For many couples looking to have a non-religious wedding ceremony, sometimes the easiest thing to do is simply to hold their ceremony and reception in the same location. This saves on travel time and hassle for all of their guests, and it doesn't strap the couple down with any religious rules or regulations they might have to meet to use a certain officiant.

# GETTING IT IN WRITING

After you've settled on your ceremony site and your officiant, get everything in writing. The best way to make sure that everyone you hire shows up on time and that your wedding day remains your wedding date (instead of having it given away to someone else by mistake) is to draw up agreements. Make sure you get a signed agreement with both the house of worship (or wherever it is you've decided to have the ceremony) and the officiant. Here are the basics of the contract:

* Name, address, phone number, fax number, and email of person/place providing services

* Date of agreed-upon services

* Location of agreed-upon services (if different from address)

* Brief description of agreed-upon services (for example, if you were booking a ceremony site, you might write down the setup for the ceremony, the number of chairs they are to provide, what decorations will be on hand, and so on)

* Time frame, if any, for agreed-upon service, such as when the officiant should show up and when he or she is done

* Fee to be paid and, if necessary, schedule of payment (for example, one third of the fee up front, one third of the fee one week before the wedding, and one third of the fee on the day of the wedding)

* Attire, if applicable (basically, what kind of clothing you want the officiant or other service provider to wear)

* Cancellation agreement (figure out what kind of refund or other compensation you would want if the officiant, vendor, or venue cancels on you)

* Don't forget to date and sign the contract with both you and your fiancé's signatures along with the signature of the person you are hiring

## Considering a Destination Wedding

One of today's hottest trends is a destination wedding. Some people argue that every wedding these days is a destination wedding because, no matter what, people have to travel to a destination to attend someone's wedding.

However, in its truest sense of the word, a destination wedding is one where everyone goes away to either a resort, a hotel, or an inn for a weekend's worth of festivities, including the actual wedding ceremony. For couples that have not put down roots anywhere, including in a house of worship, a destination wedding can be a great idea.

Destination weddings can also be a fiscally sound wedding consideration because they usually end up costing less. Most couples planning a destination wedding in someplace like the Caribbean end up honey-mooning at the destination as well. So they've paid only one set of travel expenses to get to their wedding and honeymoon.

In addition, guest lists for destination weddings are usually a lot smaller than traditional wed-dings. Not everyone can afford to go away for three or four days for a destination wedding, so these kinds of celebrations end up being smaller overall. That means a smaller price tag for the newlywed couple picking up the tab.

*And the Bride Said...*

"We discovered it would cost the same to have a wedding with 200 people in Boston as it would to have a wedding in the Caribbean with 40-50, including paying for our guests' accommodations! We are putting all of our guests up for three nights at the resort where we will be married."

Colleen, Massachusetts

One of the most popular places to have a destina-tion wedding is in the Caribbean (see Figure 3.1). The Caribbean Tourism Organization (CTO), an organization devoted to developing tourism throughout the Caribbean, has created a website where interested couples can find out everything they need to know about tying the knot on one of the more than 30 island nations that the CTO represents.

**FIGURE 3.1**

One of the most pop-ular places to have a destination wedding is somewhere in the Caribbean, such as Jamaica, which is where this couple tied the knot.

www.renaissancejamaica.com

*Websites Worth Surfing*

Look under the "honeymoons and weddings" section on www.doitcaribbean.com, the CTO's website, for the wedding requirements lists, which includes any necessary waiting periods, how much a marriage license costs, and what documents you'll need to get married in one of these locations.

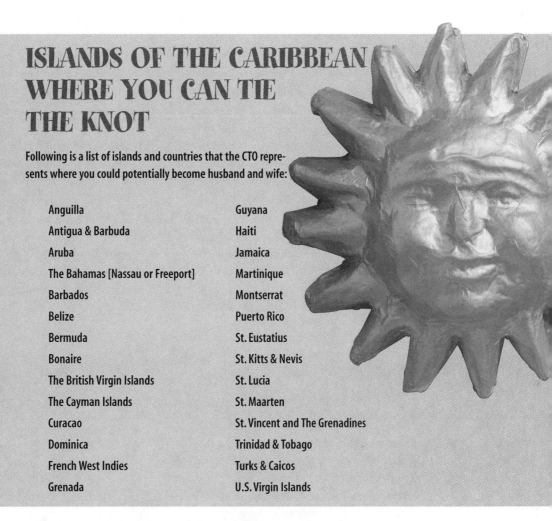

## ISLANDS OF THE CARIBBEAN WHERE YOU CAN TIE THE KNOT

Following is a list of islands and countries that the CTO represents where you could potentially become husband and wife:

| | |
|---|---|
| Anguilla | Guyana |
| Antigua & Barbuda | Haiti |
| Aruba | Jamaica |
| The Bahamas [Nassau or Freeport] | Martinique |
| Barbados | Montserrat |
| Belize | Puerto Rico |
| Bermuda | St. Eustatius |
| Bonaire | St. Kitts & Nevis |
| The British Virgin Islands | St. Lucia |
| The Cayman Islands | St. Maarten |
| Curacao | St. Vincent and The Grenadines |
| Dominica | Trinidad & Tobago |
| French West Indies | Turks & Caicos |
| Grenada | U.S. Virgin Islands |

# Choosing Your Officiant—Fast!

What's the fastest way to find an officiant for your wedding ceremony? Use the person affiliated with your house of worship. If you don't have a house of worship, here are some time-tested ways to find an officiant fast:

- **Join a house of worship.** We talked about this option earlier. If you're eventually going to be raising children in a certain religion, sooner or later you'll need to belong to a house of worship. If the timing and location of your wedding permit you to do so, join a local house of worship so not only will you have a place to get married but also someone to marry you.

- **Call your town office to see if the mayor or a local judge is available.** If you don't want someone religious to marry you, see if the town office can recommend a nondenominational officiant.

- **Use a college religious leader.** If you've decided to tie the knot at your alma mater, ask if the campus religious leader is available to marry to you.

- **Have a family friend do it.** A couple I know grew up next door to a family where the father and mother were both Episcopal priests. When she decided to get married, she asked if these lifelong friends and neighbors would officiate. Even though she was getting married outside of a church, they agreed. Might you have a family friend who can officiate at a wedding? Ask him or her to marry you.

- **Ask a nearby hotel or reception location to recommend someone.** Any commercial center that hosts weddings on a regular basis is bound to have a Rolodex filled with the names and phone numbers of officiants. If there's a facility nearby that has a good reputation, such as a hotel that consistently gets rave reviews or where you've had guests of your own stay, call and ask them for their recommendations.

# FINDING AN
# INTERFAITH OFFICIANT

If the two of you don't share the same religious background, the easiest thing for you to do might be to find an interfaith officiant. The following websites are good places to start to learn more about what constitutes an interfaith officiant—and an interfaith marriage—and to find an officiant who is right for you:

- ✳ www.dovetailinstitute.org
- ✳ www.interfaithfamily.com
- ✳ www.multifaithweddings.com
- ✳ www.rcrconline.org
- ✳ www.weddinggoddess.com

If you want to use a religious officiant and you still haven't located one, you're going to need to go on a fact-finding mission that takes you from house of worship to house of worship.

Dedicate one weekend to visiting as many houses of worship as you can find in your targeted wedding area. Of course, you should narrow down your list to only those denominations that fit with your background or current views on faith. And if you're going to stay for services, you may have to spread this task out over a couple of weekends so you won't have to rush from one church or synagogue to another.

If you're unsure of where the houses of worship are in your area, you may find the following websites worthwhile:

- www.worshiphere.org. The Worship Here website lets you search for houses of worship, in most denominations, via ZIP code.

- www.parishesonline.com.  Parishes Online is a compilation of Roman Catholic Churches across the United States. It also lets you search for parishes via ZIP code.

# Planning the Ceremony

Now that you've got your ceremony location and officiant booked, you can begin thinking about the elements of your ceremony. Although there are no hard and fast rules about how a wedding ceremony runs, there are some basics that you'll see in every wedding.

## Sample Ceremony

Here is a generic ceremony, from start to finish, that you can use when outlining your own ceremony:

1. **Processional.** This is when the bridal party enters the ceremony. Usually, the groom and his best man enter first. Then come the bridesmaids and the ushers. Next it's the flower girl, if there is one. Finally, the bride enters. One or both of her parents or a male relative can escort her, or she can walk in by herself.

2. **Introduction.** The officiant uses the introduction to welcome everyone to the couple's wedding and to talk a little bit about the couple.

3. **Readings, prayers, and songs.** If you would like to have any friends or family members participate in the wedding ceremony, this is where you would have them give a reading, say a prayer, or sing a song.

4. **Wedding statement.** The officiant uses this time in the ceremony to provide an overview of marriage, the commitment it involves, and any other historical or Biblical references to the sanctity of marriage.

5. **Vows introduction.** If the bride's father or the bride's parents are "giving her away," this is the part of the ceremony when the officiant will ask something like "Who gives this woman in marriage?" In some faiths or cultures, the officiant may insist that this question be first asked of the groom: "Who presents this man to be married to this woman?"

6. **Vows and ring exchange.** This is when the bride and the groom turn and face each other and exchange their vows, including placing their wedding rings on each other's fingers. You can write your own vows or you can use preprinted vows supplied by the officiant. You can memorize your vows or repeat them after the officiant; the choice is yours.

7. **Pronouncement.** After the vows and rings have been exchanged, the officiant may say a few words about the union your guests have just witnessed. Then he or she will pronounce you husband and wife.

8. **Special additions to ceremony.** This is where you can include any special elements that represent your heritage. It may be when a Jewish couple drinks from the same cup or has the groom smash the wine glass, or when a Christian couple lights the unity candle together.

9. **Presentation.** The officiant introduces the newly married couple to the guests in attendance.

10. **Recessional.** This is when all the participants in the wedding leave the ceremony, led by the bride and groom. It is also when guests may throw rose petals (see Figure 3.2) or birdseed, blow bubbles, ring bells, or do something else festive to hail the happy couple. (Of course, confirm with your ceremony site what types of confetti or other items are allowed to be thrown. Some facilities have restrictions on what you can and cannot use.) After the bride and groom leave the ceremony, the attendants follow, then the parents, and finally the guests.

Of course, you should work with your officiant when crafting your ceremony. He or she should have extensive experience in organizing a ceremony, and you should look to his or her expertise for ways to personalize your ceremony without making it run too long.

**tip** You can include readings from the Bible, you can ask friends or family members to sing a song (one bride had an uncle, a professional singer, serenade the happy couple with an a cappella version of "Just The Way You Look Tonight"), or you can have people recite some of your favorite poetry. The more elements you can add to a ceremony that reflect the two of you, such as a favorite song or Bible verse, the more personal your wedding ceremony becomes.

**FIGURE 3.2**
During the recessional your wedding guests may want to shower you and your new husband with good wishes by throwing something like rose petals.

www.annhamilton.com

## Blending Religious and Cultural Elements in Your Ceremony

According to statistics from various Jewish groups, nearly half of all Jewish people getting married are marrying someone who isn't Jewish. The Jewish faith isn't alone in this intermarrying trend. Plenty of Lutherans marry Catholics, Muslims marry Methodists, and so on and so forth.

Just because you're marrying someone who was raised in a different faith, it doesn't mean that you can't have some representation of your religion at your wedding (even if it's only a small one). The following sections describe some ways that you can blend your religious backgrounds into creative elements of your wedding ceremony.

### Using a Wedding Canopy

Traditionally,  Jewish couples are married under a wedding canopy or chuppah, which is a prayer shawl suspended between four poles. One person holds each pole so that the chuppah is suspended over the couple. The chuppah is supposed to represent the fragility of marriage in that, at any time, it could fall or collapse.

Hindu wedding ceremonies also include some kind of wedding canopy—usually constructed from wood instead of fabric. Here, the four poles of the wedding canopy represent the four parents who are giving away their children in marriage.

If only one of you is Jewish, you can still have the chuppah but you can make it uniquely your own by choosing a different fabric to suspend between the four poles. Instead of using a prayer shawl, you can use an antique tablecloth from one of your grandparents (it would qualify for the "old" or "borrowed" element of the "old, new, borrowed, and blue" idea that many brides weave into their ceremony). You could also choose to use a piece of tulle or fabric that matches the bride's gown (see Figure 3.3), or perhaps you'll invest in a handmade quilt for your wedding canopy, and you'll eventually use the quilt in the bedroom you'll share as husband and wife.

**FIGURE 3.3**

To add a unique element to your wedding canopy or chuppah, you can use fabric that matches your gown.

www.tanyatuckaphotography.com

Even non-Jewish couples could consider using a wedding canopy or something similar to it—especially if they like the idea of getting married underneath a symbolic house. I've seen variations on the chuppah theme in the form of a flower-filled trellis or an arbor.

## Using a Unity Candle

One of the most consistent symbols in a Christian wedding is that of the unity candle. The man and the woman each take a candle and light a third candle with each of their candles. This unified flame symbolizes the joining of two as one (see Figure 3.4).

**FIGURE 3.4**

The bride and groom each use a candle to light a third, known as the unity candle. This custom offers a superb symbol for the unity of marriage.

www.DanHarrisPhotoArt.com

Whether one of you is Christian or not, you may find the idea of combining two flames into one a wonderful addition to your wedding and decide to include the unity candle in your ceremony. Many couples include other members of their family in the unity candle lighting ceremony, such as each of the bride's and the groom's parents joining in on the lighting. Some couples that are bringing children to their marriage may also include the children in the candle lighting. However, ask your ceremony site first whether this would be acceptable; some states and/or facilities do not allow children to handle an open flame.

## Adopting a Ketubah or Marriage Contract

Another element of Jewish weddings is the Ketubah. It is a religious marriage license (as opposed to a state-issued one) for a Jewish couple. It is usually written in Hebrew.

With the increasing rate of interfaith marriages among Jews and non-Jews, a number of companies now offer various versions of a Ketubah—some in Hebrew, some in English. Usually, these marriage contracts become a decorative item that a couple will frame and hang in their home.

## Sharing a Glass of Wine

Both the Jewish and Christian faiths include the eating of bread and the drinking of wine in their religious ceremonies—think of the preparation of communion and the "kiddush" service traditionally held after a synagogue service.

Sometimes the notion of sharing a first glass of wine as husband and wife is a part of a religious ceremony. You can choose to make this symbolic act part of your ceremony, if you'd like. In many cultures mothers perform this ritual, immediately as the couple enters the wedding.

## Breaking the Wine Glass

Like the chuppah or wedding canopy, the tradition of breaking a wine glass at the end of a Jewish wedding is meant to symbolize how fragile love can be—and how with one good smash of the foot, it can be broken forever.

Some other people believe that couples break a wine glass at the end of a Jewish ceremony because they want to symbolize the permanence of getting married. That is, once you break a glass, it is forever altered—you cannot put it back together, piece by piece. The same could be said for getting married: Once you get married, you should look at it as a permanent act. Even couples with no connection to Judaism may like the symbolism behind this glass-breaking idea and choose to include the breaking of a wine glass in their ceremony.

## Decorating the Hands and Feet with Mehndi

Mehndi is the custom of decorating the bride's hands (see Figure 3.5) and feet with henna or a temporary tattoo in an ornate design. You'll find mehndi on traditional Muslim or Hindu brides. The Muslim culture regards this as a time for the bride-to-be to have two days of peaceful and quiet reflection and meditation, since once the henna is put on her hands and feet she does not leave the house again until her wedding day.

Celebrities like Madonna and No Doubt singer Gwen Stefani have shown up at special events with mehndi designs on their hands and feet, and like piercings, mehndi is seen as a form of body art. If you're marrying someone for whom mehndi is a wedding ritual—or it's a part of your heritage—it would be a wonderful nod to that legacy to treat yourself to mehndi and to proudly wear it on your wedding day. Just be sure that your mehndi design is tastefully done and that it is not offensive to the culture.

**tip** If you decide to blend traditions from your religions into your ceremony, do your guests a favor and include something in your program about what you're doing and why. By explaining each of the traditions to them, you'll make them feel as if they are more active participants in your ceremony.

As a nod to either the bride or groom's Hindu or Muslim heritage, the bride may choose to have mehndi, or henna tattoos, applied to her hands and feet for her wedding.

www.DanHarrisPhotoArt.com

# A Well-Organized Approach to Wedding Rings

Are you ready to shop for your wedding rings, also known as bridal jewelry? You'll soon discover that your choices can be overwhelming. Walk into any jewelry store in a mall or downtown, and you'll likely find display case after display case of rings. After awhile they may all look alike or you might become so overpowered by the vast selection that you can't make any selections at all.

In order to find your wedding rings in no time, you have to do some homework beforehand. I recently spoke with Bruce Pucciarello, owner of Novell Design Studio, one of the country's premier jewelry manufacturers, about what you should keep in mind before, during, and after you shop for wedding rings. Here are some of his suggestions:

- Understand off the bat that you and your future spouse do not necessarily need to find matching rings (see Figure 3.6). "Typically what leads couples that were meant to be together to find one another is their different, yet complementary, qualities," says Pucciarello. You should apply the same thinking to your ring selection. Find a ring that you each like, not one that is identical to your mate's selection. "I find that the couple that gets matching rings means that one member has acquiesced, and that's not a good beginning to a marriage."

www.novelldesignstudio

- Think about your everyday jewelry choices and use them when choosing rings. Are you a fan of sterling silver and other white jewelry? Do you like to wear overstated earrings, necklaces, and rings? You should find a wedding band that matches your personality. What about your fiancé? Does he prefer simple jewelry or does he fancy more ornate items? Suggest he keep his established tastes and preferences in mind as you go shopping together.

- Decide ahead of time whether you want to look at white or yellow jewelry. That way, when you walk into the jewelry store, you'll know that if you're only interested in platinum rings, you don't even need to look at the display cases with yellow jewelry in them. That decision alone will probably cut out half of the rings on display, which will help make the process less overwhelming.

- Try to stay away from anything trendy, such as fancy gemstones or colored metals. They may go out of fashion before your first anniversary. Instead, look for more traditional rings that you believe you'll love and still feel comfortable wearing every day for the next 40 or 50 years.

- Go to a store that has treated others you know well. Pucciarello prefers independent jewelry stores where you're likely dealing with the store's owner or the jewelry designer (as opposed to some part-time employee), who is going to be more knowledgeable not only about rings but also in dealing with customers. "Some stores would much rather sell you a $20,000 piece than the $600 ring you've fallen in love with," he says. "If you don't like how someone is treating you in the store, leave. People shouldn't take a beating from the person who is making money from you."

- Don't put off buying your rings. With all of the decision-making you face as your wedding edges nearer, you're understandably going to be feeling a lot of pressure. It's better for you to make a decision about something that's life-long, like your wedding ring, before the stress of the wedding gets too intense. Also, you should budget about two months' time for your ring—it might not take you that long to find, order, and receive one but it allows for some wiggle room.

Want to get a quick leg up on whether you prefer a platinum or yellow gold wedding band? Use your computer to zip through the websites of trade associations that represent each of these precious metals, and check out ring examples on each.

Here are the two websites I recommend:

- www.preciousplatinum.com. This is the website of the Platinum Guild International, which is an organization of platinum manufacturers devoted to educating consumers on platinum jewelry.

- www.gold.org. The World Gold Council's website is chock full of information on gold manufacturing around the world. Go directly to the "jewelry" section to learn more about yellow and white gold rings.

# Summary

I hope this chapter was exciting for you to read through. We started to talk about some very real aspects of your wedding, including finding the perfect place for you to become husband and wife and the perfect person to marry you.

In today's busy world, not everyone has time to be a part of a religious community. If this describes the two of you, then you may have had to start all over again by finding a house of worship that you might consider joining and could possibly get married in. Hopefully, with the resources I've provided, doing so was a snap. If you aren't planning to incorporate religion into your ceremony and don't wish to have the ceremony in a religious site, this chapter also offered some inventive ideas for finding the right location for your secular ceremony. And you learned a bit about the advantages of planning a destination wedding, including some great ideas for Caribbean locales.

We also talked about choosing an officiant, whether you are looking for someone within your faith, an interfaith officiant, or a justice of the peace or other officiant not connected to any religious tradition.

Once we got the essentials of where you're going to have your wedding out of the way, we got down to the business of planning your actual ceremony. I provided a very basic structure for a wedding ceremony, which you and your officiant can build off of as you blueprint the ceremony. We also talked a bit about blending religious and cultural traditions into your ceremony. I hope you found my suggestions helpful.

And then we ended the chapter on a shiny note by discussing what you need to know when buying your wedding rings.

Next up in planning your wedding: How to deal with family issues that are bound to crop up as you delve deeper into planning your wedding, including how to cope with divorced parents at your wedding. I'll also help you work through choosing your attendants and start you thinking about how you'd like your attendants to be dressed at your wedding. So let's move on to the next task on your to-do list in Chapter 4, "Planning for Attendants and Family Participants."

# Planning for Attendants and Family Participants

**In this chapter:**

❋ Choose your attendants
❋ Assign jobs
❋ Pick your colors
❋ Dress your attendants
❋ Decide on parental involvement

One of the things that makes every wedding special is the people who will be involved in it. Besides the bride and the groom, there are attendants to consider such as ushers, bridesmaids, flower girl, ring bearer, and so on. What also makes a wedding special is how much each of your parents participates in the happy day.

In this chapter, we'll talk about choosing who will be involved in your wedding—and how much. We'll also touch upon the notion of parental involvement, and the special challenges that you face when your parents are divorced.

Finally, keep in mind the timing of choosing your attendants. It's a decision the two of you should make soon after booking your ceremony and reception.

# Choosing Your Attendants

## To do list

- ❑ Talk about which people you want to be involved in your wedding
- ❑ Discuss pros and cons of certain people being attendants
- ❑ Figure out how many attendants your ceremony location can accommodate
- ❑ Ask friends and family to participate in your wedding

If you're the kind of woman who has been involved in each of your friend's weddings, either as a maid of honor or a bridesmaid, you're probably thinking that it's time to repay the favor (or the honor, as the case may be) by asking them to be in your wedding. Similarly, if you and your fiancé have stood up for each of your siblings when they got married, you're probably thinking that they should stand up there for you—and chances are they very much want to.

But put those two groups together—friends whose weddings you've been in, and siblings who've involved you in their weddings—and you're talking about the potential for a lot of attendants. Do you want 10 attendants? Do you think life would be simpler if you just have 2? Can't decide? Here are some notions to consider as you choose who will be an attendant at your wedding.

## You'll need list

- ❑ Some idea of the physical dimensions of your wedding location
- ❑ Contact information for your location
- ❑ Pencil and paper

### Deciding How Many Attendants You'll Have

Before you can figure out exactly who will be an attendant in your wedding ceremony, you need to consider your ceremony space. If you're getting married in a tiny chapel with very little room on the altar, you'll probably have to ratchet down your expectations for an oversized wedding party. On the flip side, if you are being married in a large cathedral or outside in a botanical garden, where space is not at a premium, you'll probably face fewer space limitations on the number of people who can stand up with you at your wedding ceremony.

That's why in the flowchart in Appendix B, "Planning Charts and Aids," you'll see that I suggest you choose attendants around the same time that you settle on your ceremony site. You wouldn't want to get your heart set on certain people being in your wedding, only to discover after the fact that your ceremony space wouldn't work with a wedding party of that size. Remember it will be easier in the long run to wait a bit and then ask people to be in your wedding than to ask people on a whim and then have to dis-invite them from their attendant duties.

If you're unsure how your ceremony space can accommodate your wedding party, put in a call to that location and ask the following:

1. Do you put any limits on the number of people who can stand up at the front during a wedding ceremony?

2. If not, how many people can your church/synagogue or other space accommodate along with the bride, groom, and officiant?

3. If I have a large wedding party and there isn't room for everyone to stand up front with me, where would you have them stand or sit?

4. How have you accommodated weddings with large bridal parties in the past?

## What Attendants Actually Do

In years past brides spent a lot of time making sure that their bridesmaids "balanced" out the groomsmen and vice versa. Although it's still a nice idea to have an even amount of female and male attendants, it isn't a must. What's most important is for you and your fiancé to choose people to be in your wedding that you want near to you both, rather than thinking about symmetry or other less-important issues. I suggest that you keep the following attendant duties in mind as you two decide not only on whom to ask to be in your wedding but also how many people you both actually want or need:

- **Maid of honor.** The woman  (or man) you choose to be your maid (or attendant) of honor does more than just hold your bouquet during the ceremony. He or she is the person responsible for organizing and hosting your bridal shower, accompanying you as you shop for a wedding gown, and being your right-hand person on the big day who gets you a little something to eat, gives you the thumbs up on how you look, and pretty much provides overall support. If necessary, your maid of honor can act as a witness for your marriage license. Note: if your maid of honor is married, she should be called the matron of honor.

- **Bridesmaids.** There is no hard and fast rule that says you have to have a certain number of bridesmaids in your wedding party, if any. Some brides like to make sure that they have the same number as male attendants. Nonetheless, bridesmaids are there to help out with your wedding plans, however you or your maid of honor see fit. Yes, that sort of means that they become your gophers or personal assistants, so you're wise to choose only guys and gals who will be honored (instead of burdened) to do favors and errands for you. If you have a preteen or teenage sister or cousin you'd like to honor in your wedding, you can ask her to be a junior bridesmaid. Her only real responsibility will be to walk in the wedding procession and stand up with everyone at the altar.

- **Flower girl.** Legend has it that a bride should walk into her wedding on a carpet of flower petals as a sign of good luck. That's usually why brides choose to have a flower girl—not only for the flower petals she'll throw (or bubbles she'll blow, based on your preference), but children add a delightful charm to a wedding. (However, read the section "Children in the Wedding" later in this chapter to learn more about involving little tykes in your affair.)

- **Best man.** Like the maid of honor, the best man becomes the groom's right-hand man. He is responsible for keeping the bride's and the groom's rings safe during the ceremony (if there is no ring bearer), and, if he'd like, your fiancé can ask his best man to join him as he shops for formal wear. (He's also the person who usually returns any of the men's rented formal wear the day after the wedding.) It's also the best man's duty to plan and host a bachelor party. On the big day it's often the best man who is there, with a hanky in hand, to mop the nervous groom's brow or blot his tears of joy. He is usually the groom's witness when signing the marriage license, and he traditionally offers a toast of good wishes to the couple at the reception.

- **Groomsmen or ushers.** Just like with bridesmaids, your fiancé doesn't need to choose a specific number of men to stand up for him at his wedding. Because the groomsmen's or ushers' primary responsibility is to seat guests at the wedding, it's a great job to give to his outgoing friends or family members whom he'd like to involve in your wedding in some way.

- **Ring bearer.** All the ring bearer needs to do is carry the rings into the ceremony and, if he or she has a steady demeanor, hold them until they're needed during the vows portion.

**tip** Never been a bridal attendant? If you want to get a point of view from the other side of the wedding aisle, click BridesmaidAid.com for a funny yet informative look at what goes into being a maid of honor and a bridesmaid.

## A Quick Quiz on Choosing Attendants

Before you make any hasty decisions about
whom you're going to ask to be in your wedding,
take the following quiz. By answering these questions, you and your fiancé will each have an easier time figuring out the right people to involve
in your ceremony.

> **note** Remember, there are no right or wrong answers to this quiz, and although each of these questions is geared towards the bride-to-be, the questions are also perfectly applicable to your fiancé as well—especially if he's having a hard time picking his best man and/or ushers.

1.  Who are the most meaningful people to
    each of you? You can answer this question
    in two ways. You can think about the peo-
    ple you've known the longest (siblings, childhood friends, cousins) or you can
    think about the people who've helped you through an impressionable time of
    your life (death of a parent, graduate school, first job). After you've thought
    this through, start compiling a list of these folks' names and make notations
    after each, about how they qualify as "meaningful." Granted, each scenario
    gives a different definition of a meaningful person, and only you can deter-
    mine which of your friends, family members, or work colleagues will take
    precedence in your decision-making. However, sometimes seeing people's
    names on paper like this helps to clarify your feelings about them, more so
    than just thinking about them.

2.  How many siblings do you have? If you come from a family with lots of
    brothers and sisters, the size and the makeup of your family could be the
    answer to your attendants' dilemma in one fell swoop. If you've got enough
    brothers and sisters to make up a wedding party, the easiest thing might be
    to include your siblings as bridesmaids and ushers, and be done with it. On
    the other hand if you have a lot of siblings plus a lot of friends, and you
    don't want to have a huge wedding party, you could choose to have a best
    girlfriend be your maid of honor and then have your siblings stand up as
    bridesmaids and ushers. The latter scenario lets you spread the wedding
    wealth, if you will.

3.  Which of your friends' weddings have you been in lately? If you're the first of
    your girlfriends and sisters to get married, you won't have a long list of
    "reciprocal" attendants to consider. However, if you've been a maid of honor
    or bridesmaid in plenty of weddings, you might want to take that past
    involvement into consideration as you select your attendants. But "duty"
    shouldn't dictate your choices. It's your wedding, and it should be your spe-
    cial day—not the time when you worry about repaying social debts to your
    friends and family.

4. Are there any feuds or rivalries between the people you're considering including in your wedding party? The last thing a busy bride-to-be needs to be worrying about in the weeks and months before her wedding, and on the big day, too, is playing peacemaker between two attendants who do not get along. Granted, everyone involved is supposed to act like an adult. Unfortunately, that doesn't always happen, so you can do one of two things. One, you can ask whomever you would like to be in your wedding, and then pray that everyone gets along. Or, two, you can play things safe, choosing only those attendants that you know get along.

5. What is the financial status of your potential attendants? It isn't cheap being a bridesmaid or an usher, as I'm sure you or your fiancé can attest to, if you've been in a friend's or a family member's wedding. Choose attendants that you're certain will feel comfortable absorbing the costs of travel, clothing, and accessories, and the time lost in attending the showers, rehearsals, and ceremony. If your potential attendants are at a place in their lives where time and money are at a premium—your sister is in the throes of medical school, your best friend is just starting out after attending graduate school—you may want to ask that person upfront how she feels about being a part of the wedding. Tally up an estimated total cost of all the bridesmaid's expenses and then add 10 percent. Let them know the approximate cost and make it clear to them that if for any reason they could not accept, you would clearly understand and not be offended in any way. Then give her a deadline to accept or decline.

> **note** Of course, if you do decide to exclude any meaningful folk from their attendant duties, do them a favor and let them know ahead of time. You can call or send a handwritten note that says something like, "While I would really love to have you be a part of my wedding, I was limited in my choices by financial, social, and familial burdens. However, I hope that you will still celebrate with us by being a guest at our wedding."

6. What are the family plans of your possible attendants? I can't tell you how many brides I've met who speak, with good humor, about their bridesmaid who was nine months pregnant at the time of their wedding, or the bridesmaid who, halfway through the wedding plans, announced that she was pregnant, and every few months, she had to go for yet another fitting—or expansion—of her bridesmaid gown. Many of these bridesmaids took the entire experience in stride but some confided later that they wished they could have gracefully bowed out of their duties. So don't be shy about asking any of your potential attendants if a baby is on the horizon. Let them know that you're not trying to be nosy, just cautious—because you don't want to

put them through the discomfort of standing up as a bridesmaid when, on the day of your wedding, all they'll want to be doing is sitting down with their feet up.

7. Would you be willing to choose family over friends? If you're on the fence about choosing between friends or family members to be in your wedding, my gut tells me this: you'll always be safer choosing a family member to be in your wedding. Friends can come in and out of your life as time goes by, but family is there forever. So when it comes to the attendants in your wedding, you'll be safer going with family over friends.

**note** If, despite your careful planning, you find yourself with a pregnant attendant, don't worry: plenty of dress manufacturers these days understand that matrons of honor and bridesmaids can potentially be "with child."

Check out the websites below that have many maternity attendants' dresses to offer:

- David's Bridal (www.davidsbridal.com/bridesmaids_dresses_maternity.jsp)
- Jim Hjelm Occasions (www.jimhjelmoccasions.com)
- Nordstrom (www.nordstrom.com)

## Other Ways to Involve Special People in Your Wedding

Sometimes you just can't have everyone you want to be involved in your wedding actually stand up as an attendant. That doesn't mean you have to completely shun the special people in your life. There are plenty of non-attendant responsibilities that you can assign your friends and family so that they feel like they're a special part of your wedding as well. Here are some of those responsibilities:

- Overseeing the guest book
- Handing out programs at your wedding ceremony
- Doing a reading during the ceremony
- Singing or playing music at your ceremony
- Handing out flowers to grandparents as they arrive at the ceremony
- Acting as the liaison with the photographer and videographer, and your guests
- Distributing bubbles, birdseed, or whatever you've chosen to have your guests use to "shower" you with good wishes at your ceremony

## Children in the Wedding

Some of the sweetest pictures I've ever seen from weddings are those that include the adorable flower girl or the shy ring bearer. There's nothing like the presence of children to bring a down-to-earth quality to your wedding. In addition, there's nothing like children to add an element of unpredictability to your wedding.

In the middle of the procession, your flower girl may decide that she needs to go potty—and call out to her mother to let her know that she needs to go the bathroom *right now*. Or your ring bearer may decide that the walk down the aisle is too frightening for him to complete and so he goes into a crying fit or temper tantrum in the middle of the church. That's not to say that all children will behave badly at a wedding, but you should take the following childlike qualities, if you will, into consideration when weighing the pros and cons of having children participate in your wedding:

- **Personality type.** No matter how cute your wallflower niece is, she might be terrified by the sheer number of people staring at her as she walks down the aisle as the flower girl. That's why you should match the child's job, if any, with his or her personality type.

## AND THE BRIDE SAID...

"I asked my very outgoing 6-year-old niece to be my flower girl (well, actually bubble girl). She had no problem leading the procession of the wedding and stopping at each aisle to blow a stream of bubbles for the guests. On the other hand my more laid back 8-year-old niece did a fabulous job being out of the spotlight as the attendant who was responsible for holding the gown's train. She wasn't interested in being the center of attention, and I knew that. All she had to do was keep her eyes on my train—and not on the guest's faces, which would have surely unnerved her. I'm glad I was able to include both girls in the ceremony."

Carly, Pennsylvania

- **Age.** If you don't want to worry about multiple bathroom breaks for your flower girl or ring bearer, don't choose a child who has just finished potty training (anywhere between ages 2 1/2 and 4 1/2). If you don't want to worry about leaking diapers, avoid having a toddler be in your wedding. Basically, although very young children look adorable in pictures, in real life they can be a handful. If you're set on having children in your wedding, you may want to choose older children who are less likely to be cranky, because they didn't nap, or don't need potty breaks every 15 minutes.

# Choosing Your Wedding Colors

For many brides the color or theme they choose to represent their wedding becomes the be all, end all, for everything from flowers to invitations to bridesmaids dresses. For other brides, colors aren't a big deal and don't dictate every decision. Regardless of where you stand on your color choices, having a hue in mind is helpful when thinking about things like table linens and what color outfit your attendants will wear. So how important are colors to you? Do you consult an interior designer or all the latest home fashion magazines before deciding which color to paint your living room? If so, then you're probably going to want to settle on a wedding color quickly and let it guide you in all your wedding selections. For our purposes now, you'll need to have a color in mind when thinking about how you want to dress your attendants.

If color isn't that important, you should still have a palette in mind when choosing items for your wedding. For example, by now you've chosen the place where you're going to get married, and the date when you'll become husband and wife. The time and place of your wedding can be very powerful parts of your color decisions, and you should use both elements when looking at attendants' attire.

What should you keep in mind when considering colors?

- **Time of year.** Love hunter green but you're getting married in June? You might want to go with a more appropriate summer shade that's still in the green family, such as mint green or celadon. Think baby pink is the bomb but you're tying the knot in December? Your best bet is to go with a more vibrant version of pink that is more reflective of the season. Why not consider fuchsia?

- **Setting.** Make sure that the colors you choose represent where it is you're getting married or having your reception. For example, a wedding ceremony held outside in the middle of fall is going to command colors that are very different from a Saturday night summer affair held in a high-end hotel. (The former wedding would be looking at foliage-like hues of red, yellows, golds, and oranges whereas the latter wedding would likely go with more classic, sedate colors, such as black and white,  white and red, or white and gold.)

- **Colors you favor in everyday life.** Not having your wedding at a time when colors are obvious, such as fall or Christmas? Then I suggest you think about what some of your favorite colors are. If you still can't decide, look to your wardrobe, your home, and your decor, and see which palettes you tend to favor again and again. For example, if you were to come to my house and look at my walls, my furniture, or the clothes in my closet, you would see that I'm a big fan of blue and green. My dining room is a federal blue while my bedroom is a sage green. One of my favorite shirts is baby blue whereas the jewelry I tend to wear the most has a sort of blue-green hue to it. With these color-choice patterns in mind, you would have an easy time figuring out that my wedding color was either blue or green, and you would be right—it was forest green.

- **Shades that flatter most skin types.** Although you may be thinking about your colors in terms of table linens, flowers, and invitations, there is an even more important consideration when it comes to wedding colors: how good your favorite shade is going to look on your bridesmaids. I definitely want you to pick a color that you like for your wedding, but please do your attendants a favor and don't choose an unflattering color. What are some unflattering colors? Yellow comes to mind because it tends to make most people look jaundiced. Other colors don't look great based on a person's ethnicity—green may make an olive-skinned person look even greener, or red will clash with a ruddy complexion. Rather, go for shades that tend to flatter everyone, and if you're not sure what those are, just watch the news for a couple of days and notice what color clothing broadcasters tend to wear—and which tends to look great on them. My guess is you're going to see a lot of blue and pink—all great colors to fall back on for bridesmaids. Also, when in doubt, you can go with black—seemingly every girl's favorite (and flattering) shade.

# Dressing Your Attendants in a Flash

## To do list

- ❑ Choose wedding attire for your attendants
- ❑ Tell your attendants about your choices
- ❑ Purchase or make arrangements for buying clothing and accessories

After you've decided whom you want to be involved in your wedding, you're going to have to address the issue of what they're going to wear. This is a decision you should make soon after choosing your attendants. You want to give yourself plenty of time to consider your attendants' attire, especially given that it takes most retailers of bridesmaid dresses between six and eight weeks to get the dresses in the store.

Then you should budget a month or so for fittings. In fact, you should budget at least four to five months to find, order, and receive your maid of honor's and bridesmaids' dresses. Suggest that your fiancé follow the same timeline for ordering formal wear for his attendants. While plenty of manufacturers and retailers can deliver dresses and tuxes in six weeks or less—good to know if you're planning a last-minute wedding—you should allow yourself sufficient time to shop around.

> **tip** If you've decided to dress your attendants in matching outfits, make sure that you order them all at the same time and from the same store. Because dye lots on fabrics can vary over time, you'll have better luck with perfectly matching dresses if the same store puts in the order in one fell swoop.

# You'll need list

❑ A list of physical characteristics (size, skin/hair/eye color) of your bridal attendants

❑ A computer and Internet access

## Outfit Options

Today, you have multiple options for bridesmaid's outfits as well as usher attire. You can choose to dress your attendants in matching garments to keep with tradition or you can mix and match their outfits. Here are three attendant attire options, and their pros and cons:

- **Matching dresses.** Brides continue to love the idea of having their attendants wear matching versions of the same dress. Ever wonder why brides favor this option? Legend has it that, in ages past, brides dressed their maids in matching outfits—and in a dress similar to their own—for a simple reason: That way, should any evil spirits show up at the wedding ceremony to harm the bride, they wouldn't know which woman standing up front was the bride. Legends aside, there are pros and cons to having your attendants wear matching dresses. Matching dresses create a uniform appearance for your bridal party, which looks great in pictures. However, not every woman looks good in the same dress silhouette. If you have attendants of various sizes, I would recommend that you begin your search by having your larger attendants try on dresses first. Usually, a style that looks good on a bigger body will look just as good on a smaller body. Then you can order the dress accordingly. The following figures illustrate some of the options for these choices.

**FIGURE 4.1**
**FIGURE 4.1**

Choose a matching dress style that compliments attendants of all sizes.

www.alfredangelo.com

**FIGURE 4.2**

With two carefully placed spaghetti straps, you can find an age-appropriate and matching dress for your youngest attendant and your bridesmaids.

www.alfredangelo.com

- **Mix-and-match separates.** One of the hottest trends from formal-wear designers is the idea of mix-and-match separates for the bride's attendants. These separates could include sweater sets with skirts, shell tops with pants, blouses with skirts, or some other combination that results in a uniform look among your attendants. The pros of the mix-and-match look are the versatility it offers your attendants. The cons? Well, like some dresses, not every shirt or skirt flatters every figure. So if you're having bridesmaids of varying sizes, take that into consideration as you choose your separates for them to wear.

**FIGURE 4.3**

These mix-and-match separates are just slightly different in nature, but not so much so that they don't look great together.

www.davidsbridal.com

**FIGURE 4.4**

A crisp white blouse paired with a traditional skirt looks great for a more casual wedding.

www.alfredangelo.com

- **Complementing outfits.** For the bride who is looking to give her attendants a little bit of freedom with their outfits, complementing attire is the way to go. Here's how it works: the bride chooses a color and/or a fabric she favors and asks her attendants to keep the color/fabric in mind as they shop for an outfit. Or she selects a dress style that is available in a variety of colors, and asks her attendants to choose a color they like to wear. One bride I know did this and ended up with bridesmaids wearing the same dress but one wore lavender, another wore baby blue, and a third wore mint green. Together, they looked lovely. This option allows the attendants to find whatever kind of outfit or color that they feel comfortable in. Now that's a pro. The only con could be that you've chosen a color/fabric which isn't widely available, and that will make outfit shopping much more challenging for your attendants than if you'd told them the style number of a certain dress you want them to buy, and sent them off to the store. Or you've chosen a dress you like and left color choices up to your attendants. Then two women end up wanting to wear the same color and you need to figure out if that will work for your vision of your bridal party.

**FIGURE 4.5**
Dresses of varying lengths and color can complement each other nicely.

www.davidsbridal.com

**FIGURE 4.6**
The only parameter that this bride gave to her five attendants was that they should all dress in pink or coral. The fabric and style was up to them.

Courtesy of Beckie Thompson

# HOW TIME OF DAY MAY AFFECT HOW YOU DRESS YOUR ATTENDANTS

One of the reasons that I insisted that you set the time and day of your wedding before making any other decisions is because the time of day that you have your wedding can affect every choice you make, including how you dress your attendants, both female and male. Following are some rough guidelines, based on the time of day you say "I Do," for the kinds of clothing you and your fiancé should be looking at for the bridesmaids and groomsmen. Keep in mind that while these guidelines have tradition in mind, many of the rules of wedding etiquette have relaxed, now that we're in the twenty-first century. So use this information as a rule of thumb. In the end I would recommend that you make clothing decisions based on your preferences and personality.

❋ **Daytime wedding.** For a formal or semiformal affair held during daytime hours, your attendants should wear a floor-length dress or skirt. Your groomsmen or ushers would likely wear one of these jacket options—a stroller jacket or a tuxedo with vests that match or complement the bridesmaids' dresses. For an informal wedding during the day, you'll have more flexibility in dressing both your women and men. For your female attendants you can choose strappy, cocktail length dresses, and you can dress your groomsmen in light- or dark-colored suits (depending on the season). I've even seen some couples have fun with their informal daytime wedding by having their men wear blue blazers and Bermuda shorts!

❋ **Evening wedding.** For starters an evening wedding is considered to be one where the ceremony begins after 6:00 p.m., regardless of the time of year. Lucky for you there isn't much of a difference in how you dress your maid of honor and bridesmaids for a formal or semiformal evening affair. You'll still want to stick with floor-length gowns, dresses, or skirts. Now as far as the groomsmen go, it's tuxedoes all the time for both a formal and semiformal evening wedding. For an informal evening event, your female attendants should still stick with more formal-looking dresses and men will do just fine in dark suits.

**note** Don't know your tuxedo from your stroller jacket? Log onto the website of a men's formal-wear shop, like After Hours (www.afterhours.com). You can scroll through page after page of men's clothing and get a better sense of styles the two of your prefer.

Websites Worth Surfing

## Researching Bridesmaid Attire

Before you hit any stores to find your attendants' garb, do your homework first on the Web. Log on to the Internet and do a search for bridesmaid attire. Know some designers that you like? Add their names into the search and see if they have anything in their collection that tickles your fancy. Keep in mind that many dress designers include their website address in their advertisements. As you look through bridal magazines and find dresses that you like, make a note of the URL, compile all of those addresses in one place, and devote one lunch hour to previewing dresses for your attendants.

## Where to Shop

Not only do you have numerous options for dressing your attendants, but also you can choose from a variety of sources for purchasing the outfits. Here are some bridesmaid attire shopping options to consider:

- **Bridal salon**—Nearly every shop that sells wedding gowns sells clothing for your maids. One of the benefits of buying your gown and attendant attire in the same location is you can often negotiate a discount when you purchase everything together.

- **Formal-wear shop**—The store that all of the teenagers go to for their prom gear may also be a great place for you to look for fabulous frocks for your bridesmaids. Unfortunately, if you're looking for a dress during prom season, you may find the store to be overrun by giggling young girls.

- **Department store**—Although many department stores have gotten out of the bridal gown business, they've continued to keep their evening wear departments alive and well. That's where I would suggest you head when scoping out your attendants' outfits.

- **Catalogs**—There are plenty of mail-order businesses that may not sell bridesmaid dresses, per se, but you'll find that their dress selections are comparable to what you would find at a specialty store. If you're looking to dress your maids in a more casual way, such as in matching sundresses, and you've got attendants living all over the country, a catalog may be the most convenient way to go.

- **Internet seller**—An e-tailer will offer you many of the same benefits as a catalog, and in fact, you'll find many of today's catalogs online. One of the benefits of shopping via the Internet is you can actually email links from various dress websites to your bridal attendants so they can check out selections, even if they don't live close by.

Want to get a desktop preview of your bridesmaid dress options? Click on the websites of these dress manufacturers and national retailers for a quick tour of gowns and separates you may want to dress your attendants in:

> www.alfredangelobridal.com
>
> www.davidsbridal.com
>
> www.jcpenney.com
>
> www.jcrew.com
>
> www.karenwarrenclothing.com
>
> www.nordstrom.com

- **Retailer**—Many chain stores carry dresses that would easily work in a less-formal wedding setting. For example, on recent visits to The Gap, Banana Republic, Chico's, Laura Ashley, Ann Taylor, and Talbot's, I saw plenty of dresses, plus twin sets and skirts, that a bridesmaid could have worn to a wedding and no one would have been the wiser. Best of all, many of these retailers have kids' sections attached or kids' stores affiliated with them, so you might even find clothing for your youngest attendants here, too.

- **Sample sale/trunk show**—If you live in or near a city where designers hold sample sales or trunk shows, you may have great luck finding inexpensive dresses for your attendants. Keep in mind that when it comes to sample sales, you won't often find large quantities of garments (because these are, in fact, the samples that the designers originally used to interest stores in their wares). So if you're having a large bridal party, this option may not be for you. However, a bride who will only have one or two attendants might just strike fashion gold at a sample sale or trunk show.

**tip** Bridesmaids on a budget? You may want to look into visiting consignment or resale shops to see if they have any frocks in stock that would work well for your wedding. Also, there are a number of online versions of the neighborhood consignment shop, including Glamour Closet (www.glamourcloset.com). A former multiple bridesmaid started this business as a way to get some good use (and some money) out of all the bridesmaid dresses that were cluttering her closet. You may also want to check online auction site eBay for bridesmaid dresses or even free site craigslist.com for dress options.

# AND THE BRIDE SAID...

"My bridesmaids have very unique personalities, along with very different body types. I really wanted them to feel beautiful that day, and to look as unique as they all are. I also wanted my wedding to be colorful and something people would remember. So I decided to allow them all to choose their own dress for the wedding. Picking out the dresses together was such a fun experience, and the girls were thrilled to have a choice in what they wore. In addition to the dresses being unique, I spent months selecting just the right necklaces for each girl, which were their gifts for standing up with me. My dress shop was so helpful and encouraged me throughout the process of selecting different gowns. Every other bridal salon strongly discouraged me from executing idea, but I knew it would work. When it all came together, I just cried when I saw my attendants. Many people at the wedding told me that it was like being at a runway show, and that they couldn't wait to see the next dress!"

Beckie, Michigan

## Choosing Footwear and Accessories

As someone with hard-to-fit feet, it has always been painful to have footwear dictated to me by a person who doesn't understand the special challenges I face each time I go out to buy shoes. Your attendants could be the same way—one could have wide feet, another could have super narrow feet, another could have really big feet and another may have extremely tiny feet.

Just as today's bride has the option not to dress her bridesmaids in identical dresses, so it goes with footwear. Although dyeable shoes are great for matching garb, they're not a must. If you're looking to save time and make the lives of your attendants easier, let them have some leeway with their shoes. Give them a sense of what you're looking for, such as color or style, but then let them buy affordable, comfortable shoes that they like.

**FIGURE 4.7**

If you really want to do your attendants a favor, let them buy shoes that they'll truly wear again, like these strappy sandals from Payless Shoe Source.

www.payless.com

If you're having a super-formal wedding where everything's got to match, you should probably look into dyeable shoes so you'll have uniformity right down to your attendants' feet. Your attendants will like knowing that in today's fashion-forward wedding world, dyeable shoes aren't just boring pumps anymore. Stores like Payless stock dyeable shoes in either satin or crepe in a number of different styles—including open-toe slings, platform shoes, and strappy sandals. Best of all they're affordable (less then $40) and Payless can dye your shoes in 1 of 64 shades and get them back to you in only 10 days.

Now as far as bridal accessories go, I would suggest that you try to buy your headpiece and any jewelry that you or your attendants are going to wear at the same store where you order your dresses. You'll do a better job of matching everything or making sure that your headpiece, handbag, and necklace looks good with your gown if you can try them on altogether. True, you may pay a bit more for these items at a bridal salon, but you'll save time and have peace of mind by taking care of your clothing and your accessories in one stop.

Many brides like to give their attendants the gift of jewelry—specifically, jewelry that she wants them to wear at the wedding—so watch closely and see which necklaces and earrings your attendants seem to favor. Then, either when they're not looking or on another day, buy those sets for them. The best time to give them those gifts is at your rehearsal dinner.

**tip** One of the best gifts you can give your attendants is the gift of their attire. If you've asked them to be a part of your wedding, you can pick up the tab for their outfit. It's a generous thing to do, but also a logical choice, given that you've asked them to wear this specific outfit for your wedding. Also, if for some reason your bridesmaids don't like the dress or shoes you've chosen, you won't add insult to injury by asking them to pay for them.

## Keeping Track of Your Attendant Shopping

With all that's on your to-do list, you'll want to make it as easy as possible to keep track of all the clothing and accessories you need to look at, consider, and arrange to have your attendants buy for your wedding. To that end I've created this handy chart that will help you keep everything in order, from start to finish.

## Details on Attendants' Attire and Accessories

| Attire | Style Number/ Designer | Store Info | Price | Payment Details | Order Date | Pick-Up Date | Notes |
|---|---|---|---|---|---|---|---|
| Dress | | | | | | | |
| Accessories | | | | | | | |
| Shoes | | | | | | | |
| Notes | | | | | | | |

# Getting Your Parents Involved

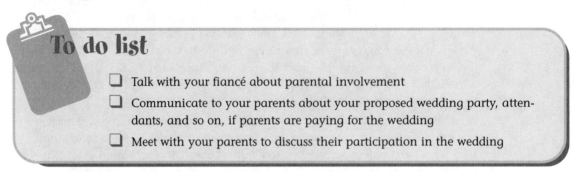

## To do list

- ☐ Talk with your fiancé about parental involvement
- ☐ Communicate to your parents about your proposed wedding party, attendants, and so on, if parents are paying for the wedding
- ☐ Meet with your parents to discuss their participation in the wedding

Your parents may have set ideas on how they will be involved in your wedding ceremony and which members of your family they expect you to include in the wedding party. Chances are you may not see eye to eye with your parents, and so you're going to need to talk things out about how you (not they) see your wedding party taking shape.

## Talking with Your Parents About Plans

I suggest that you book a weekend day with each of your parents to have the "talk" about what role they'll play in your wedding and who you're planning on inviting to be in your wedding party. To avoid conflicts you're going to need to talk everything out with your parents. Even if you have set ideas of what you want with your bridal party, give your parents the courtesy of at least hearing them out on their ideas and preferences, if they have any.

Make the time to sit down over a weekend meal, or talk on the phone if you live far away, to discuss attendants and such. You'll want to make sure that you're all on the same page with these issues, and being upfront and honest is the best way to accomplish this task, and to avoid any family feuds down the road.

Just as I've said that talking about money can be a delicate affair, the same can be true when discussing parental involvement in your wedding. That's why I want to offer this piece of advice: Before you sit down to talk with both of your sets of parents about money issues related to the wedding, decide ahead of time what elements of your wedding are important to you both (and are non-negotiable), what elements you'd be willing to be flexible on, and what elements you couldn't care less about—and are willing to fork over total control to your respective parents, if need be. The reason I want you to choose your battles ahead of time is it will help you avoid having a battle over every little detail of your wedding, especially if your parents are picking up the tab.

## Dealing with Divorced Parents

Although later chapters deal with the specifics of how to word an invitation or arrange seating when one or both of you has divorced parents, what I want to discuss now is the importance of talking with your divorced parents about your wedding plans. You need to let them know, right away, that you will do everything in your power to avoid creating any situation in which they will be uncomfortable; of course you won't try to force them to sit or dance together if they choose not to. I'll repeat that—let them know ahead of time that it is not your mission to make your wedding an uncomfortable situation for them.

That said, you also need to state that although you will do your best not to put them in an awkward situation, sometimes things happen and people who are no longer married may find themselves standing next to each other or somehow in close proximity at a wedding. If your divorced parents have an amicable relationship, this won't be a problem. Otherwise, you need to let them know that you expect them to behave like adults and not to make a scene at your wedding. If one of your parents doesn't think he or she can act accordingly, you're going to have to ask that parent to stay home.

I know that's a tough thing to say but you must say it. Unless you want squabbles sucking up all your planning time, you're going to have to take a stand and let your parents know that you're the focus of your wedding day, not them.

If you both have divorced parents and are wondering how you can fit four sets of parents into roles usually played by two, here are some suggestions:

- Have the parents that raised you walk you down the aisle. That is, if your mom and dad split long ago and you spent your formative years living with your mom and stepfather, then I think you would do right to honor them both by having one or both of them escort you to the altar.

- See if your divorced parents would be willing to put aside their differences and both walk you down the aisle.

- If you are close to both sets of parents, you may have your mother and stepfather walk you partway down the aisle, then have your father and stepmother walk you the rest of the way.

- When it comes to honoring one of your divorced parents, you may choose to have your mother stand up as your matron of honor and his father as the best man.

- For first dances, you can dance with your father and then your stepfather, or you can forego first dances altogether to avoid any awkward moments.

# Summary

If you're anything like me, you grew up thinking that your best friend from childhood would be your maid of honor and you hers. That would make everything so simple when it came time to plan your wedding. But then life got in the way, perhaps you grew apart, you developed new friendships, and now you may find yourself on the fence about whom to include in your wedding.

This chapter presented you with suggestions that you can use to help look at the special people in your life and to see which of them are the right ones to include in your wedding. Unless you're looking to have the world's largest wedding party, you're going to have friends or family members that you had wanted to include in your wedding party but just couldn't. That's why I gave you ideas on how to involve special people in your wedding in roles other than those of the attendants.

I also suggested you consider some issues involving the use of children in your wedding—are you prepared for potty breaks during your processional?—and the role family can play in your wedding party.

Speaking of your wedding party, as a modern bride you have tons of options on how to dress your maid of honor and bridesmaids. I talked about mix and match separates, complementary outfits, and even the notion of letting your maids choose their own footwear. Only you will know which clothing options will work for your wedding but I hope that the suggestions I've offered help you to make decisions without too much stress and concern.

Finally, I talked a bit about your parents and how to discuss your proposed wedding party members and plans with them. In addition, I provided some ways to deal with divorced parents.

In Chapter 5, "The Words, Music, and Flowers That Bring Your Ceremony to Life," we're going to start talking about the various elements that are going to liven up your wedding—choosing invitations, flowers, and music. In addition, this chapter will give you valuable pointers and tips for hiring the people who will capture your wedding forever—the photographer and the videographer.

# The Words, Music, and Flowers That Bring Your Ceremony to Life

**5**

One of the tasks on your to-do list from the last chapter was choosing your wedding colors. I'm sure that you used that information when thinking about what outfits you wanted your maids to wear at your wedding. Now you'll put your color choices to good use as you start to think about other elements of your wedding where color plays a big role—namely the flowers and your invitations.

We're going to cover a lot of ground in this chapter. In addition to flowers and invitations, we're going to discuss writing your vows, organizing your wedding program, and figuring out what kind of music you'll play at your ceremony. Also, you'll learn about choosing a photographer and videographer who will do a fabulous job capturing all of the images of your special day. Oh, and this chapter also explains how to arrange for the most important aspect of your big day—getting you to the chapel on time. So you don't end up driving yourself (or driving yourself crazy), we'll talk about nifty wedding-day transportation options, ranging from classic cars to trolleys.

# Invitations in a Jiffy

## To do list

- ❑ Choose invitations appropriate for your ceremony
- ❑ Select paper color, ink color, and font
- ❑ Word the invitation message
- ❑ Buy postage stamps

If you think about it, a wedding invitation serves a very simple purpose—to invite people to a wedding. However, brides-to-be often spend an awful lot of time fretting over what their invitation should say, what paper it should be printed on, or what color ink they should use. There's no need to worry about the minutiae. If you approach your invitations systematically, you'll have them chosen, written, and sent in a jiffy.

**caution** Remember when ordering invitations that you don't need as many invitations as people on your guest list. You may be inviting four people from the same family who live at the same address. That means that you can send them one invitation for the entire household. If you don't keep this information in mind, you'll end up over-ordering invitations.

## You'll need list

- ❑ Number of households you're inviting
- ❑ Color swatch to match invitations

## The Elements of an Invitation

Regardless of what your invitation ends up looking like, there are some common elements to a wedding invitation that you'll need to keep in mind. Each element imparts different yet critical information about your wedding to your guests, and those elements include the following:

- **Ceremony invitation.** This provides the particulars of the wedding ceremony—who is getting married, when they're getting married, and where they're getting married.

- **Reception card.** This tells your guests where and when the wedding celebration will occur. For a reception that immediately follows the ceremony and is being held in the same location as the ceremony, many couples choose to add "Reception to follow" at the bottom of the invitation and don't need to enclose a separate reception card. However, if you're having your reception at a different location, you should include a reception card that tells where and when your reception will occur.

- **Response card.** This is how your guests will RSVP to your wedding. The response card should include a line for the guest to write in his or her name so you'll know from which guest you're getting an RSVP. You should also have a place for the guest to check "Will attend" or "Will not attend," and definitely include an RSVP-by date so you receive responses in a timely manner. If you're taking RSVPs by email, which many of today's couples do, you can include the RSVP-to email address on the response card as well.

- **Response card envelope.** You should pre-address this envelope to your home address or your parents' home—whichever address will serve as your wedding-planning headquarters. It should also arrive with sufficient postage on it so your guests can't use the excuse "I couldn't find a stamp" as to why they didn't RSVP to your wedding on time or at all.

- **Directions.** A map or driving directions will tell your guests how to get to the ceremony and, if the reception is being held in a different location, how to get to the reception as well. It's perfectly acceptable to use a computer-generated map, such as the ones you would find on Switchboard.com or MapQuest, but do your guests a favor by double-checking the map before you include it in your invitation. Internet map services don't always include the most direct or efficient way to get from point A to point B. Make sure that you're not sending your guests on a wild-goose chase.

- **Inner envelope.** This holds all the elements of your invitation together. It is also where you write the names of the people you're specifically inviting to your wedding—which may not be the same names as those that appear on the outer envelope, which is the envelope you use to mail the invitation set. Let me explain.

  If you were inviting your cousins Jane and John Smith to your wedding, and you were also inviting their children Joshua, Jake, and Jennifer, you wouldn't address the outer envelope with all of those names. That would be too cumbersome. Instead, the outer envelope should say something like "Jane and John Smith" or "Mr. and Mrs. John Smith" and then their address. However, on the inner envelope, you would write "Jane, John, Joshua, Jake, and Jennifer Smith." This lets the Smith family know that all five of them are invited to your wedding. On the other hand, if your inner envelope said "Jane and John Smith" only, your cousins Jane and John would know (or should know) that only the two adults are invited to your wedding and that they should schedule a babysitter for the time and day of your wedding because the kids aren't invited.

- **Outer envelope.** This is the envelope in which the actual invitation set is mailed. It's where you'll write the person's name and mailing address and on which you'll put your postage stamp.

# SAVE-THE-DATE CARDS

Everybody today is busy, so make sure that you give your guests plenty of advance warning about your upcoming wedding. That doesn't mean that you should send your invitations out super early, though. Rather, as soon as you set your wedding date, you should create and mail out Save-the-Date cards. These are exactly what they sound like—a card that asks your wedding guests to save the date of your wedding so that when your invitations arrive later on—usually six to eight weeks before your event—it won't come as a surprise. RSVPs are not necessary with Save-the-Date cards. They simply act as a heads up for your guests.

Save-the-Date cards are traditionally less formal than invitations, so go ahead and save yourself time and money by making them yourself, if you're tech savvy. You can buy paper stock at your local Staples or office supply store and create them on your computer. You can even send them as postcards, if you'd like. Or if you'd rather leave the printing to someone else, visit your local Kinko's or Sir Speedy shop, or a similar online operation, and have the store whip up simple Save-the-Date cards that you can get into the mail right away, so your guests can mark their calendars accordingly.

## Choosing the Colors, Paper Stock, and Ink

You've already chosen your wedding colors, so now when it comes to your invitations, you should have an easier time making decisions. By keeping your wedding colors in mind, you'll automatically limit your choices and save time as you search for invitations.

How much or how little of your wedding colors you use in your invitations is entirely up to you. You can do something as simple as using a sheer invitation overlay, such as a piece of vellum, in your wedding color, whereas the rest of your invitation is a neutral color. Or you can design your entire invitation, from paper stock to borders to ink colors, around your wedding colors.

## Choosing the Right Invitation

Keep in mind that your invitation is supposed to communicate subtly to your guests what kind of an event you're having. An invitation for a Friday night wedding, on white paper with black ink, would tell an invited guest that it's going to be a pretty formal affair.

Two related elements that dictate what kind of wedding invitation you'll choose are the time of day and the setting of your wedding ceremony. A daytime garden wedding needs a different invitation than a Saturday night black-tie affair or a barefoot, beachfront wedding in a tropical setting. After you consider time of day and setting, you can automatically overrule invitation options that just don't fit that scenario.

Okay, so what kind of invitations work best for different kinds of weddings? Here are some suggestions:

- **Black tie/evening.** Most weddings held after dusk have a formal aspect to them, especially if they're on Saturday night—the most popular time of the week for a wedding. So how do you communicate a black-tie event in your invitation? Well, first, you can include "black tie preferred" on the bottom of your invitation, so your guests aren't confused about the event's dress code. Second, you can send out an invitation that reflects the formal nature of your event. That would be an invitation printed on white or ecru paper with either black or a metallic type.

- **Weekend-day wedding.** A daytime wedding is almost always less formal than a nighttime one. For example, proper etiquette says that a man should never wear a black tuxedo to a daytime wedding—even a formal one. The only exception would be a Roman Catholic ceremony with a full mass. These are usually held during the daytime and are considered to be a formal ceremony. If this describes your wedding ceremony, you should use the guidelines for a black-tie affair. So if you're having a weekend daytime wedding, your invitations should look less formal too. That's not to say that you can't choose white or ecru paper if you'd like—just go with a less formal ink color, such as the color you've chosen for your wedding. If you've chosen black and white as your wedding colors, you could go with a red ink, which complements black and white nicely.

- **Casual.** An afternoon wedding in a garden or a beachfront wedding done in bare feet begs for an invitation that reflects the more casual nature of your event. I would suggest going with a paper stock that perhaps is reminiscent of your setting—a flower-filled card for the garden wedding or a sandy-colored card stock with the shadow of a shell on it for your beachfront wedding— which will do a wonderful job of communicating the atmosphere of your upcoming nuptials to your invited guests.

Let me tell you how I planned my wedding invitations with my colors in mind. My husband and I chose forest green as our wedding color, and one of the reasons we made that choice was because of our wedding's setting—outdoors in my grandfather's backyard. To reflect the casual nature of this Sunday morning affair, we chose white invitations with a floral border. We had the invitation printed in green ink and enclosed them in an envelope with a green interior. The invitations ended up being so pretty that we had one framed as a decoration. More importantly, our invitations communicated with our guests that we were having a casual event. So when our guests showed up wearing sundresses with hats and Bermuda shorts with jackets, we knew our invitations had done their job communicating this information.

### Designing Ethnic and Religious Invitations

When it comes to your invitations, the one exception to the ink color or time of day rule is when you're having an ethnic or religious ceremony.

For example, a person of Asian descent may want to have the wedding invitations reflect his or her heritage with recognized symbols from his or her background. In addition, for many Asian countries, red is the color of good luck and weddings (not white), so it would be perfectly appropriate to use red paper or red ink on your invitations.

Your wedding colors shouldn't prevent you from including colors or symbols from your ethnic or religious background, if having them be present on your invitation is important to you and your family. Remember: this is your wedding and you should choose an invitation that you feel is fully reflective of the kind of wedding you're planning. And if your wedding will include elements of either of your ethnic or religious heritages, then by all means include relevant symbols or colors in your invitations as well.

## Choosing a Font

Fonts define the lettering style you use in your invitations—or any printed items, for that matter. Different fonts can communicate a different message, regardless of what the words say. Although there are thousands of fonts to choose from, each font falls into one of two categories—serif or sans serif.

**tip** When assembling your invitations, do not, I repeat, do not, include a cute little card that has information about your gift registry on it. A wedding invitation is not the place to communicate this information. However, you can include somewhere in your invitation information about your wedding website, if you have one. And if you do have a wedding website, it's perfectly acceptable to have a link on your wedding website to more information on your gift registries, including the stores where you've registered your preferences. Sites like weddingchannel.com and theknot.com can help you get a wedding website up and running in a snap or at least be a uniform place where your guests can go to get details of your wedding, including where you've registered.

Serif fonts are those that have curly-qs or wavy elements to them. Sans serif (literally without decoration) are more straight, up and down fonts that don't have any little tails or waves on letters like "y" or "f."

When you look at traditional wedding invitations, you'll notice that they're often printed with a serif font that almost looks like script. A more contemporary wedding invitation might have a sans serif font.

Keep fonts in mind as you plan the look of your invitation. Although there are no hard and fast rules about fonts, it's good to know which fonts tend to be used with which kinds of events most often, so you can choose just the right font to reflect the formality or informality of your affair.

**tip**

Before you buy postage stamps for your invitations, bring a complete invitation set with you to the post office. You want to make sure you know exactly how much postage each invitation will need, either based on weight, shape, or size—for example, oversized envelopes often need more postage than their smaller counterparts as do oddly shaped invitations. It's critical to check postage ahead of time so that your invitations don't end up being returned to sender (you!) for insufficient postage. This would cause a real time drain in your planning because you'll need to resend all your invitations if you didn't get postage right the first time around.

## Wording Your Invitations

How you word your invitation communicates some very important information to your guests—who is paying for the wedding (those people's name or names usually comes first) and the marital status of the bride's and the groom's parents.

So you don't spend a lot of time fretting over how to word your invitations, here are phrasing options for some of the most common scenarios you'll find at today's weddings:

- **Bride and groom are paying for their wedding**

    *Betty Ann Bride*
    *and*
    *Gary John Groom*
    *request the honour of your presence*
    *at their wedding*
    *Saturday, the twenty-third of September*
    *two thousand six*
    *at ten o'clock in the morning*
    *St. John's Church*
    *Indianapolis, Indiana*

- **Bride and groom, and both of their parents, are paying for the wedding**

*Betty Ann Bride*
*and*
*Gary John Groom*
*together with their parents*
*Mr. and Mrs. Bob Bride*
*and*
*Mr. and Mrs. George Groom*
*request the honour of your presence*
*at their wedding*
*Saturday, the twenty-third of September*
*two thousand six*
*at ten o'clock in the morning*
*St. John's Church*
*Indianapolis, Indiana*

- **Bride's parents are paying for the wedding***

*Mr. and Mrs. Bob Bride*
*request the honour of your presence*
*at the marriage of their daughter*
*Betty Ann*
*to*
*Gary John Groom*
*son of Mr. And Mrs. George Groom**
*Saturday, the twenty-third of September*
*two thousand six*
*at ten o'clock in the morning*
*St. John's Church*
*Indianapolis, Indiana*

- **Groom's parents are paying for the wedding***

*Mr. and Mrs. George Groom*
*request the honour of your presence*
*at the marriage of*
*Betty Ann Bride*
*daughter of Mr. And Mrs. Bob Bride**
*to their son*
*Gary John*
*Saturday, the twenty-third of September*
*two thousand six*
*at ten o'clock in the morning*
*St. John's Church*
*Indianapolis, Indiana*

* optional, but nice touch.

# DIVORCED PARENTS AND INVITATIONS

Having divorced parents means you have to do some creative wording with your wedding invitations. The names of people who are no longer married should never appear together on the same line of a wedding invitation. So instead of Mr. and Mrs. Bob Bride, the invitation would read Mrs. Bella Bride and Mr. Bob Bride; or instead of Mr. and Mrs. George Groom, the invitation would read Mrs. Grace Groom and Mr. George Groom. Alternatively, you may choose to refer to a divorced mother by the title "Ms." instead of "Mrs." if she prefers.

If either parent has remarried, you can include their new spouse's name alongside their own on the invitation.

- **Bride's parents are divorced and are paying for the wedding\***

*Ms. Bella Bride*
*and*
*Mr. Bob Bride*
*request the honour of your presence*
*at the marriage of their daughter*
*Betty Ann*
*to*
*Gary John Groom*
*son of Mr. And Mrs. George Groom\**
*Saturday, the twenty-third of September*
*two thousand six*
*at ten o'clock in the morning*
*St. John's Church*
*Indianapolis, Indiana*

*\* optional, but nice touch.*

- **Bride's parents are paying for the wedding but the groom's parents are divorced**

*Mr. and Mrs. Bob Bride*

*request the honour of your presence*

*at the marriage of their daughter*

*Betty Ann*

*to*

*Gary John Groom*

*son of Mrs. Grace Groom*

*and*

*Mr. George Groom*

*Saturday, the twenty-third of September*

*two thousand six*

*at ten o'clock in the morning*

*St. John's Church*

*Indianapolis, Indiana*

- **Bride and groom have divorced parents, stepparents, and are paying for the wedding themselves**

*Betty Ann Bride*

*and*

*Gary John Groom*

*together with their parents*

*Ms. Bella Bride*

*and*

*Mr. and Mrs. Bob Bride*

*and*

*John and Grace [Groom] Smith*

*and*

*Mr. George Groom*

*request the honour of your presence*

*at their wedding*

*Saturday, the twenty-third of September*

*two thousand six*

*at ten o'clock in the morning*

*St. John's Church*

*Indianapolis, Indiana*

## Do-It-Yourself Invitations Versus Using a Stationer

Now that you know what your invitations should look like, here's how to figure out how to get them done. You have two choices: you can go the do-it-yourself (DIY) route, or you can hire a stationer to print the invitations for you. Read on to learn which method might work best for you and your fiancé.

- Are you and your fiancé tech savvy? Do you like to be hands-on with every-thing that you do? Is time not an issue in the weeks and months before your wedding? Are you looking to cut costs on your invitations? If you answered "yes" to most of these questions, DIY is definitely the way to go for your invi-tations.

  You can write and design your invitations on your personal computer, print them out on specialty card stock that you've purchased for the task, and get them ready to go without leaving the comforts of your home office. Most per-sonal computers today come with a range of fonts—the Mac that I use, for example, offers about 75 different fonts—so you can create invitations that look as if they were professionally made with typefaces that only invitation companies once had access to. If you have a color printer, you can even have fun with color on your invitations by using a colorful ink choice for your font or by creating fancy borders.

- Are you and your fiancé time-starved? Does the idea of creating anything on your computer freak you out? Are you a traditionalist who has everything professionally printed? Does your family expect you to have engraved invita-tions? If you answered "yes" to most of these questions, forgo DIY invitations and go the traditional route with a stationer. Most stationers need at least a month to print wedding invitations, so keep that in mind when you place your order. Also, look to work with a stationer with a good reputation around town or that is affiliated with one of the recognized companies in wedding and events planning business, such as Carlson Craft or Hallmark. They have catalogs with all types and styles (including ethnic) of invitations to choose from, and they can usually turn around invitations in as little as two weeks.

If you're interested in creating DIY invitations, you can shop for card stock in brick-and-mortar stores or visit their online sites. Here are two good sites to shop:

- www.paperdirect.com. As the name implies, Paper Direct specializes in paper stocks of various shapes, sizes, and colors. The company has an extensive wedding collection with invitations in traditional as well as off-beat shapes and sizes.
- www.staples.com. Most Staples stores have a decent selection of papers that you can use to make wedding invitations. However, keep in mind that Staples tends to stock only papers on the traditional side such as white and ecru paper.

## Custom Versus Semi-Custom Invitations

If you're turning to a professional for your wedding invitations, you'll be dealing with either custom or semi-custom invitations.

A *custom invitation* is exactly what it sounds like—an invitation that is made just for you. This option is usually the most creative and labor-intensive way of getting invitations made, and it can be the most costly. You should budget about two months before your invitations need to go out (or about four months before your wedding) for selecting, proofing, and printing your custom invitations. And you should budget between $10 and $30 per invitation for a custom invitation. (So if you do the math and are ordering 100 invitations, you're looking at $1,000 to $3,000 spent on your invitations.)

A *semi-custom invitation* is one where you can change some of the elements, such as the wording, the font, or even the paper stock. But what keeps the cost on these lower is the fact that the printer has a template or a set selection of elements to work from. Companies like A Papier in Los Angeles will do semi-custom invitations that look as if they're custom done. "We might add on a ribbon or pressed flowers," says owner Alyson Bravo. When working with a company like A Papier, you can expect to pay $6 to $12 per invitation set (or $600 to $1,200 for 100 invitations), and you'll usually have your invitations in hand about two weeks after you've signed off on the final proof.

You can use larger companies for semi-custom invitations as well, such as a local Hallmark stationer, which will have catalogs for you to choose from, or an online printer like VistaPrint.com. Understand, though, that once you start leaning towards the mass-produced semi-custom invitations, you will pay less (VistaPrint.com can do 150 invitations for about $60) but you'll also have a lot fewer choices.

## Steps to Ordering Invitations

Once you've found the company that will be printing your invitations, you usually have to select four elements of your invitations up front: the typeface, the color of the ink, the type of paper, and the kind of printing. (The two most common types of printing are engraving and thermography. In engraving, the words are literally pressed into the paper. This option can add a couple of dollars per invitation set to your bill and adds at least two weeks to your turnaround time. Thermography applies type as raised ink on the paper surface; it looks like engraving, but is faster and more economical.)

Next, you'll need to supply the printer with the particulars of the wedding—the names, dates, and places of the important people. If you're ordering from an online printing company, you'll usually click through screens where you can enter this information. If you're working with a semi-custom printer at a stationery store or a custom printer like A Papier in Los Angeles, you'll fill out a content sheet, which is like a questionnaire of the who, what, and when of your wedding.

After that, you'll decide what kind of language you want to use on your invitation. With an online company, you'll be able to see how your invitations will read using formal, semiformal, and casual language. This is usually instantaneous as you click from screen to screen. With traditional printers you may have to look at how others have worded their invitations and see which language you prefer (you'll look at samples in a catalog) or the printer will fax you proofs with different kinds of language used. "It depends on the social level they are trying to convey," says Alyson Bravo, owner of A Papier. "Are they trying to go with something really formal or more Bohemian, where they're saying something about two families coming together."

Finally,  you'll get to proof the invitations you've selected to make sure the wording is correct, the font is right, and that there aren't any grammatical errors. Again, with an online printer, you'll get a proof instantaneously, which you'll need to print out, check over, and sign off almost immediately. With a semi-custom or custom printer, you'll receive a faxed proof in a few days, and expect that you'll have a couple of back and forths with the printer.

In order to properly proof, Bravo of A Papier suggests you do the following:

- Check everyone's names and make sure they're spelled correctly
- Use a ruler to read each line of text to check for errors
- Read the invitations backwards, word by word.
- Say the text out loud.
- Ask two people to proof the invitations as well. "Find one person familiar with the event and one who isn't," suggests Bravo. "The former person can point out any discrepancies in details that you may not have realized, and the latter person can comment on flow."
- Mark any changes clearly in dark ink and block letters so the printer can see them when you fax it back.

You should expect to go through the proofreading process with every version of your invitation. On

**tip** Traditionally, wedding invitations are addressed using hand calligraphy, a gorgeous albeit time-consuming and expensive option. (Most calligraphers need a minimum of two weeks to address your invitations.) If you're looking to save time and money on your invitations, consider using a calligraphy-like font from your computer to address your invitations. You can create a mailing list of names and addresses, which will be a great time-saver when you're writing thank-you notes. Also, you can print names and addresses on clear labels so as not to detract from the invitations. If you're not computer savvy, you can always use your neatest handwriting to address your envelopes—or ask a friend or relative with neat handwriting to do the addressing.

average a couple will have three versions before finally getting the perfect proof. Then it's off to the printer and, depending on the printing process and how detailed your invitation is, you can expect to receive your semi-custom invitations in two weeks or your custom invitations in three to four weeks.

# INVITATION IDIOSYNCRASIES

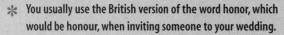

Keep in mind that there is a certain formality to invitations, regardless of how casual your wedding is going to be. Here are some tips to remember:

✳ You usually use the British version of the word honor, which would be honour, when inviting someone to your wedding.

✳ You spell out the date of the affair and put the numerical date, spelled out, before the month.

✳ You spell out the year of your affair, so 2006 would be two thousand six.

✳ You do not write a.m. or p.m. on invitations. Instead you use "in the morning," "in the afternoon," or "in the evening."

✳ You include the full, legal name of the bride and the groom. So while my name appears as Leah Ingram on this book cover, on my wedding invitation my name appeared as Leah Jaclynn Ingram, my full legal name. (And yes, if you've noticed, I didn't change my name.)

## Practical Ways to Get Postage Stamps

If you're busy like I am, usually the only time that you can get to the post office to buy stamps is when everyone else can—during your lunch hour, when the line can snake out the door. With a wedding to plan, you probably don't have the time to spare waiting in line, which is why I would recommend buying the postage stamps you'll use on your invitations via the Internet. (Timesaving advice aside, I still stand behind my suggestion of visiting your post office in person to check on the postage requirements of your invitation.) The United States Postal Service will let you order special-occasion stamps (such as the LOVE stamps many brides use on their invitations) on its website (www.usps.gov). For a nominal fee, you can have those stamps delivered to you.

# Writing Your Vows and Your Program

## To do list

- ☐ Write your vows
- ☐ Design and outline your ceremony program

It used to be that all the bride and groom had to do for their vows was "repeat after me"—that is, repeat exactly what the officiant told them to say. Similarly, years ago a simple program for a wedding was all you needed. It commemorated the wedding date, told you the order of the ceremony, and it made nice filler for a scrapbook. Not any more.

Today's brides and grooms want to have a hand in everything for their wedding, including their vows and their ceremony program. Here are ways you can write both in no time.

## Vows in a Cinch

Before you put pen to paper or fingers to the keyboard, stop and ask yourself: do I really need to write my vows? Start out by asking your officiant to fax, email, or read to you over the phone the typical vows that this person uses at ceremonies. Upon hearing or reading them you may have just stumbled upon the perfect words that your fiancé and you will say as you become husband and wife. If so, you've just saved yourself a tremendous amount of time and energy on your vows because you don't have to write any of them.

However, if after seeing or hearing your officiant's standard vows you still want to add your own ideas to them, follow these suggestions so you don't get overwhelmed by the idea of writing your vows:

- Keep it as simple as possible. Remember that you're writing words that you're going to be saying in front of a lot of people. There's no reason to go into some long and involved explanation of why you love this person or how you met. Just express your feelings for each other, in the easiest way possible, and that's it.

- Borrow from literature. If there is a particular passage in a book, poem, or Shakespearean play that expresses your feelings for one another, by all means use it in your vows. You wouldn't be the first bride and groom to do this. Sometimes hearing something familiar, such as a sonnet, makes your vows more meaningful for each other and for your guests because they're recognizable.

- Compare your vows. If you've written paragraph after paragraph that describes your feelings for your future husband whereas he has only written a sentence or two, you're going to need to balance out your vows. You want both sets of vows to be approximately the same length; edit the vows as necessary to make them so.

- Remember your setting. If you're being married in a religious ceremony, you should let your officiant see your vows ahead of time as a courtesy. With that in mind you should avoid saying anything in your vows that could be offensive to the clergyperson who will be leading the ceremony.

- Read your vows out loud ahead of time. Sometimes words on paper sound just fine when you read them silently. But then you go to speak them and boy do they sound awful. That's why I always recommend that you say your vows out loud so you can hear how they sound and make sure they sound okay. Also, when you read them, use a timer. I would suggest keeping your vows portion to less than five minutes per person, if that. You don't want to bore your audience with your personal thoughts about each other that seem to go on forever.

## Planning Your Program

At today's weddings the ceremony program has taken on a life of its own. Some include photographs; others include trips down memory lane about how the bride and groom met. While that all sounds like an interesting document to look at, when it comes down to it, it's unnecessary. Here are the basic elements you can include in your program; if you keep them in mind, you won't get bogged down putting together your program.

1. Personal statement. Offer a brief welcome or introduction from the two of you, and thank your guests for joining you that day.

2. Order of the ceremony. Outline exactly what your guests can expect to occur during the ceremony. You should include specific readings—and the names of people who will be doing them—along with musical selections.

3. Explanations, if necessary. If you're having a religious ceremony that will include elements that not everyone understands, you can create a glossary of sorts at the end of your program that explains potentially confusing portions of your ceremony to your audience.

4. Special recognition. This is where you can list the people who are participating in your ceremony and their responsibilities. You can also use this section of your program to mention any special relatives (living or deceased) or other friends whom you wanted to include in your ceremony but couldn't.

# Choosing Ceremony Music

There is a reason you tend to hear the same musical selections over and over again at wedding ceremonies—they work. That means that not only are the selections popular but also, for whatever reason, their tempo, words, and arrangements fit well in a wedding setting.

There's no reason that you have to reinvent the wheel as you choose the music for your ceremony. The easiest way to save time on your musical plans is to stick with the tried and true. However, there's nothing wrong with adding in one or two personal favorites to your musical selections, as long as they work in your wedding setting. Just don't pick something that is so obscure that you can't find sheet music for your musicians.

Just remember that music plays a certain role in your wedding and that you need to plan for three main areas of your wedding: pre-service music, the processional/recessional, and ceremony music. Here are suggested songs for each.

## AND THE BRIDE SAID...

"We decided to have our musicians play one of our favorite Enya songs at our wedding. We figured it was a perfect selection for a ceremony. Well, we were wrong. The song itself on the CD sounds great, but the musicians just didn't do it justice."

**Wendy, Iowa**

## Pre-Service Music

The music that you have playing as your guests arrive at your ceremony should be calming yet welcoming. Here are some musical pieces that many people have used as pre-service music. These selections can be done instrumentally or vocally, as appropriate:

- "Ave Maria"
- "Jesu, Joy of Man's Desiring"
- Pachelbel's "Canon"

## Processional/Recessional Music

Many of the selections for the processional (when the wedding party walks into the ceremony) are interchangeable with the recessional (when the wedding party leaves the ceremony). Make sure you choose music that is easy for folks to walk to. That means finding selections with an even beat and a not-too-fast tempo. Here are a few popular selections:

- Beethoven's 5th Symphony or "Ode to Joy"
- "Prelude in C Major"
- "The Prince of Denmark's March"
- "Suite Gothique"
- "Wedding March"

**tip** When choosing ceremony musicians, see if they have a website. Those that do usually include on it their repertoire, which is a listing of all the songs they know how to play. Not only will this help you determine if this musician will be able to tackle the tunes you want to hear at your ceremony, but also will give you a good sense of the common songs that couples include at their ceremony.

## Ceremony Music

You may want to add some musical selections to your ceremony, just as you would readings, to further personalize your ceremony. Many couples pick popular ballads that a friend or family member can serenade them with during the ceremony. Others pick songs that are somewhat reflective of their religious background, such as the song "Sunrise, Sunset" from "Fiddler on the Roof" at a Jewish wedding.

Here are some suggested songs that work well as a vocal piece during a ceremony. Of course, if there is a current tune that is a favorite and which words and music would lend itself to a wedding, then by all means add it to your wedding ceremony as well. Also, you'll want to stick with songs that describe your love for one another or something else that is relevant to your wedding. For example, if you're having a destination wedding in Jamaica, it would be very cool to add Bob Marley's reggae tune "One Love" to your musical selection.

- "Have I Told You Lately"
- "Let It Be"
- "Unchained Melody"
- "Wedding Song (There is Love)"
- "The Wind Beneath My Wings"

Thanks to today's digital technology, you may be able to plan all of your ceremony music without leaving home. There are two websites I know of that catalog popular wedding tunes and with the click of a mouse (and the right software, such as QuickTime or Real Media Player) you can hear them on your computer. They are

- The University of Virginia's Music Library, which not only includes snippets of wedding tunes but also resources for finding sheet music. Find it at www.lib.virginia.edu/MusicLib/guides/ wedding.html.

- The Piano Brothers from Minnesota, a pianist duo that specializes in "easy-listening" piano music that's perfect for weddings. You can hear online samples from their CDs at www.pianobrothers.com.

**tip** If you're feeling unsure about what musical selections to choose for your wedding, preview some songs ahead of time. There are a number of wedding-music CD compilations out there that let you hear various versions of popular wedding songs. That way when someone mention's Pachelbel's "Canon," you'll be able to hear the tune in your head because you've listened to it on CD.

## Ceremony Musicians

One of the best places to find musicians to play or vocalists to sing at your ceremony is through your house of worship. Many churches and synagogues have active musicians and choral groups that would likely be available to perform at your ceremony. And we're not just talking about blue-haired ladies playing the organs. I've been to houses of worship whose congregants have formed jazz quartets and soft-rock bands and which bring a unique element to ceremonial music. So ask and ye just might find great musicians for your wedding under the same roof as where you're having your ceremony.

Another option for ceremony musicians is through the band that you hire to play at your reception. This option is especially cost effective when you're having your ceremony and reception in the same location. Because the band will have to be there at a certain time to set up anyway, perhaps the bandleader will "loan" you a pianist or guitar player or other instrumentalist for your ceremony—and not charge extra for it.

**caution** Whatever you do, don't make up your mind ahead of time about the exact combination of musicians you'd like to have at your ceremony without consulting a musical professional first. You may like cellos, violins, and harps but a music expert may counsel you against going with all strings and instead adding in instruments from different families. Or perhaps your budget can't support a string trio or quartet so you should think about a soloist or duo instead.

Regardless of where you find your musicians, you should budget about six months before your wedding to start your search, and definitely keep your ceremony locale in mind. Otherwise, your musician won't match your setting. So, for example, an outdoor ceremony would lend itself well to "softer" duos, such as a flute and cello, whereas an indoor ceremony in a larger space would benefit from musicians that can provide a "bigger" sound, such as a brass quartet.

Prices can range greatly with ceremony musicians. Some charge by the hour; others have a set fee. And as I mentioned earlier, if you're "borrowing" a musician from your reception band, you may not be paying anything extra for their services at your ceremony. All in all, it isn't out of the question to spend in the ballpark of $500 for your ceremony music.

# Ceremony Flowers in a Jiff

## To do list

- ☐ Research florists
- ☐ Meet with various florists
- ☐ Decide on styles for bouquets, boutonnieres, and decorations
- ☐ Choose your blooms

When it comes to the romance of a wedding ceremony, it's often the flowers and other decorations that take center stage. A bride who walks into a church holding a cascading bouquet of white flowers can look absolutely angelic. Or when a couple becomes husband and wife under a trellis of fresh flowers, they look like something straight out of a Hollywood romance.

Romantic images aside, the real challenge with wedding flowers is not letting them overwhelm your planning time and budget expenditures. You're surely going to have tremendous choices when selecting your bouquet, deciding on your blooms, and arranging your centerpieces. In this section, I'll help you figure out the most cost- and time-efficient ways to find the right flowers for your ceremony and your attendants as well as for your reception tables.

## You'll need list

- ☐ Color swatches
- ☐ Diagram of spaces to be decorated with flowers
- ☐ List of participants who'll be wearing flowers

## Finding a Fabulous Florist

Like all vendors you'll hire for your wedding, you should ask around for recommendations for florists that have served others well. You want to hear things like, "The flowers this florist made for me lasted for days," or "He really knew how to work wonders within my budget," or "She was so great to work with that I can't wait to have another event so I can hire her again."

When you've got the names of some florists to consider, start making appointments to visit them. You definitely want to meet face-to-face with this person and not only to see if you like her. When you visit a working flower shop, there are some things that you should look for that will tell you whether this is a shipshape operation:

- First, what does the place look like when you walk in? Was there someone to greet you? Does the store look neat and orderly? Is the sales staff pleasant? Or is everyone running around in chaos and no one even noticed that you walked in the door? Obviously, you want a business that fits the former description, and you want to run far away from a business that fits the latter description—if there's chaos on the retail level, you can only imagine how crazy things must be behind the scenes when they work with brides like you.

- Second, what do the flowers in the store look like? Is everything bright and perky, or are there dead and wilting blooms scattered around? A top-notch florist brings in flowers on a daily basis—if not by visiting a local flower market or wholesaler than by delivery truck. If you visit a florist that looks as if the flowers have seen better days, find another florist.

- Third, when you sit down to talk to the florist, does he listen to your ideas about color preferences and floral likes and dislikes, and offer ideas on how he can work within your budget? The best florist is one who takes his customers' ideas and budget and gives them what they want, within reason. You can't expect a florist to give you $10,000 worth of flowers if you've only got a $1,000 budget to work with. Conversely, you don't want a florist who only suggests $10,000 worth of flowers if you've made it clear that your budget is only $1,000.

## Bouquets and Boutonnieres

It's understandable why so many brides develop a sentimental attachment to their bouquets: they are probably the loveliest bunch of flowers they'll ever hold in their life. But a bridal bouquet is more than just a collection of flowers—it's an extension of your wedding ensemble. You should choose a bouquet that works well not only with your wedding gown but also with the setting of your wedding.

There are two popular kinds of bouquets for a bride to carry. One is cascading, which is exactly what it sounds like—a selection of flowers that seems to cascade down from the bride, like water going over the falls. This elaborate bouquet works well with a formal wedding gown or a more ornate wedding overall. The other popular bouquet is hand-tied blooms. These usually feature a tight bunch of short-stemmed flowers held together with a ribbon.

Similar to the hand-tied bouquet is a nosegay, which is just a fancy word for a small bouquet. It's usually what the bride orders for her attendants. Given that corsages aren't as popular as they once were, brides have started giving nosegays to their mothers and grandmothers as well.

As far as flowers for the men in the wedding, there is the boutonniere, which is usually a single bloom that complements the flowers in the bride's bouquet and which is pinned to a man's lapel.

## Decorating with Flowers

One of the easiest ways to make quick decisions about the flowers you'll use in your decorations is to stick with the choices you've made for your bouquets. If you're going with a hand-tied bouquet of Gerber daisies, have your florist make centerpieces featuring the same blooms as well as decorations for your ceremony. And they don't have to be elaborate decorations either. For example, she can cut the heads off of the Gerber daisies and float them in a pretty bowl along with tea lights for a simple yet elegant centerpiece. Similarly, she can tie Gerber daisies to the pews at the church or put them in buckets or baskets that line the aisle.

## In-Season Blooms

One of the best ways that a florist can suggest working within your budget is to go with in-season blooms. That means that he'll steer you towards flowers that are abundantly available at the time of your wedding. Not only will this help you save money on your arrangements, but also it will ensure that your florist won't have a hard time finding your favorite flowers.

## Month-by-Month Chart

The following is a random sample of flowers that are available by month, based on information from the California Cut Flower Commission (CCFC):

| Month | Blooms to Choose |
| --- | --- |
| January | Daffodil, violet |
| February | Daffodil, violet |
| March | Daffodil, forsythia, lilac |
| April | Daffodil, dahlia, daisy |
| May | Dahlia, daisy |
| June | Dahlia, daisy, marigold |
| July | Dahlia, daisy, marigold |
| August | Dahlia, daisy, marigold |
| September | Dahlia, daisy, marigold |
| October | Daisy, gladiola, hydrangea |
| November | Daisy, gladiola, hydrangea |
| December | Gladiola, Christmas eucalyptus, poinsettia |

## Year-Round blooms

Flowers that used to be available only for a few months during the year are now available year-round. That's because many of the flowers you see in stores were grown in countries with warm climates, like New Zealand or South America, when it's cold in the United States. If any of these flowers are your favorite, you're in luck—you can get them readily at any time of the year.

- Chrysanthemum
- Gerber daisies
- Lilies
- Sunflower
- Tulips

**tip** Roses are also available year-round. But if you're having a February wedding, you may want to hold off on including roses in your arrangements. According to the California Cut Flower Commission, of the approximately 1.2 billion roses that are sold each year, 130 million of them are sold around Valentine's Day. So not only might you have a harder time finding the roses that you like for your February wedding, but also you will surely pay a premium because of its popularity on Valentine's Day.

# Hiring a Photographer and Videographer

When you think about it, your wedding photographs and video are the two things from your wedding that are yours to enjoy for a long time afterwards. The food you serve, the band you hire and even the space you use for your reception are all about treating your wedding guests well. Sure, the bride and groom go away from their wedding with lots of gifts, but it will be their wedding photographs and video that they'll look back on for years to come.

I'm not suggesting that you blow a huge portion of your budget hiring the most expensive and fanciest photographer or videographer on the planet. Rather I want you to be thoughtful in how you approach this hiring decision. Its outcome will be with you for the rest of your life in the form of your wedding album and wedding video.

Before you can hire your wedding photographer, you need to ask yourself: what do I want from my wedding photography? Are you looking to have traditional group shots with everyone posed? Are you more interested in having candids of everyone at the wedding? Or would you like an artsy effect to your wedding photographs? How you answer each of these questions will determine what kind of wedding photographer you hire—a traditional photographer, a candid photographer, or a photojournalistic photographer. Read on for an explanation of how each approaches photographing a wedding.

## To do list

- ❑ Familiarize yourself with the styles of photographs and photographers you might want for your wedding
- ❑ Consider what services/results you might want from a videographer
- ❑ Determine what images you want captured from your wedding
- ❑ Assign a family member to work with the photographer/videographer

## Traditional Photographer

A traditional wedding photographer is going to capture images from your wedding in a very standard way. He'll likely pose you at your ceremony with various members of your family and your clergy. He'll do the same at your reception, including taking table shots of all of your guests. Much of what this photographer gets on film is staged. For the bride and groom who are not comfortable in front of the camera, this kind of photographer may work best. That's because you know when he or she will be snapping your picture, you'll get all of your posed shots out of the way and then you can go on to enjoy the rest of your wedding without more picture-taking hanging over your head.

## Candid Photographer

A candid wedding photographer is probably going to mix things up a bit—he or she will do some posed shots, like a traditional wedding photographer would, but this kind of photographer will spend most of the time capturing candid interactions of your guests along with you and your new husband. If your idea of how you'd like your wedding photographs to look mimics the kind of photographs you'd see in a newsmagazine or newspaper, a candid photographer is right for you.

A candid photographer is a good choice for a couple if they want to work with someone who won't be in their face throughout the wedding, with camera in hand. It takes a talented photographer to capture an entire wedding without getting in the way of the guests or the bride and the groom, so when you check your potential candid photographer's references, make sure you ask things like, "Were you even aware that the photographer was around and taking pictures?" and "Did your photographer pester your guests" and "Were you pleased with the resulting photographs?"

**FIGURE 5.1**

A candid wedding photographer will capture private interactions at your wedding, such as the flower girl looking up to the bride.

www.mccory.com

## Photojournalistic Photographer

A photojournalistic photographer is more of an artistic photographer than a photojournalist—the latter being the kind of photographer who shoots events for newspapers and magazines. Unfortunately, too many photographers have co-opted the term "photojournalistic" without really understanding what it means or the kinds of photos clients expect to see.

"To truly shoot photojournalistically you don't get the photos of people interacting," explains McCory James, a Denver photographer. "It actually relates more to the actual setting of the wedding, such as taking pictures of a flower girl's basket, the ushers standing next to a doorway. It's more the environment than just the people." Photojournalistic pictures can also include candid interaction but done in a creative way, such as a picture of crying mother of the bride photographed through a frame of the crook of someone's arm. When McCory is photographing the wedding party, "I might tell the groomsmen to pick up the bride, and then let them figure it out from there. I get the fun of what they're doing while capturing the wedding party."

**tip** Regardless of what kind of wedding photographer you decide to hire, here's a must during the interview process: make sure that you see pictures from a wedding, start to finish. Even the most amateur photographer can get one or two good photographs of a wedding, but only a pro can get excellent quality photographs, image after image, throughout an entire wedding. If a photographer you're meeting with seems hesitant to show you more than his "best of" album, move on to another photographer.

Savvy wedding photographers let you see their portfolios online. One such photographer is Florida-based Dan Harris, who impressed me with his extensive website that includes his entire portfolio of recent weddings from start to finish. That means that any couples interested in hiring Harris can check out his work via the Web whenever it's convenient for them. For a look-see, visit his site at www.danharrisphotoart.com.

## Wedding Videographer

As you shop for your wedding photographer, you may discover that he or she also offers videography services. That would be a time-saver indeed. However, sometimes you need to hire a separate company from the photographer to do your video.

www.mccory.com

S

o what do you need to keep in mind when hiring a videographer? Here are some points to consider:

- See a rough cut. Just as you would ask to see wedding pictures, start to finish, when interviewing a wedding photographer, you should do the same with your videographer. So ask to see a rough cut of someone's wedding video so you can get a sense of how well (or poorly) this person can capture a wedding before he or she adds in any special effects.

- Make sure you see videography in a setting similar to your wedding. The last thing you want to do is hire a wedding videographer who doesn't know how to shoot in natural light for your outdoor, daytime wedding. Although most pros are well versed in the use of both natural and artificial light, not all videographers are, so make sure the person you hire is.

- Talk to recent brides and grooms who have used this videographer. Of course, you want to hire a person who can shoot great video, but more importantly, you want to hire someone who will be a pleasure to work with. If couple after couple tells you how obnoxious this videographer was, you should find another one to shoot your wedding.

- If you're having a small wedding, don't let the videographer talk you into a multiple camera setup. A videographer only needs more than one camera when he or she is dealing with an oversized wedding with many players to film. For a wedding of less than 100 folks or so, you should be fine with only one camera.

### Getting the Pictures You Want

So you're feeling pretty good about the photographer and videographer you've decide to hire. Great. Now you've got to make sure that each gets the shots you want at your wedding. And while your photographer and videographer may be talented, they're not psychic. So if you're going to end up with pictures and video of the important people and moments at your wedding, you have to put together a shot list.

In addition to putting together a list of the specific things at your wedding and people you want them to capture, you should assign one family friend or relative to work with the photographer and another to work with the videographer. Make sure you choose your photography and videographer "liaison" wisely—someone who knows most of the members of your family. That way when the photographer's shot list says "Capture Aunt Bertha and Uncle Max swing dancing," your cousin will be able to guide your photographer to the right swing dancing couple on the dance floor.

Type up your shot list at least a few weeks before your wedding (a few months before is even better) so you can circulate it to the important people in your life. Let each of your parents look the list over, so that if you've forgotten anyone important, you'll have time to add those folks to the list. In addition, make sure you deliver the list to the photographer and videographer a few weeks in advance so he or she can plan accordingly for his time and the amount of film or footage he or she will need to have on hand. Also, make sure you bring an extra copy of the shot list with you on the day of—just in case the photographer or videographer has forgotten it.

# Wedding-Day Transportation on the Double

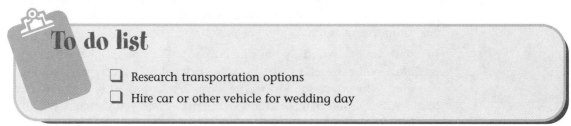

## To do list

- ❑ Research transportation options
- ❑ Hire car or other vehicle for wedding day

## You'll need list

- ☐ Size of bridal party
- ☐ Details of wedding plans
- ☐ Timeline for wedding day

It wouldn't be a wedding without the bride and groom. That's why you want to make sure that you secure reliable wedding-day transportation that not only gets you to the chapel on time but also gets you to and from the reception without any major issues.

The best way to find reliable transportation is to ask recent brides which company they used and what their experience was like. In addition, ask your reception site, wedding planner, or a reputable hotel in the area what transportation company they would recommend. Hopefully, the same business name will keep coming up (with positive reviews all around), and then you'll have a good sense of which company to call. Remember: your wedding is not the time to open the Yellow Pages and randomly pick a limousine company. Sure you can find plenty of reputable and reliable limousine companies in the phone book, but you should only hire one that has treated people you know with respect and courtesy—and will treat you and your wedding party the same way on your big day.

## Off-beat Transportation

There's no rule that says that a bride has to arrive at her wedding in a white limousine. Here are some creative, alternative modes of transportation to get to your wedding and reception:

- Vespa scooter
- Trolley
- Horse and buggy
- Funky modern car, such as a PT Cruiser or VW Beetle, or classic car
- On foot

**FIGURE 5.3**

A white limo isn't the only way to arrive at your wedding. It's perfectly acceptable for the bride and her wedding party to travel on foot.

www.mccory.com

# LODGING FOR YOUR GUESTS

Many couples feel the need to block out a bunch of rooms in a hotel for their guests to stay in at their wedding. This is especially true for a wedding being held in a city where very few guests live or in a location that will be exclusive to your wedding, such as a resort. Sometimes, though, your guests may want to shop around to see if they can get a better rate at a hotel of their choosing. So before you spend a ton of your money holding rooms for your guests, give them the option to price their own hotel rooms and let them see if they find lodging that is more within their budget. That way your guests won't feel as if they have to pay more than they're comfortable spending to stay in a hotel for your wedding.

Want to get a sense of what comparable hotel rooms will cost guests coming to your wedding? Dedicate a lunch hour to surfing the Net for websites that allow you to book hotel rooms online. Some of these include Travelocity.com, Expedia.com, and Hotels.com.

# Summary

Wow! Did we ever cover a lot of territory in this chapter. I hope that you feel as if your wedding plans are coming together nicely. They should be.

By now you should have decided what your invitations are going to look like and how you're going to word them. And hopefully you have a better sense of the role invitations play in your wedding—and what role they don't play (namely, asking people to give you gifts).

I hope that you've made progress on your vows and your ceremony program as well, and that after thinking about all of your flower options, you've come up with the blooms that will look best and make you the happiest on your big day. In addition, have you thought about how you're getting to your wedding (walking, riding a scooter, catching a cab?). You should have begun looking into all of that by now.

Finally, if you took my advice, I'm sure you've found a fabulous photographer and videographer who will capture your wedding and help create memories that will last a lifetime.

In Chapter 6, "Your Reception Done Right," we get to talk about the nitty-gritty of your reception, including where you're going to have it. This is also the time to have some delicious fun with your wedding plans and taste various caterers' menus and wedding cakes. Yum. We'll also start working on your seating chart, which you likely won't be able to finalize until a few weeks before your wedding when all of your RSVPs are in. But it doesn't hurt to start thinking about your seating arrangements ahead of time so that you're not left at the last minute, finagling where everyone is going to sit at your reception. By planning ahead, you'll have less stress at your reception and overall on your big day.

# Your Reception Done Right

**W**hile the "I Do" part of your ceremony is where the importance of your wedding lies, the reception is where you're probably going to spend the lion's share of your money—and your planning time. Unless you plan special events for a living, such as a conference planner or a public relations professional, you probably have no idea what goes into entertaining hundreds of people at your wedding. Well, in a word (or two)—a lot.

The good news is this: If you've been following this book's chapters in order, you've already taken care of some of the reception planning. Back in Chapter 4, "Planning for Attendants and Family Participants," you figured out your wedding colors and then chose appropriate flowers. You also gave some thought to what centerpieces to use on the tables at your reception, so that's done. Now, you've got to make arrangements for the reception itself, including choosing the space where you're going to have your reception—along with the food you'll serve. Finally, you'll create your menu, choose what your wedding cake will look (and taste) like, and finalize your seating arrangements.

## In this chapter:

* Selecting your reception site
* Hiring a caterer
* Planning your menu
* Choosing a wedding cake baker
* Finalizing seating arrangements

## To do list

- [ ] Consider options for a reception location
- [ ] Plan special arrangements for special locations and situations

# Choosing the Perfect Place for Your Reception

There are any number of places where you can hold your wedding reception, and any number of factors that can affect your decision. Your budget will play a big part in where you hold your reception as will the size of your guest list. The time of year will also affect your decision—I wouldn't recommend an outdoor wedding in the middle of winter, although if you're willing to put up heated tents at your favorite park, I guess you really can have a winter wonderland wedding outside.

Your expectations of your wedding reception will also determine where you hold your reception. If you've always dreamed of an intimate dinner party as your wedding reception, you'll likely look at restaurants versus catering halls when checking out reception sites. Similarly, if you want a say in everything about your wedding— from the decorations to the table linens to the way the dance floor is set up—you'll probably do better booking a raw space, such as a metropolitan loft or museum space, rather than a hotel. (Hotels and catering halls may not offer as many possibilities as an empty space that you can decorate from the dance floor on up.) The following sections help you consider the possibilities along with the pros and cons associated with different location types. You also learn about a few special considerations you'll need to keep in mind when you make certain choices.

**tip** By now you've figured out when you're getting married and at what time of day. Well, the day and time of your wedding can go a long way towards narrowing your reception choices. If you're having a Sunday morning or Sunday afternoon wedding, you could plan to have a brunch or afternoon tea reception, respectively. Likewise, a wedding held after 5:00 p.m. begs for a dinner party, and a destination wedding in a tropical location is perfect for a tropical feast featuring local fare. You don't have to spend a lot of time stressing out over what kind of reception to have—just look at the calendar and the clock and plan appropriately.

# You'll need list

- ☐ Estimate of number of guests
- ☐ Budget allocation for reception

## Location, Location, Location: Considering Your Options

Not sure exactly what kind of location you want for your reception? Check out these site suggestions and see if any is right for you. Keep in mind that many, if not all, of these spaces can usually accommodate your wedding ceremony as well. So if you're looking to combine your event under one roof, these will all be great possibilities:

- **Hotel ballroom/banquet hall.** A space like a hotel ballroom or a banquet hall in a catering space adds an air of elegance to a reception. It's the perfect place to hold an evening affair, especially if you've got a large guest list. One of the benefits of a hotel or banquet hall is that they are used to doing special events and will have everything you need on hand to seat and feed your guests. That means that when you book the space, the price will include tables, chairs, linens, silver, glassware, and so on. Some spaces even include centerpieces and candles, which lets you cross a few more things off your "to-do" list.

- **Country club.** A country club offers a bit of flexibility that is perfect for a day-into-evening event. If your reception begins before sundown, you can invite your guests onto the patio or out onto the lawn for cocktails and hors d'oeuvres. Then as nighttime comes everyone can move inside for dinner and dancing. Like a hotel or banquet hall, a country club should come fully equipped with tables, chairs, china, linens, and more, which will make your overall planning easier.

- **Museum, mansion, gallery, private home, public park, or loft space.** Each of these locales offers a "raw" space, if you will, that lets the bride and groom plan a reception from a blank slate. You're choosing the location based on its existing ambiance—great art on the walls, hip decor and high ceilings, or whatever design elements that appeal to the two of you. Then you'll build on that existing ambiance to create a reception that reflects your individual and combined personalities. That's really cool for a creative couple with specific ideas of how they want their reception to take shape, but it's also an option that can become overwhelming and pricey.

Every location has its own costs, of course, but the following table gives you some idea of the costs associated with a few sample locations within the United States. These costs are for comparison only, and may not represent the current rates of the listed locations.

| Kind of Space | City, State | Rental Fee | Party Size | Extras |
|---|---|---|---|---|
| 1840s Ballroom/renovated loft-like space in Inner Harbor historic building | Baltimore, Maryland | $3,000 Sat. p.m.; $2,500 Fri.–Sun. (not Sat. p.m.); $2,000 Mon.–Thurs. | 250 | Includes 200 chairs, 20 tables, and dance floor. |
| 27,000-square-foot Gothic-Tudor mansion turned fine-arts center | Atlanta, Georgia | $4,000 Fri. p.m.; $7,000 Sat. p.m.; $5,000 all day Sunday | Flexible | Fee includes cooking equipment, plus chairs, tables, and two pianos. |
| Historic home owned by local historical society | Chicago, Illinois | Ranges from $3,400 to $4,250, based on day and season | Up to 600 | Can rent tables and chairs onsite. |
| City parks | Dallas, Texas | $15/hour | Varies | Nothing else included. |
| 5,000-square-foot loft space in cast-iron building | New York, New York | $200-$500/hour | 250 for cocktails; 150 seated | Includes kitchen and sound system. |
| Botanical garden | St. Louis, Missouri | $250 weekdays; $650 weeknights; $1,200 weekends | 125 inside; 175 outside | Must use specific caterer. |
| Living museum space | Sturbridge, Massachusetts | $1,500 to $2,000 | 125 to 220 | Discount offered on Friday and Sunday. |
| 37-room home of former beer baron | Milwaukee, Wisconsin | $750 for three hours only | About 125 people | Can rent piano, tents onsite. No candles. |
| Fine arts academy | Philadelphia, Pennsylvania | $3,000 | Up to 150 | Fees discounted 10 percent January, February, March, July, and August. |
| City parks | Seattle, Washington | $350 to $450 | Varies | Expect to pay an additional fee to serve alcohol. |

- **Private restaurant.** Have a favorite place where you love to eat? And are you planning on having a small wedding and reception? Then why not book your preferred eatery for your reception? Many times a restaurant can offer a cost- and time-effective option for receptions on the smaller side and, like a hotel or banquet hall, will provide all of the items you need to serve your guests a meal—china, linens, glassware, flatware, and so on.

- **Public park, botanical garden.** Garden receptions can be a dream come true for a couple on a tight budget—the fee to rent a public park or botanical garden is usually nominal, if not a "pay what you wish" donation to the non-profit that manages the space. It's also an excellent option for larger weddings where you'd like a bit of flexibility and do not want a space to limit you.

# GETTING A WEDDING CONSULTANT FOR FREE

Busy couples would probably be wise to hire a wedding consultant to help them plan their wedding. But did you know that you can get a planner without actually hiring one? There are two ways you can covertly get a planner for free. You can book your reception at a hotel or you can book a caterer with wedding planning experience.

In the former situation, the banquet manager at the hotel will become your de facto wedding planner. He or she will handle every detail of your wedding if you ask him or her to do so. "I can be really involved if you want my help," says Julie Atkinson, director of weddings and special events at the Chicago City Centre Hotel. "I've worked with tons of vendors, and I will only recommend the ones that are timely and professional." Atkinson is quick to point out that she does not receive kickbacks or commissions from vendors. She also reminds couples that with your wedding, like so many other things in life, you get what you pay for.

What about the caterer with wedding planning experience? It's not so far out as it might seem. You may think that your caterer can only bring food to your reception table, so to speak, but ask him or her and you may be surprised to find out that the catering company can also secure tables, chairs, linens, or any other items you might need for your reception—and all at cost. By asking about this extra option, you may have just saved yourself a lot of time when planning your wedding reception—and not incurred too many extra costs.

## Special Considerations

Don't forget to plan for any special considerations your location choice might present. Although some museums or private homes have tables and linens onsite, for example, you're probably going to have to bring in everything else to make your reception a reality—including cooking equipment, china, and more. If the two of you are busy and have little time to deal with all these planning details, this reception option may not be right for you. On the other hand if you're having a small reception, the scaled down nature of a gallery or private home may be worth the extra investment of time to personalize your reception that much more.

Planning an outdoor wedding? You can't trust mother nature—she may just decide to rain on your wedding. That's why I always advise couples planning an outdoor wedding to tent it. If Murphy's Law holds true, when you don't get a tent, it will rain cats and dogs, but if you get a tent, you'll have a beautiful sunny day. (Murphy's Law seems to favor weddings.)

A tent is smart insurance for your outdoor wedding, regardless of the location, and don't skimp on it. Also, like the "raw" space of a museum, a public park likely won't provide any of the necessities you'll need for your reception. So while the rental fee for the park will be cheap, plan on watching your costs add up as you arrange for the tent, tables, chairs, linens, and more.

> **note** Keep in mind, though, that if your budget will allow for you to hire a party planner or wedding consultant, he or she could probably save you time and work wonders with a space such as a museum, gallery, or private home.

> **tip** While it will still be a few weeks until you know exactly how many people will actually attend your affair, you can gauge a rough headcount, in case any of your vendors ask for this figure. Here's what you do: take your guest list and subtract 10 percent. That's because, on average, 10 percent of people RSVP "no" or approximately 90 percent of your invited guests end up coming to your wedding.

## Rental Fees

To give you a sense of how much rental fees can add to your reception price tag, here is a smattering of costs you can expect to incur when you need to secure tent, tableware, and more for a wedding with 150 guests. Again, these costs are rough estimates, based on a sampling of costs around the nation:

- Tent: $3,000 minimum
- Indoor and outdoor lighting: $2,000
- Dance floor: $3,000
- Ballroom chairs: $900

- Tables: $200
- Tablecloths and other linens: $600
- China: $750 per course
- Flatware: $450 per course
- Glassware: $450 per course
- Portable bathrooms: $2,000 each

> **tip**
> If you have your heart set on having candles at your reception, such as in the centerpieces, ask about this option upfront. Some reception sites do not allow for "open flames" and therefore do not have an open-flame permit. That means, no candles, no Sterno (to keep buffet food warm) and, obviously, no smoking. The last thing you need to happen is to find out at the last minute that your beloved votive-candle centerpieces won't work or, worse yet, that the fire marshal is on his way to shut down your wedding, because of the presence of candles.

# Hiring a Caterer Quickly and Painlessly

## To do list

- Consider off-premises versus on-premises caterers
- Investigate favorite restaurants as a source for caterers
- Check caterers' websites
- Follow up on caterers' references
- Try caterers' tasting menus

Your heart probably told you that your fiancé was the right man for you, and perhaps your calendar told you the right time of the year for the two of you to be married. But when it comes to hiring a caterer for your wedding reception, you're going to have to rely on your gut and your taste buds to make this delectable decision.

Why your gut? Because the caterer is going to have to feel like the right person to you—someone who you'll want to work with on planning your reception menu for however many months it takes to plan your wedding. Why your taste buds? Well, the fare he or she cooks up should be delicious to you and to your guests. You wouldn't hire a band without hearing their music or a photographer without seeing his or her photographs. Well, you should never hire a caterer without tasting his or her food.

# You'll need list

- ❑ Estimate of guest-list numbers
- ❑ Budget information
- ❑ Internet access/computer

## Off-Premises Versus On-Premises Caterers

As you begin to investigate caterers, you'll need to get up to speed on how different companies work. You'll quickly discover that a business is either an off-premises or on-premises caterer. Let this chart help you figure them out—and figure out which option is right for your wedding reception.

| Off-Premises Caterer | On-Premises Caterer |
|---|---|
| Not affiliated with any one reception locale. | Usually the exclusive caterer for one or more reception places, such as hotel, museum, mansion, or country club. |
| Allows couples to choose any vendor they want to use for their reception. | May be restricted to using a certain wedding-cake baker, florist, or other vendor that is affiliated with the reception space. |
| Offers more menu flexibility, based on experience. | Menu limitations are a reality, especially with reception locales that offer only a handful of menu options. |
| May have more hidden costs associated with it, especially if you ask your off-premises caterer to secure rentals (such as linens, dishes, flatware, glasses, and so on) for the reception. | Fixed costs based on prepricing plans from reception locale. Usually one size—and one price—fits all. May be more cost efficient for some couples. |

## Restaurants Are a Good Place to Start

You'll need to find your own caterer if the reception space you've decided on doesn't provide one for you, or if you've decided to go with an off-premises caterer instead of the in-house offering. Where do you look for a caterer? Many restaurants do catering on the side, so if there's an eatery you favor, ask it first. It's a good place to start because you've had personal experience not only with their food but also with their wait staff and their prices.

## Searching Online

Although I would never advise hiring a caterer cold out of the phone book, an online version of the good old Yellow Pages is a great place to get started in your quest for a caterer—and an excellent use of a lunch hour.

I recommend visiting a website like Switchboard.com, where you can plug in the business category you're looking for (caterer) and the city and state where you're going to have your reception. Then when companies come up, you can search within the results using the Find option on your computer (Ctrl+F) to narrow your choices.

For example, just like in traditional Yellow Pages ads, companies will add information in their Switchboard listing that lets you know if they specialize in weddings, corporate events, or the like. Many will also include their cuisine specialties, so if you are interested in serving ethnic dishes or fusion fare, you can type in these keywords to produce a list of caterers that are associated with those types of cuisine. Many of these caterers will offer a website address so that when you're done looking on Switchboard, you can switch over, if you will, to their websites and investigate further—all without leaving your desk.

## References Are a Must

Know somebody who makes great food because you've eaten at his or her restaurant? Or did your friend have a fabulous caterer at her wedding and you'd like to serve the same food at yours? Although personal experience counts a lot in your search for a caterer, what counts even more is hearing that the caterer is great to work with. That's why no matter how great someone's food is, you must check his or her references before signing on the dotted line.

I always advise couples to speak to at least three couples who've used this caterer (or any other vendor, for that matter) and make sure that they've used this company within the past 6 to 12 months. Then you can feel confident that any reviews you hear relate to the company's current staff.

Once you've got another couple on the phone or have their email address, here are some of the things you want to ask about the caterer:

- Was the caterer easy to work with?
- Did the caterer work with your initial menu ideas?
- Did the caterer work within your stated budget?
- Was the caterer able to readily suggest adequate substitutions for the more expensive items on your menu?

- How was the caterer's staff to work with?

- What, if anything, would you change about how you were able to work with your caterer?

- If you had to sum up your experience with this caterer, what would you say?

- If your sister or best friend was getting married, would you recommend that she use this caterer? If so, why? If not, why?

- What else should I know about this caterer before I consider hiring him or her?

## Taste Testing

Now that references have checked out, you can get down to the business of actually sampling each caterer's fare. I mean, if a caterer doesn't feed you something delicious when you're interviewing him or her, you can't be confident that this company will feed your wedding guests great food. Any caterer you're considering should have no problem putting together a tasting menu for you.

Before you visit the caterer, though, have a sense of the kind of menu you want to serve at your reception. It wouldn't make any sense for someone to feed you pork tenderloin as a sample when you're thinking about Italian food for your main course. When my husband and I visited the caterer we eventually hired for our reception, we'd told her ahead of time that we were interested in having a Sunday brunch menu. So during our visit she fed us all brunch-appropriate foods: zucchini bread, banana muffins, and strawberries dipped in chocolate.

Besides letting your taste buds be the judge, there's another important aspect about meeting with your caterer and having him or her serve you food—this meeting will allow you to see firsthand how the caterer handles presentation. Did the caterer have a table fully set with china, silver, and glassware, along with flowers and candles, where you and your fiancé could sit for your tasting menu? Or did you have to pull an office chair up to his desk, where he proceeded to serve food on paper plates with plastic forks? You can tell a lot by first impressions; this is especially true for your caterer. If he's so laissez-faire about impressing a new client—and that's before he has your business—how much more laid back and potentially sloppy will he be on the day of your wedding?

You really want to hire a caterer who wows you with his presentation and whose food knocks your socks off. Also, he or she should be a nice person to deal with and willing to brainstorm menu ideas that are within your budget. If you find someone with neither of these qualities, use your napkin to dab the corners of your mouth (the caterer did supply napkins, right?), politely excuse yourself, and move on to a different caterer.

# Planning a Menu and Choosing a Baker in No Time

There's no need to agonize over the menu of food you'll serve at your wedding reception. And choosing a good wedding cake baker doesn't have to take forever (or cause you undue anxiety). In this section of the chapter, you learn fast tips for handling both of these arrangements quickly and efficiently.

# You'll need list

- ❑ Estimate of guest list
- ❑ List of caterer's specialties
- ❑ Time, day, and location of reception
- ❑ Budget allocation for food and cake

## Making Menu Decisions

There are likely four factors that will affect your menu decisions: time of day of your wedding reception, your budget, your caterer, and your favorite foods. If you keep them in mind, you'll have an easier time planning your menu.

- **Time of day.** This affects your menu in a very simple way—if you're having a late morning or early afternoon weekend reception, you wouldn't serve a full dinner to your guests—it would be out of place. Rather, your menu would probably resemble something you would find on a restaurant's brunch or lunch menu. Similarly, your guests might look askance at a buffet table featuring omelettes and muffins during a nighttime reception. So if you let the time of day guide you in your menu selections, planning should be a snap.

- **Your budget.** This will help you determine your menu based on simple dollars and sense. If you're trying to be frugal with your food choices, you're likely going to choose less expensive menu items, such as chicken, pasta, or other selections that best reflect the timing of your reception and your budget allocations. On the other hand, if you have a limitless budget, you may choose to expand your menu to include a sushi bar, expensive cuts of meat, or fancy pastries for dessert.

- **The caterer's predetermined specialty.** You may have hired your caterer based on some predetermined specialty that you knew that this caterer had, such as kosher meals, Italian feasts, or seafood bonanzas. If you stick with what your caterer knows and does best, not only will you have an easier time determining your menu but also you likely won't have any unpleasant surprises (either culinary or monetary) down the line. So if your land-locked caterer isn't well versed in seafood selections yet you insist on having a menu that reflects your Gulf of Mexico upbringing—including all the coastal cooking you loved as a kid—you may not like how he serves seafood or the price he charges to cook a meal that's out of his element.

- **Your favorite foods.** Sticking with your favorite foods as you plan your wedding menu is always a good idea. If you serve your guests what you love to eat, you're going to feel really positive about the menu you've created. So don't let a caterer talk you into serving foods that you're not familiar with or that you don't like, just because he or she thinks it's a good idea or because that's the kind of food your caterer likes to make and serve. Although it's okay to add one or two different elements to your menu, your best bet is to serve something you like. Besides, we're looking to save time here and if you have to go back to culinary school to understand the suggestions your caterer has offered, your menu-making will end up becoming a time-consuming task.

## What You Need to Know About Wedding Cake Bakers

What do you need to know about wedding cake bakers?

- Ask your caterer first if he or she specializes in wedding cakes. Not all do but someone who has mastered the skill of wedding cake baking and catering a wedding would be a great find indeed. If your caterer isn't a master cake baker, he or she may be able to recommend someone who is.

- Your corner bakery may have the best wedding cake baker around. Many bakeries can create cakes that would rival even the best caterer's—and likely for a lot less money, time, and hassle than going with the cake baker that all the celebrities use.

- A wedding cake is nothing like a birthday cake. You're probably used to paying peanuts (or close to it) whenever you get a cake to celebrate someone's birthday. Well, if you budget between $500 and $2,000 (or more) for your wedding cake, you won't have sticker shock when you start adding up the details of your ideal wedding cake.

- Some wedding cake bakers don't bake cakes at all. Many brides and grooms look to cut costs by having a fake cake for their cake-cutting ceremony. If serving your guests the real deal is no big deal to you, you will definitely save time and money by ordering a fake cake. That is, the top layer of the cake will be real—it's what you'll use for your cake-cutting ceremony—but the rest will be decorated Styrofoam. Just keep in mind that if you go the fake cake route, you still have to come up with another dessert to serve your guests. Some frugal couples order a plain sheet cake (with a birthday cake-like price tag) and serve that instead. The guests are none the wiser.

- Make sure your cake baker shows you a selection of cake toppers to choose from. If he or she doesn't have any or you're not happy with the choices on hand, you're going to have to find an appropriate cake topper on your own.

**caution** In my opinion, a great wedding cake baker always has a photo album of cakes baked for previous brides and grooms. Bakers should be so proud of confections they've made in the past that they're compelled to put together a collection so future clients can see photographic examples of their work. That's not to say that a great cake baker might not have photos to show you, but I'd be cautious if that were the case. Ask for references and follow up on them.

# THE LOWDOWN ON CAKE-CUTTING FEES

If you fall in love with a cake baker that isn't affiliated with your reception site, you might encounter the notion of cake-cutting fees. That's because if your wedding cake was part of your reception package plan and you're asking the site to cut someone else's cake, they will likely charge you a "courtesy" fee of something like $1.50 or $2.00 per slice. I think this is pretty cheesy but that's the way the industry runs. However, just because this is standard operating procedure, it doesn't mean that you can't question it. So do so, as soon as you find your caterer. Ask straight out, "If I bring in my own wedding cake, will you charge me to cut and serve it?" Not all caterers will and if yours agrees not to, get that all in writing so you can save yourself time down the line of hassling over unexpected cake-cutting fees on your bill.

# Speedy Seating Arrangements

## To do list

- ❑ Create alphabetical guest list based on RSVPs
- ❑ Design seating arrangement

## You'll need list

- ❑ Reception RSVPs
- ❑ Location site plan with table sizes
- ❑ Paper and pencil/pen/marker

If you've never planned an event before, you have no idea how time-consuming planning seating arrangements can be. But like anything else with your wedding, if you approach the task logically and thoughtfully, you'll get through it in no time. Here's how you can do your seating arrangements speedily, after all of your RSVPs have been received:

1. Start by creating an alphabetical list of all of your guests. That means that if you've invited three people from the same family, you should list each person's name separately. This list will give you an accurate head count.

2. Second, seat the people that will be the easiest to place, such as the bride and groom (natch!), your parents, and your bridal party.

3. Next, seat people that would naturally go with those you've already placed at tables. This should take care of a good chunk of your list.

4. Finally, use family relations, long-standing friendships, or similar backgrounds/interests to find seating for the remaining people on your guest list.

> **tip** If you can, see if your reception site or caterer can provide tables that vary from the standard "round table for 10." You may find that certain groups of people do not go together naturally in 10s but rather in 4s, 6s, or even 14s. By having some flexibility in your seating arrangements, based on table size, you may save yourself time in planning your seating arrangements.

5. Plan to have two extra tables on your seating chart for any overflow, last-minute additions to your guest list or simply to offer your guests flexibility should they choose to move their seat.

## AND THE BRIDE SAID...

"To make working out seating arrangements easier, we wrote down the names of all of our guests on little pieces of paper, and moved them around until we found the perfect place for everyone to sit. This saved us from writing down names and then erasing them from the seating chart."

Maria, Michigan

## Summary

At this point, you should be feeling really good about your reception. It should be coming together nicely, and I'm sure will add wonderfully to an already great day.

If you followed my advice up to this point you should have secured the perfect spot for your reception, found a caterer who can wow even the pickiest eater in your family, and put together a menu that's sure to be divine. And did I mention your wedding cake? I'll bet that by now you've selected a great baker who is going to give you the best dessert you and your guests have ever tasted.

Speaking of wedding cakes, we talked a little bit about cake-cutting fees, which you might end up having to pay if you booked a cake baker not affiliated with your caterer or reception site. It's a stupid rule, I know, but one that the industry has allowed to become commonplace at weddings. Oh, well. Finally, I helped you figure out a fast way to finish your seating arrangements. Then, after your RSVPs are all in, you should be able to get the task completed lickety-split.

Because the reception will comprise the largest portion of your wedding budget, it's no surprise that the reception will comprise more than one chapter in this book. In Chapter 7, "Entertainment and Extras for Your Reception," I'll discuss the basics on your decorations and entertainment for your reception. That includes a bit more on centerpieces, favors, and gift tables along with whom to hire to entertain your guests. It's all very cool stuff.

# Entertainment and Extras for Your Reception

**7**

**In this chapter:**

* Finding musical folks to entertain your guests

* Figuring out your wedding favors

* Choosing extras that make your reception even better

* Understanding why you should insure your wedding

People have come to expect certain things at wedding receptions—catching up with old friends, dining on terrific food, and enjoying great music. That's why one of your tasks now is to figure out the right entertainment for your wedding reception. It may sound like an overwhelming item on your to-do list, but it doesn't have to be.

Remember how we tapped into the time of day and setting of your wedding when figuring out things like what kind of food you were going to serve at your reception? Well, you can use those same clues to make your entertainment decisions easier.

Read on to learn which entertainment options are right for your reception, and then how to find the actual people who will do the entertaining. Then you'll decide on the favors you'll need to secure for your guests, how you're going to handle gifts at the reception, and all the other extras that could easily slip through the reception-planning cracks.

# To do list

- ☐ Decide what kind of entertainment you want
- ☐ Begin screening entertainment companies
- ☐ Hire your band, deejay, or other musician
- ☐ Put together your suggested song list

# Expedient Ideas on Entertainment

Before you can decide who will be providing the entertainment for your reception, you need to figure out which entertainment option makes the most sense for you. As I mentioned, time of day and location of your reception will have a lot to do with the entertainment choices you make. If you're having your reception on a weekend morning in a public park, having a band rocking out or a deejay spinning tunes would be very much out of place. So if you're having a more laid-back reception, you should choose more laid-back entertainment. Maybe you want to hire a jazz trio for light background music or a classical guitarist.

**tip** You could even opt for the easy, economical entertainment option my husband and I went for at our reception—a five-CD player, filled with five of our favorite albums, and playing on "shuffle" for the four hours of our reception. Not only did our CD-based entertainment plan save us money, it saved us time, too. All that it required was two friends of ours spending 20 minutes that morning wiring the tent with mini-speakers so everyone could hear the tunes throughout the day.

## Matching the Entertainment to the Event

See which of these scenarios best fits your reception, and then you'll have an easier time deciding on the perfect entertainment for your event:

- **Late morning, early afternoon, or mid-afternoon reception held outdoors.** The timing and setting of this kind of reception really begs for more subdued entertainment. You can absolutely hire live entertainment but you may want to go with a company that can promise music that will match the feel of your wedding. Also, an outdoor wedding is less likely to have a traditional dance floor—and therefore traditional dancing—so you want music that isn't about breaking a sweat on the dance floor. I might recommend finding musicians or a deejay who specialize in classical, jazz, or soft rock versions of popular tunes. Or you can hook up a mechanical musical system, such as the CD player I used at my reception, and choose CDs of jazzy, classical, or quieter music. That way, when your guests are mingling while sipping mimosas, Bloody Marys, or other early-afternoon cocktails, they won't have the mood shattered when the deejay or band breaks into the latest Nelly tune. However, should you feel like having barefoot dancing on the lawn or beach (depending on your locale), you could always plan to have your entertainment break out the livelier tunes a little later in the reception.

- **Late morning, early afternoon, or mid-afternoon reception in a hotel or banquet hall.** You'll have more flexibility with your music options at an indoor reception held at this time of the day. Your reception space is likely to have a dance floor, and you'll probably want to encourage your guests to go out onto the dance floor and enjoy themselves. However, you can mix things up a bit with the deejay or band that you hire for your reception. You can have more mellow music playing during your cocktail hour, and then you can have them break into the dance tunes when regular food is being served. You'll

> **tip** I wouldn't recommend the CD system for music at a hotel or banquet hall because the space is likely to be too large—unless it has an existing sound system you can easily hook your CD player into and you have the mastery to do so. However, if you're having your reception in a smaller space, such as a gallery or a private room at a restaurant, your simplest option for music may be the CD player, just a few live musicians, or a deejay.

have a great deal of flexibility with an indoor reception held later in the day. People expect to dance at these kinds of events, and so you should choose your band or deejay accordingly.

- **Late afternoon or evening reception held outdoors.** Chances are your outdoor event that goes into the evening is likely to have the same atmosphere as an indoor event held in a more traditional reception space, such as a hotel ballroom. In addition, I'll bet that an outdoor evening event is going to be held under an awning or a tent, where having a dance floor would be par for the course. You probably want to book entertainment that will allow for dancing, something wedding guests come to expect with a late-day celebration. Again, the only exception to this entertainment rule would be if you're having a super small reception in an outdoor space that just doesn't lend itself to dancing, such as the patio of a restaurant or country club.

- **Late afternoon or evening reception held in a hotel, banquet hall, or other indoor space.** Your entertainment choices for this kind of reception are almost identical to an outdoor wedding held in the evening. Your guests are likely to expect some kind of dancing—and your space is surely going to have a dance floor—so book your entertainment accordingly.

## Choosing Between a Deejay and a Band

Demographics—your age and your gender—may affect your entertainment choices in more ways than you're aware. Answer the following questions to help you narrow down your entertainment possibilities:

- How old are the two of you? Not that age is the defining factor in choosing your entertainment, but according to Julie Atkinson, the director of weddings and special events, at the Chicago City Centre Hotel, younger couples tend to skew towards hiring a deejay whereas older couples lean towards bands. So if you guys are younger and know that the majority of your crowd will be younger, and therefore more responsive to a deejay, that may be the best entertainment choice for your reception.

- Which one of you has the most say in your music decisions? I always advise couples to split wedding-planning responsibilities according to their skills, hobbies, and professional training. So if your husband-to-be is the music connoisseur whereas you're fine with whatever happens to be playing on the radio, chances are your fiancé will want to have more of a say in finding your entertainment. And if your fiancé is like 90 percent of the grooms that Atkinson deals with, he'll go with a deejay. On the other hand if you're the music lover and are the one charged with booking the entertainment, chances are you'll go with a band.

> **tip** During the course of the average four-hour affair, a deejay or band can only play about 80 songs, if that. So don't waste time putting together an intricate song list of hundreds of tunes. There's no way your entertainment will be able to play everything—unless you're willing to extend your reception six or more hours!

Still unsure of what kind of entertainment is right for your reception—and you don't want to spend any more time worrying about it? The following chart will help you compare and contrast the services of a deejay versus a band:

| Deejay | Band |
| --- | --- |
| Because he/she plays recorded music, you'll get authentic songs from your favorite artists. | A well-rehearsed band can do spot-on renditions of your favorite songs but there's always the chance of their improvising a bit. |
| Can bring a youthful exuberance to an event. | Having live entertainment brings a certain sophistication to a reception. |
| Usually can handle all kinds of musical requests from the bride and the groom, as long as the deejay has an extensive library of CDs and records. | Some bands specialize in certain musical genres so if you're looking for a band to play songs from across the musical spectrum, make sure you hire a band with a versatile repertoire. |
| May add in gimmicks to entertain your guests, such as handing out rubber chickens during the "Chicken Dance." Great for a celebration with young children present. | Less likely to do any gimmicky things, such as handing out props. |
| Can be a more affordable option for a couple on a tight budget. Fees usually run in the hundreds of dollars, but go up exponentially with extra people, props, or gimmicks that the deejay brings to the party. | The bigger the band, the larger the price tag. Bands can easily cost into the thousands of dollars. However, for a reception and ceremony that occur in the same location, you may be able to "borrow" a few band members for free to play your ceremony music, making the band more economical. |

## Booking Entertainment on the Double

Whether you've decided on a deejay or a band, you'll approach hiring your entertainment similarly. Here are some ways to do that on the double:

1. Start by asking for references. Because you've already booked your reception space and caterer by now, ask someone associated with either or both for recommendations for reliable deejays or bands that have served past clients well. Are you using a wedding consultant? Maybe he or she can recommend someone to provide your entertainment. Similarly, ask any friends or neighbors if they've hired someone recently to play for a wedding or bar/bat mitzvah, and see if you begin hearing any of the same names. Also, have you been to any special events and experienced an entertainment company firsthand? Be sure to give them a call.

2. Make an appointment with the deejays or bandleaders that come highly recommended. You always want to meet your deejay or bandleader firsthand before working with him or her. If you're working with a company that represents multiple deejays or bands, you may have to settle for meeting with a

company rep on your first get-together—and then later on you can narrow down your choices for the bandleader or deejay.

3.  See your potential deejay or bandleader in action—either live, at a special event where you can pop your head in, or captured on video or DVD. Make sure if you're watching a recording of his or her performance, it's from a recent gig. Band performers can come and go, so you shouldn't make a decision based on musicians who are no longer with the band. Some entertainment companies may have streaming video on their website, which will give you a good preview of what they have to offer, but I would still ask to see videotapes of recent performances, regardless of the video quality.

> **note** Why is it so important to see the deejay or bandleader in action? A person's personality in an office can be very different from his or her personality up on stage or with a microphone in hand. You want to make sure that this person's performances mesh well with your idea of an entertainer.

4.  Always ask for additional references. Even if someone you know referred you to this company, you should speak to three or four other couples who used this deejay or bandleader. Again, make sure that the references are from recent events, for the above-mentioned reason—it won't do you any good to hear rave reviews about someone who is no longer working with that company. Any company that won't supply references is, in my book, not worth working with. In fact, it's a red flag, and you should find someone else to provide the entertainment at your wedding reception.

5.  When you settle on the bandleader you love or the deejay of your dreams, get his or her name in writing—in the contract you draw up for their services.

Plan to dedicate at least one weekend day to visiting bands and deejays—ideally, when they're on location and performing at someone else's wedding. If that's not possible then arrange to have them send you a videotape or DVD of recent performances. Better yet, see if they have streaming video on their company website, which will allow you to review their performances without ever leaving home.

> **tip** The National Association of Mobile Entertainers has more than 25,000 deejay members, all of who are dedicated to providing clients with great entertainment at a wedding. You can search the association's website at www.djkj.com for member deejays near you.

# WHAT TO PUT IN A CONTRACT WITH YOUR ENTERTAINMENT

You should always get everything in writing with every vendor you hire for your wedding, including your entertainment. Here are specifics that you should include in the contract you draw up with your deejay or bandleader:

- The name of the deejay/bandleader
- Fee you will pay
- Number of people you've contracted to be there (that is, if you've negotiated a fee based on six people and eight show up, you only have to pay for the six)
- Time the person is to arrive
- Length of event
- Amount of time he or she will be providing music—and number of agreed-upon breaks, and for how long
- Kind of clothing you expect him or her to wear

## Putting Together Your Suggested Song List

There are certain times during your reception when you may want to have your deejay or bandleader play certain songs. That's why it's important to put together a song list, along with a road map for your event. Keep in mind, though, that many entertainers find a song-by-song outline for an event very restrictive, and it may hamstring your entertainment. A bandleader or deejay can often read the mood of the crowd on the spot better than you can anticipate their dancing needs in the days and weeks before your event, when you'll likely be putting together your song list.

So instead of wasting time putting together 80 or so songs for him or her to play, do this: outline specific songs you want played when, such as the father-daughter dance or your first dance

**tip**  About two weeks before your wedding, meet with your bandleader/deejay and map out your reception. At this point you can hand him or her your suggested song list and point out when certain songs should be played, such as a first dance. You don't want to hand him or her that list on the day of—or give him or her a quick rundown of your reception on the spot. That doesn't give the deejay/bandleader sufficient time to plan for your event.

together as husband and wife. Then give your deejay or bandleader an idea of the kind of music you want them to stick with along with the kind of music you want them to stay away from. This will give your entertainment a better sense of the songs to prepare to play plus give them the freedom to improvise a little bit, should the crowd respond well to the disco tunes you asked for or shy away from the country songs you really wanted to hear.

# SAVING MONEY ON ENTERTAINMENT COSTS CREATIVELY

A deejay can cost anywhere from $300 to $1,300 or more. A band will cost double or triple that price. But you can cut your entertainment costs in a few ways:

- See if you really need live entertainment for the entire portion of your reception. You may be able to get away with recorded music for your cocktail hour and save an hour's fee from your deejay or band.

- If you don't anticipate dancing at your wedding, don't even bother paying for live entertainment. A CD-player hooked into your reception hall's sound system, with some of your favorite CDs in it playing on shuffle, will provide sufficient background music.

- If you won't have dancing but like the idea of having live entertainment, keep your costs simple by bringing in a duo or trio instead of a full ensemble to play light music while your guests eat. Hiring 2 or 3 musicians will definitely cost less than 8 or 10.

- Once you've booked your band, see if you can "borrow" some of the musicians to play music at your ceremony. While this won't save money on the reception portion of your entertainment costs, it will be a smart financial move for cutting your ceremony music costs.

- Live near a music school or a college with a stellar music department? See if there are any existing musical groups there that have experience playing at special events like a wedding reception. Student musicians will surely charge less than professionals.

# Gifts and Favors

## To do list

- ❏ Plan for your gift table
- ❏ Decide on your favored favors
- ❏ Buy favors

Now that you have the entertainment portion of your plans out of the way, you should start thinking about where you'll have your guests put the gifts they bring to your wedding. You also need to decide what gifts (namely favors) you'll give your guests to thank them for attending your wedding.

If you live in a location where guests rarely bring physical gifts to a wedding, such as the Northeast, where cash is king, don't assume that you can get away without having a gift table of some sort. Chances are some of your guests will be coming from somewhere else, where it's okay, if not expected, that you bring a wrapped gift to someone's wedding. And the last thing you want to be doing on your big day is scrambling around figuring out a secure place to put your gifts. Also, if you're getting money gifts, you're going to need a place to put them as well.

## Great Gift Table Ideas

You definitely want to dedicate a space at your reception for gifts. I would recommend talking with your caterer or banquet manager about setting aside a table near the entrance of your reception for gifts. You don't have to spend a lot of time decorating your gift table—just put a pretty tablecloth over one of the round tables from your reception or, if you're having a small reception, a card table, and call it a day.

For gifts of money, which you're bound to get from at least one person on your guest list, I wouldn't bother with a money purse. That old-fashioned idea tends to cause a lot of stress for the

**tip** One of your maid of honor's responsibilities is taking care of the safe delivery of your wedding gifts, once the reception is over. (Encourage your bridesmaids to help her out, if she needs assistance.) Make sure that you work out a game plan with her ahead of time so she'll know where she's bringing the gifts. This could be back to your home (don't forget to give her a spare key or the alarm code for your home security system) or to your parents' house. If you've had a destination wedding, far away from anyone's home, make plans in advance for a local shipping center (Kinko's or Federal Express, for example) to work with your maid of honor the next day to safely ship all of your gifts back to your home.

bride, who is responsible for carrying it around at her reception. Instead, invest in a pretty birdcage, wire mesh basket, or some other clever container at a craft store and place it on the gift table. You may even want to stuff a couple of empty envelopes in the container to give guests the idea that, ah ha, this is for gifts in small envelopes (money). By doing so you won't have all of your guests coming up and handing you envelopes when all you want to be doing is eating, mingling, or dancing with your new husband. Plus, by having a designated place for smaller (and easier to lose) gifts in envelopes, you'll be less likely to misplace them.

# You'll need list

❑ Favors for guests
❑ Container for money gifts

## Finding Favors Your Guests Won't Throw Out

Giving your guests favors as a thank you for attending your wedding is a lovely idea. Unfortunately, many times these favors end up getting left behind or thrown out, because brides choose items that are less than spectacular. Here are some favor ideas that I'm sure your guests will love, use, and enjoy after your wedding:

- Small boxes of chocolate. What person is going to turn down a box of chocolate truffles or a similar confection that you've placed at his or her seat?

- Cookies baked in the shape of a wedding cake, bouquet of flowers, or some other wedding-theme novelty. Have your names and wedding date iced right onto the cookie.

- Picture frame that doubles as a place card. I've seen gorgeous pewter frames that brides have used to notify guests where they're going to be seated at the reception—and as a favor. Also, do your guests a favor and tell them that the frame doubles as the favor. For example, if the place card says "Leah Ingram, Table 7," put in small writing underneath, something like "Please take this frame home as a token of our appreciation for joining us on this special day."

- Freshly potted plants. With an outdoor or warm-weather wedding, you can get away with freshly potted flowers. For a Christmas-time wedding, you can select Christmas cactuses, which have a terrifically colorful flower on them. These plants will do double duty as a centerpiece/decoration and then will become your guest's favor as well. Like the picture frame mentioned above, you should put some kind of notification on each reception table that lets guests know that you'd like to have them take the greenery home as a token of your appreciation.

- Colorful clusters of candy. You can play into your wedding colors by putting together bags of similarly colored confections, such as jelly beans, to give to your guests as favors. Not only will they add a colorful touch to your tables, but they'll be delicious, too.

- Candles. Again, a cluster of candles on your table will add an air of elegance to your centerpieces, and then they can do double duty as guest's favors. I would recommend choosing candles, like the candy, that match or complement your wedding colors.

# FAVORS WITH A LOCAL FLAIR

A fun and creative way to find your favors is to choose something that is symbolic of where your wedding is behind held. Some such associations are obvious—such as offering gifts of pecans for an Alabama-based reception or cheese at events held in Wisconsin. But here are some other examples you may not have thought of:

Arizona: A box of cactus candy.

Colorado: Something featuring aquamarine, the state gemstone.

Hawaii: Why not give your guests fresh-flower leis?

Idaho: This state has more white pines that any other state and is also home to tremendous supplies of silver. You can use either for inspiration when choosing favors.

Kansas: Go for a little movie memorabilia and tap into your inner Dorothy from *The Wizard of Oz* for ideas.

Kentucky: You can hand out miniature Louisville Sluggers to all of your guests.

Maine: LL Bean is Maine's venerable shopping institution and is a great place to find favors for your guests.

Maryland: Look to the Baltimore Orioles (the bird or the team) for favor ideas.

**Minnesota:** Did you know that one of Minnesota's official foods is the blueberry muffin? You can provide little baskets of mini blueberry muffins for your guests to take home.

**Missouri:** Mark Twain was inspired to write his classics while living in the show-me-state. Why not give your guests a collection of Mark Twain's writing as a gift to remember your Missouri wedding by?

**Montana:** Fly-fishing is big in Big Sky country, so angle for favors that fit this theme.

**New Hampshire:** You can have fun with your favors at any New England wedding, including New Hampshire, by giving your guests small jugs of locally produced maple syrup.

**New Jersey:** How about giving your guests a CD from New Jersey's prodigal son, Bruce Springsteen?

**New York:** A number of regions in the Empire State produce wine, so a bottle of local vintage spirits would make a great favor.

**Ohio:** You can get a rock-and-roll favor at the <u>Rock and Roll Hall of Fame in Cleveland</u> or pick up pretty baskets from the Longaberger Company, based in Newark, Ohio.

**Oklahoma:** This state has the largest number of Native Americans living anywhere in the United States, so find favor inspiration in something Native American.

**Pennsylvania:** You can't go wrong with Hershey kisses as your favors.

**South Carolina:** Your guests are sure to love sweetgrass baskets, a local craft from the low country.

**Tennessee:** Go with anything blues (born in Memphis) or country-inspired (thanks to Nashville), and you have a great musical favor.

**Utah:** Called the Beehive state, you can find your favor inspiration in anything having to do with bees, such as beeswax candles.

**Washington:** Seattle is a big coffee town, so why not give java as a gift to your guests?

# Extras for Your Reception

## To do list

- ☐ Buy single-use cameras
- ☐ Stock up on paper stock
- ☐ Make place cards
- ☐ Make table cards

Beyond centerpieces, favors, and your gift table, there are still some items you may want to add to your reception. These extras include single-use cameras, which your guests can use to photograph their perspective of your wedding. You also want to make sure that you put aside time to create place cards and table cards so your guests will know where they're supposed to sit.

## You'll need list

- ❑ Single-use cameras for reception tables
- ❑ Card stock
- ❑ Calligraphy pen
- ❑ Computer and printer

## Using Single-Use Cameras

If you're worrying that your reception tables won't look substantial enough, you can always place a handful of single-use cameras on each table. Not only will this give a fun look to your tables, but it will also give your guests something extra to do during the reception. Plus, by providing single-use cameras for your guests, you'll have another benefit: in the end you'll get additional photos of your wedding, taken from many different perspectives. Sure, single-use cameras may not give you the same quality pictures as your professional photographer, but sometimes your friends and family are able to capture special moments at your wedding that would have passed your photographer by.

## Making Place Cards for Your Guests

After spending time with your speedy seating arrangements from the previous chapter, don't forget to create place cards for each guest and then table cards for each table.

If you've hired a calligrapher or stationer to handle all of the printed matter for your ceremony,

**tip** These days most couples do one of two things with seating at their reception—they have open seating, which means guests can choose to sit anywhere they'd like, or they assign guests to a specific table, which I've referred to as assigned seating. But in its truest sense assigned seating means telling a guest specifically in which seat and at which table you would like him or her to sit. Weddings are rarely this formal anymore, so I wouldn't lose sleep doing more than giving guests notification of which table you'd like to have them sit down at during the reception. Also, most modern wedding guests understand that when they arrive at the reception, they will look for their name on a place card, which will direct them to the table assignment. There's no need for you to spend time beforehand placing each and every place card at a specific seat throughout the reception space. That's why I suggested that you have one table at the entrance to your reception devoted to these place cards. It's where guests know to look to find out where they are sitting.

you can ask him or her to tackle place and table cards as well. If you're tech savvy you can create these cards yourself on your computer and print them out on special paper stock that you've purchased for this very reason.

Here are the basics of what you'll need to put on your place cards:

- Person's name
- Table where he or she is sitting
- If you use picture frames to hold the place cards that double as your favors, include this on the place cards as well: *Please take this picture frame home as thanks for joining us on our special day.* Don't forget to do the same if you're giving them greenery, candles, or another item already on the table as their favor.

Make sure your caterer or banquet manager sets aside a table for place cards. You don't want to spend time on place cards, only to discover there's no place to put them out at your reception.

Confirm with your caterer, banquet hall manager, florist, or whomever is creating your centerpieces for you that there will be space in or near the centerpiece for a table card. What good is a table card if guests can't see it?

**tip** Want to have some fun with your table cards and seating assignments? Instead of giving each table a sequential number, why not give them names that relate to your favorite musician, author, or some other meaningful item in your life? You can name the tables based on nearby towns, different kinds of wine (merlot, chardonnay, zinfandel), or favorite sports teams. These will surely be a conversation piece for all of your guests.

**tip** *Using Your Lunch Hour* Make a list of all the vendors you still have to call and dedicate a lunch hour to contacting them. This could be the deejay or bandleader that you have one last question for, the company that's making your place cards, or a favored charity that you've decided to include in your wedding plans, with donations made in your guests' honor.

# MAKING YOUR WEDDING BENEFIT A GOOD CAUSE

If you happen to wait until the last minute to find favors for your guests and are feeling stumped for a creative idea, why not "give" favors that benefit a good cause? I've known plenty of couples that decided to forego traditional favors in favor of donations to a favorite charity instead. If you decide to go this route, you can make a notation on everyone's place card that you've made a donation in each guest's name to such-and-such charity. Or you can create a card that says just this, which you'll place at every table.

There are more ways to make your wedding benefit a good cause beyond making donations. You can also

- Donate leftover food from your reception to a food bank.
- Donate your flowers to a nursing home or hospital, where the people there are sure to enjoy the pretty blooms for days after your event.
- Hold your ceremony or reception in a place where the proceeds of your wedding fees will benefit a good cause. This could be a local museum, park or nature conservancy.

There are two websites that can provide great ideas on making your wedding benefit a good cause, including charities that you can make donations to in lieu of favors.

- www.idofoundation.org. The I Do Foundation is based in Washington, D.C. and not only suggests charities that you can donate to, but also stores that you can register with that will donate a portion of your gift proceeds to good causes.
- www.marriedforgood.com. This site offers a comprehensive list of the country's top-rate charities, one of which you may decide should be the beneficiary of your wedding.

# Insuring Your Wedding

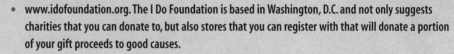

## To do list

- ☐ Investigate wedding insurance
- ☐ Buy an insurance policy

As I'm sure you're aware of at this point, weddings can be costly affairs. With the average wedding in the United States setting the average couple back $22,000 or more, there's a reason you'll want to insure your event—it makes perfect sense.

Wedding insurance can help you avoid losing any deposits or fully paid-for vendors should certain circumstances prevent you from walking down the aisle on your appointed day. And besides being a smart investment, wedding insurance doesn't have to cost a huge chunk of change. For just a couple of hundred dollars, you'll be able to insure your entire wedding. Of course, I'm not an insurance agent and I don't sell insurance policies. So call yours and ask him or her about what it would take to insure your wedding. It may be the best money you'll spend on your special day.

# You'll need list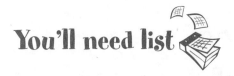

- ❑ Wedding logistics (date, location, number of guests)
- ❑ Wedding budget information

For a good overview on what you should look for in a wedding insurance policy, log on to www.wedsafe.com, a company that provides wedding and liability insurance for special events. Even if you don't buy your policy through Wed Safe, I recommend spending time on the website so you can educate yourself on the importance of wedding insurance and what you need to know as you investigate a policy for your event.

# Summary

With everything that we've covered in this chapter, your reception planning should be done. Finished. Complete. That's a great feeling, isn't it?

You should be proud of yourself because by now you've hired your entertainment. You had the chance to compare and contrast the services of a deejay versus live musicians, and based on the kind of wedding you're planning, plus the timing and location of it, I'm sure you've hired the best entertainment for your big day.

We also got your favors squared away, including reviewing ideas for favors that your guests will actually enjoy, use, or even eat. Yes, I'm a big fan of food-oriented favors—and I hope I presented some ideas for locally available food and other items that might work well for your wedding reception.

This chapter also dealt with some nitty gritty stuff, like making sure you don't forget place cards for your guests—or a table to put them on at your reception. And speaking of tables we also talked about setting aside a table for your gifts and providing a clever receptacle for gifts in envelopes.

Finally, I gave suggestions on how you can make your reception benefit a good cause—either by making donations in lieu of traditional gifts, or by donating items from your reception (food, flowers) to worthy causes afterwards. And I touched upon the topic of insuring your wedding, and why that's one detail you don't want to let slip through the cracks.

In Chapter 8, "Taking Care of the Bride," we let you, the bride, take center stage. This chapter is all about taking care of yourself—how to find a dress you'll love, figuring out how you want to wear your hair on your big day, getting your makeup done just right, and why, in the middle of all this crazy shopping around, you need to schedule a day to pamper yourself. So, as you turn the page and move on to the next chapter, I can't help but say, "Here comes the bride…"

# Taking Care of the Bride

**8**

With all the details of your wedding ceremony and reception taken care of, now it's time to turn to you, the bride. You could say that we've saved the best for last, in that now we're going to focus on taking care of you.

In this chapter, we'll hone in on your dress-shopping needs, find the perfect dress for your big day, and make sure that the whole experience of buying your dress doesn't take up too much time.

In addition to finding you a fabulous dress, we're going to help you figure out how to wear your hair on your wedding day and what kind of makeup you should plan to wear. Full disclosure: I'm a strong believer in hiring a professional to do your hair and makeup on your wedding day. I figure with all you have on your mind, the last thing you should worry about is whether your hair isn't cooperating or your mascara is clumping just a bit too much. So I'll help you find a pro to do your hair and makeup in a jiff. Of course, if you're a DIY (do-it-yourself) bride and are determined to do your hair and makeup yourself, don't worry: I've offered tips to help you in this regard as well so that in the end, your hair and makeup will look fabulous, too.

# Finding and Choosing Your Wedding Gown

## To do list

- [ ] Research dress styles in magazines and online
- [ ] Determine the kind of dress you're looking for
- [ ] Choose and list stores that have the style of dress you've chosen
- [ ] Find a dress that matches your body type and complexion
- [ ] Purchase your dress

If you're like most women, you've had a vision in your head since you were a little girl of what you were going to look like on your wedding day. For years, because I was a *Little House on the Prairie* fan as a kid, I assumed I would get married in a dress like Laura Ingalls could have worn. Of course, when I grew up and started shopping for gowns, I had to let my adult fashion sensibility take over, lest I look like an idiot in a late-19th century homespun wedding gown.

But having a strong vision of the kind of dress I liked helped me to focus my shopping efforts. With minimal research, I was able to plan to visit only stores that stocked the styles I liked, so I didn't waste time visiting shops that didn't carry my style. In no time, I had the dress of my dreams.

In this section, you'll read a number of ideas for making your wedding-gown shopping experience less stressful and more productive. You'll learn how to choose a dress that fits with the location and event you've planned, as well as one that flatters your body shape and coloring. And you'll learn how to organize your search so that you can find the perfect dress in short order.

## You'll need list

- [ ] Computer
- [ ] Internet access
- [ ] Tear sheets of dresses you like
- [ ] Date book for making appointments

## Choosing a Dress That Matches the Formality of Your Wedding

Although many rules of etiquette have relaxed when it comes to weddings, you may find the following suggestions helpful to keep in mind as you shop for your dress:

- **Formal wedding**. You want to wear a floor-length gown with a train and a long veil. A formal wedding would be a ceremony that comprises a high-noon Roman Catholic mass, a wedding held at an elite country club, or a wedding ceremony that begins after 5:00 p.m.

- **Semiformal wedding**. You may also wear a floor-length gown but you may decide to forego the train. When choosing a veil, go with a shorter length. A semiformal wedding is probably the most common type of wedding ceremony and reception that people have. The kinds of weddings that fall into this category include pretty much all ceremonies held in a house of worship.

- **Informal wedding**. You can wear a three-quarter's length gown, or you can choose a cocktail dress or dressy suit. When it comes to informal weddings, there are no rules about how the bride should dress. You can rest assured that your wedding qualifies as informal if you're holding it in an informal location, such as at a garden, in a fire hall, or on the beach.

Most sticklers for wedding-fashion etiquette will tell you that you must choose a white or off-white gown for a formal or semiformal wedding. While that may be true in certain social circles, some folks feel that the length of the gown and its design have more to do with its formality than the color. When in doubt get second or third opinions on the dresses you try on to make sure that your first and second choice dresses fit with the formality of your occasion.

**tip**
Certain houses of worship have restrictions or suggestions on the kinds of wedding gown they "prefer" their brides to wear. For example, some conservative religions may require that the bride cover her shoulders during the ceremony. Always check ahead of time with your religious officiant to see if there are any rules you need to keep in mind when shopping for your gown.

## Organizing Your Dress Shopping

To approach your dress shopping in an organized fashion, stock up on bridal magazines and start ripping out advertisements and other pictures of wedding dresses that you feel might look good on you. These tear sheets will come in handy as you plan your dress shopping excursions—when you find a designer you like, you can usually look on the company's website to find a store near you that carries that designer's wares.

Once you've got designers and shops narrowed down, you can plan your shopping trips accordingly. This way you won't waste time. If possible, try to choose stores that are located near one another, so you can cluster your shopping in two- and three-store bursts. This will help you approach your dress shopping efficiently.

Keep in mind that most stores carry a variety of designers, and you shouldn't limit yourself only to trying on dresses by a single company. Chances are if you like a certain kind of dress, you'll find a number of designers that might make similar dresses. By keeping an open mind you may find a dress that fits your body (or your budget) better than you'd originally planned.

Let your fingertips do the walking on your keyboard one lunch hour, and use website addresses from bridal gown advertisements to locate stores near you that you might want to visit to try on dresses. Then, once you've got your list complete, tap into Mapquest or a similar Internet map program to plan your upcoming gown excursions so that you make the most of your shopping time.

You may find the dress of your dreams at the first shop; you may find it after the 50th dress you've tried on. Throughout it all keep an open mind—a dress that looks awful on the hanger might look fabulous on your body and vice versa—and don't settle for a dress that doesn't seem perfect to you.

> "When you go dress shopping, you will have to get undressed in front of different people, so be sure to prepare yourself both mentally and physically! Wear nice, comfortable underwear that will look good under a dress, and try to bring a strapless bra with you. The stores might offer you one, but usually your own is more comfortable. Try to do your hair a bit and wear some makeup so that you feel as pretty as possible when you look at yourself in the mirror in these gowns."
>
> Julie, Massachusetts

## You'll need list

- [ ] Neutral-colored underwear
- [ ] Shoes with a heel
- [ ] Digital or Polaroid camera
- [ ] Maid of honor for shopping companionship

## Preparing for Your Shopping Expeditions

"You can't buy a wedding gown like you would a sweater or a pair of jeans," says Nancy Aucone, president and founder of The Wedding Salon, an upscale bridal shop in Manhasset, New York. That is, you can't approach this purchase casually or without forethought. To help you prepare for your walk down the many bridal shop aisles, here are some important pointers to keep in mind:

- Call first to see if you need an appointment. There's nothing that will burst your bubble like walking into a bridal store you've been dying to visit, only to discover that there's no one there to help you.

- Expect hands-on service. You know how sometimes it feels like salespeople are hovering when all you want to do is shop by yourself? Well, when you're buying a wedding gown, you should prepare yourself for one-on-one service, and, if you have to, try to enjoy all the attention salespeople are willing to shower on you.

- Dress yourself comfortably and appropriately for a long day of shopping. The average bride-to-be can spend three hours in one shop alone! So wear comfortable clothing and shoes that are easy to get in and out of, undergarments that won't embarrass your mother and which won't stick out underneath a gown, and don't forget to do a little something with your hair and makeup. You won't get a real sense of how you could potentially look on your wedding day if you spend your shopping day walking around with bed head and dark circles under your eyes.

- Take along tear sheets from magazines so you can show the staff at the bridal salon the kinds of dresses you'd like to look at first. But don't become wedded to those dresses only. "Tear sheets are a good place to start," says Aucone, but she prefers it when brides come to her store with an open mind to a variety of silhouettes. "Often brides who come in only wanting to try on straight, simple dresses leave having purchased a dress that's at the opposite end of the spectrum than what she originally thought she'd like," adds Aucone.

- Bring reinforcements whose opinions you trust, but don't bring too many girlfriends along. You know the old saying that too many cooks in the kitchen can ruin the soup? Well, the same could be said for gown shopping—too many girlfriends can ruin the experience.

- Speaking of the experience, stick with shops that come highly recommended from friends and family. "Our business is 75 percent referral," says Aucone. "You shouldn't shop at a place that doesn't make it a pleasant experience."

- Find out ahead of time if the shops you'll be visiting will let you have someone snap a picture of you in the dresses you try on. Some stores don't allow photography on the premises because they don't want to risk you taking a picture of the gown to a custom-designer who can make a knock-off. But if you can take pictures, do so. This will help you remember the gowns that you liked the most and decide, once and for all, which gown you'd like to wear on your big day.

- Don't shop on an empty stomach. Have a little nourishment in you before you hit the racks, or you may end up like some of the too-nervous-to-eat brides that Aucone has seen faint in the dressing room.

## Trying on Wedding Dresses

I have to admit that I'm a bit prejudiced against traditional bridal shops that only stock sample-size dresses. This practice prevents brides without a sample-size body (usually a 6 or an 8) from trying on their wedding gown for real before ordering it. I don't think you should have to invest hundreds, if not thousands, of dollars in a garment you've never seen on yourself, save for holding the dress on a hanger up to your body.

That's why I feel more comfortable shopping in stores that stock many different sizes of wedding gowns and special occasion dresses, like David's Bridal. (I know for a fact that this chain carries sizes 2 to 26 in its stores.) You'll also find a variety of sizes in department stores, where you can check out evening wear or prom dresses for alternative wedding dress options. You can also visit outlet shops and resale shops for last season's wedding gowns at a discount. If you need to get your gown pronto, you'll save time—and your sanity—by avoiding the whole gown-ordering scenario.

What it all boils down to is this: try on lots of dresses so that when you finally buy your wedding gown, you'll feel confident that you've chosen the best dress for you. Sure, you can gaze at dresses in wedding magazines and at online sites, but you won't really know the dress that's right for you until you try it on. Touching and feeling a garment that's as important as a wedding gown is an experience you really can't duplicate over the Web. I hope that by approaching dress shopping in such a sensible fashion, you'll be able to find the perfect dress for your big day.

**tip** Invest in a strapless corset to bring with you on your shopping trips. When it comes to wedding gowns, sometimes a regular strapless bra won't suffice for shaping and supporting your body. That's why most bridal shops keep strapless corsets on hand for customers to use, but be forewarned: they may or may not have one that fits you well. So you may find yourself swimming in a too-big bra or squeezed up to your neck in one that's too small.

**tip** If you need a wedding gown fast and have decided to buy a store's sample or one off-the-rack, make sure the store lets you thoroughly inspect the dress before buying it. Take it outside or into a brightly lit lobby so you can see how the fabric looks. Are there any stains? Did the lace or embroidery tear in any places? Does the dress need to be cleaned ahead of time? If you find that your dress is in less-than-perfect condition, see if you can't negotiate a deal with the shop—either to have them knock some money off the price or give you a deal on cleaning and restoration.

# GETTING A GOWN IN A HURRY

According to research from the Association of Bridal Consultants, most brides take about 10 months to buy their wedding gown. In my book that is way too long to be thinking about anything related to a wedding, let alone a dress. But given that many women custom order their gowns, I'm not surprised that it takes 10 months.

Some brides don't have the luxury of waiting 10 months to get their dresses, though. They may be getting married 3 or 6 months after they became engaged, and so they need a dress fast. In this instance buying a wedding gown from a shop with a large inventory of styles and sizes or one that offers dresses off-the-rack is probably a time-crunched bride's best bet.

What will happen is this: The day you go to the store to buy your gown, you will likely be trying on the actual gown that you'll wear as you walk down the aisle. On the other hand, when you order a gown based on a sample, you may not be able to actually try it on, especially if you're not a sample size (size 6 or 8). Instead, you'll have to imagine yourself wearing the dress and won't actually get to see it on your body until after it's been ordered and paid for.

Whether you buy a gown from inventory or order one, the dress will probably need some alterations to make it fit your body perfectly, unless you're extremely lucky. But even alterations shouldn't put a dent in your planning timeline—I can't imagine that they would take more than a week or two, which should work just fine for a last-minute bride planning a wedding in no time.

## Choosing a Wedding Gown That Works with Your Body

With magazine pages and online photos in hand and your wedding's formality, setting, and season in mind, you're off to a good start in figuring out the kind of wedding gown you'd like to wear. But you should keep other ideas in mind as you shop—specifically your physical assets and liabilities.

Use the following chart to find the most flattering wedding gown you can. Keep in mind that if you're tall and slim, you can wear whatever wedding gown you like—everything is going to look fabulous on you, so you can probably skip this chart all together. If you're like the rest of us, the info in this chart can help you choose a gown that makes the most of your own personal beauty.

**tip** Can't figure out an A-line dress from a sheath gown? Many bridal manufacturers and retailers include dress specs on their websites to help you understand this brave new world of wedding-gown lingo. I especially like the line drawings on the David's Bridal website (www.davidsbridal.com), which not only explains which kind of dress looks good on what kind of body but also offers photographs of each kind of dress so you can get a good sense of what they look like in real life.

| Body Type/Attributes | Kind of Dress to Look for or to Avoid |
|---|---|
| Ample hips, bottom, and legs | An A-line is good for concealing a pear-shaped physique. Also, if you're smaller on top, you should try on strapless dresses as well. They do a good job of highlighting your assets and covering your liabilities. At the same time avoid a puffy skirt, which will make your hips and thighs look even bigger. |
| Short stature | If you want to appear taller, go for an A-line dress, which can give the illusion of height; avoid a dress with too much detail or a big skirt—it can overwhelm a petite bride. |
| Boyish figure, petite chest | Look for a fitted dress that will play up curves, such as one with a corseted bodice, but avoid sheaths or anything that's too sexy. A top with a built-in padded bra or underwire can enhance a small bust as well. Also, a girl with a boyish figure will look fabulous in a halter-style dress. |
| Fuller figure | Again, look for an A-line dress. Avoid any body-hugging fabrics that could be less-than-flattering on you. |
| Big bust | Look for a dress with a halter top design or one with three-quarter-length sleeves. Both are flattering. Big-busted brides should avoid a strapless gown—you may fall out of it—or a dress with a deep-V neckline. |

## Choosing the Color of Your Gown

Even though my cousin Cara was a first-time bride in her 30s, she didn't wear the wedding gown of a first-time bride. Instead of going with a traditional white dress, Cara chose a more modern gown—an ivory dress with spaghetti straps and multi-colored embroidery all over that allowed the dress to perfectly complement the garden setting of her wedding.

I'm not surprised that Cara made such an off-beat choice for her wedding gown. Once you start visiting bridal gown shops, you won't be either. On a recent trip to one such shop, I found wedding gowns that were anything but white—there were gowns with white and beige beading, some with ice-blue details and others in a rosy hue. In fact, some modern brides wear wedding gowns that are red, yellow, or even green.

There's no rule that says that you have to wear a white or off-white wedding gown. White gowns can be unflattering—many women look washed out in a white dress—so you should feel perfectly comfortable choosing a nontraditional shade for your gown. Or you can go with just a bit of color, such as a baby blue or platinum accent to your skirt or veil, which will give a formal-looking gown a very fashion-forward feel.

## Steps and Timeline for Choosing a Custom-Ordered Gown

Despite the advantages of buying a gown that they can try on, many brides choose to buy custom-ordered gowns. Nancy Aucone offers these steps to buying a custom-made gown:

1. Start shopping for your wedding gown one year before your wedding.

2. Plan to place your dress order at least six months before your big date, and expect to pay 50 percent of the dress's price at that time.

3. Between three and four months later (sometimes sooner), your dress will arrive. The salon will call to schedule your first fitting.

4. Make sure that by the time your dress arrives you've found a pair of shoes to wear with it. Even if they're going to be dyed, you'll need to bring the "raw" shoe with you to the first fitting.

5. At your first fitting, the salon will ask that you pay the balance on the dress. At this point in time, they'll measure your body so they can cut the dress (i.e., alter it) to fit you perfectly, including the length with your shoes on. Once you've paid for your dress in full, the salon will let you take a picture of yourself in it, and they'll give you a swatch of fabric that you can use to show your florist or whomever needs to match items to your dress. At this point you should look at veils, headpieces, and any other accessories to match your dress.

6. About one month later, you'll go for a second fitting to see how the alterations panned out. If you've lost or gained weight, a seamstress will tweak your dress accordingly.

7. Usually two weeks before your wedding, you'll go for an additional fitting.

8. The week of your wedding, you'll have your final fitting. It will be at this final fitting that you'll learn how to put your veil on, how to work your bustle (your skirt), and to practice walking in your dress.

**note** Keep in mind that this timeline and these suggestions are for a bride with plenty of time to shop for her gown. Most bridal shops can work on an expedited basis and can turn around a custom-ordered gown in as little as 30 days. However, you'll pay significant rush charges for this faster service.

**caution** Whether you buy off-the-rack or order a custom-made dress, once you have it finally cleaned, pressed, and properly hung before your wedding day, leave it be. You don't want to try it on one last time, and risk getting makeup or coffee on it. Also, keep your gown away from any pets (perhaps in a locked closet) that may want to "investigate" the dress and ruin it in the process.

**tip** Be sure to wear your wedding-day shoes around the house (on carpeting!) from time to time. You want to make sure that they are comfortable enough for you to have them on for your entire wedding day. If it turns out they're not comfortable, return them (thus the advice to wear them on carpeting only) and invest in another pair of more comfortable shoes.

**tip** Before you wear your new wedding-day shoes, take a piece of sandpaper and scuff the bottoms. This will prevent you from sliding around on never-worn shoes.

9. After your final fitting, you'll pay the balance on the alterations and for any additional accessories you may have purchased to go with your dress.

10. The bridal shop will do one last pressing of your dress and stuff it to keep its shape. You'll arrange for a time to pick up the dress, usually the day before the wedding. Once you get your dress to your home or hotel room, store it carefully in a closet or other protected place and leave it alone.

# ACCESSORIES CHECKLIST

There's more to shopping for your wedding than just buying a wedding gown. You need to get all of the goodies that go along with being a bride. So you don't end up shopping for a headpiece or a pair of stockings at the last minute, here is a list of all the accessories you'll need to buy or borrow for your big day:

- Headpiece, hat, or veil
- Jewelry
- New shoes (make sure they're comfortable)
- Stockings or pantyhose
- Stole or shawl (if you're having a winter wedding)
- Gloves (if you prefer)
- Handkerchief
- Bridal purse

# Choosing Hair and Makeup Styles and Stylists

## To do list

- ☐ Determine whether you'll do your own makeup and hair or hire a professional
- ☐ Research makeup artists in your area
- ☐ Schedule trial runs with makeup artists
- ☐ Book your makeup person
- ☐ Consider hairstyles that complement your face

One of the most important things for a bride to keep in mind about her hair and makeup on her big day is this: she should choose a hairstyle and makeup palette that not only complements her but also that reflects the importance of the event.

"This is what I come up against a lot of times—brides who say, 'I don't wear makeup,'" says Lorraine Altamura, a makeup artist in Yonkers, New York, who has more than 20 years of experience doing both bridal and celebrity makeup. "Well, the truth is you're going to have to wear a little bit of makeup on your wedding day or you're going to look washed out in your pictures.

"Another thing I come up against is brides who say, 'I always wear my hair straight.' Well, you aren't going to the office today, and I'll tell them that there's no such thing as a mousy look for brides in my book. I let them know that there are ways to do a less-is-more approach with makeup, ways to use makeup to enhance your look without piling it on, and to do the same with a hairstyle."

What Altamura says every bride should be trying to achieve with her bridal-day hair and makeup is "a classic look that stays true to your own identity. However, brides need to understand that a little more makeup or classic style of hair might be a marvelous change for their wedding day."

In this section, you'll consider a number of important factors when deciding on the best makeup and hairstyles for your wedding day. You learn how to determine whether to do the styling yourself or to hire a professional stylist, and how to go about finding and choosing the best stylist. You also discover a few good tips for booking your stylists and scheduling a practice run to make sure your makeup and hair will be perfect on the day of your wedding.

## Finding a Hairstyle That Complements Your Face

Before you fall in love with one kind of hairstyle for your wedding day, keep this in mind: The shape of your face and the size of your neck will affect your hairstyle decision more so than what all the fashion magazines are showing for hairstyles. Here are Lorraine Altamura's suggestions for matching a hairstyle with your face shape:

- An oblong face needs to look less long. You can accomplish this by creating width with your hair on the sides of your head. So even if 1980s big hair comes back in style by the time of your wedding, do not add volume to the top of your head. That will make an oblong face look even longer. So will straight-down long hair—it will accentuate the face's length. Instead, you need to create width on the sides of your face with volume, such as with curls or layers.

- With a wider, more round face, you want to have a little height on the top and have pieces of hair hitting the face to frame it. You do not want to make the face seem even wider, such as by pulling the hair back tightly. You need long vertical hair to diffuse the roundness of the face.

- The inverted triangle face has a bigger forehead and a pointy chin. The worst kind of style you can wear with this shape face is straight-across bangs—it will accentuate the shape of the triangle. What helps to reduce the appearance of the forehead is soft waves on the side of the face. It contours nicely. Also, you want to choose a hairstyle that fills in the gap between the ears and the collarbone, to help reduce the size of the chin, but don't go for really long hair—it will drag the chin down. If you want to wear your hair up, get tendrils to come down but remember: tendrils don't always need to be curly—they can be wispy, too.

- A bride who has a long slender neck and is self-conscious about it should wear her hair down. Hair up or short hair will only make her neck look longer.

- If a woman has a thick, short neck and wants to mask it a bit, she should speak to her hairstylist about choosing a hairstyle that frames and contours her neck.

A good place to research various hairstyles is right at your local hair salon. Most salons have books in their waiting rooms that showcase various short, medium, and long hairstyles. So take a few minutes before your next hair appointment and see if you can find any wedding-day hair ideas in those books. Also, if you visit your local bookseller, you're likely to find magazines devoted entirely to hairstyles. These can be a good resource as well. Finally, good old wedding magazines are a great place to look for hairstyle ideas. Check out the online version of such magazines as *In Style Weddings* for the up-to-date wedding-day hair options.

**tip** When your hairstylist places your headpiece, make sure he or she centers it on your head. A headpiece worn too far back won't show up in pictures and one worn too far forward will look imbalanced and as if it's tipping off your head.

# HEADPIECES IN A HURRY

It's easy to find the right headpiece for you, once you know your face shape. Keep these tips in mind, and your shopping will be snap.

- If you have a long chin, you don't want a pointy tiara. It will be like having a triangle on the top and the bottom of your head.

- If you have a round face, stay away from round crown pieces because they will only accentuate the roundness of your face.

- When in doubt, go with a headband-style headpiece—it looks the best on most face types.

## Making Decisions About Makeup

You can't get away without wearing any makeup on your wedding day—everyone needs a little extra makeup to look good in photographs or under bright lights. However, you want to make sure that, at the end of your makeup application, you still look like yourself.

"If you feel comfortable with how you look, you'll come across looking the most beautiful in your photos," says Rachel Weingarten, a noted beauty and trend expert in New York City who is also a former celebrity makeup artist and co-founder of Air Kisses.com.

Weingarten also points out that the amount and color of makeup you choose to wear should reflect your wedding location, timing, and formality. So if you're having a more formal affair, here's how your makeup should play out:

- Wear more dramatic makeup overall
- Go for darker, smoky eyes
- Choose a deep-colored lipstick

If you're having a casual, laid-back affair, you might want to approach your makeup this way:

- Wear makeup that is more natural and glowing
- Choose subtle colors for eye shadow, blush, and lipstick
- If you're getting married on the beach, bronzer on your face and gloss on your lips may be all you need as far as makeup goes.

Here are some tips to keep in mind when thinking about makeup for your big day:

- Now is not the time to try anything drastic, such as experimenting with false eyelashes if you've never worn them.
- Make sure that you play up your best feature. "If you are known for gorgeous sparkly eyes, use eye color that enhances them," says Weingarten.
- In playing up one feature, don't forget about other features on your face. You need balance to make your makeup look its best. So if you're doing up your eyes with smoldery eye shadow, don't forget about lips, or your face will just fade.

Even with that good advice in mind, though, you still have to decide whether you'll do your own makeup on your wedding day or whether you'll leave that to a professional. Both choices, as always, offer their own advantages and disadvantages. Regardless of which option you choose, you should definitely schedule a practice makeup session. That way, you can decide ahead of time how you'd like your hair and makeup to look. The information and advice in this next section of the chapter will help you decide which choice is right for you.

### Do-It-Yourself Makeup

For some women there is only one option for wedding-day makeup and that's doing it themselves. It may be that you've never had your makeup done professionally and you're just not comfortable with the idea of working with a makeup artist for your wedding-day look. Or perhaps you're overly concerned that you'll end up looking artificial and inhibited with someone else doing your makeup. Or maybe your budget simply won't allow for such an expenditure.

> **tip** Pack yourself a touch-up kit for your makeup that includes the lipstick you used and some translucent powder. That way, you'll have everything you need to do touch-ups throughout the day—something you'll have to do, even if you've had your makeup done professionally.

Whatever your reasons for wanting to do your makeup yourself, here are step-by-step tips to great wedding-day makeup, courtesy of Rachel Weingarten:

1. Layer your makeup. Don't put on a heavy coat of pancake makeup and think it will stay all day. There are a lot of things to keep in mind beyond foundation. If you have dark spots near your eyes or discolorations on your face, you need to find a good concealer and get it as close to skin color as possible.

2. When applying cover-up to any dark circles under your eyes, don't overdo it—you'll end up with white circles that will make you look like a raccoon in your pictures. Instead, dot the concealer on, starting at the inner corner of your eyes. Tap it with your fingertips to blend. Use the same application method with concealer on other parts of your face, such as with a pimple.

3. Next, put a light base on your face with a good foundation. Most makeup artists like to use their fingers to apply makeup because the temperature of their skin will heat up the foundation so it blends better on the face.

4. After foundation apply translucent powder to set your makeup. You can use either a big fluffy brush or a cosmetic sponge.

5. Next, move on to your blush. While a cream blush will look good in photos because it lasts, it's not right for the bride with oily skin. It could clog the pores and it's more likely to wear off faster, so stick with powder blush

instead. Don't apply blush as a stripe of color. Instead, dot the apples of your cheeks (the round parts that form when you smile) and then blend it in.

6. Focus on your eyes next. Start by putting foundation on your eyes, just like you do the rest of your face, and set it with pressed powder applied with a big fluffy brush. This will create a base for your eye shadow to help it last longer.

   As far as colors go, women with lighter skin should go for a pale pink or gold-hued eye shadow. A woman with darker skin should choose a darker bronze color for her eyelids. If you cry a lot, definitely use waterproof mascara.

7. Finally, do your lips. Don't forget to put foundation on your lips—it will help your color last longer. After foundation, outline your lips with a neutral-colored lip pencil; then use it to fill lips. Blot lips with a tissue. Then put on lipstick color, blot, and then a drop of gloss on bottom lip. And voila, your lips are done.

So you've decided on DIY makeup for your wedding. Great. Now you've got to get up-to-date on the latest makeup techniques. Dedicate a weekend to visiting various makeup counters at your local department store so you can find the makeup you like and want to use for your wedding and so you can get a free makeover. See if your maid of honor can join you with a video camera in hand. That way she can record the steps the makeup artists use to make you look gorgeous, and you can review the tape later so you can brush up on your techniques.

**tip** To find the right color blush for you:
- Think pinks or pale apricot for light skin colors.
- If you have somewhat sallow skin, go with a coral-colored blush.
- For darker skin take your blush up a notch with burgundy

**tip** If you decide to do your own makeup, make it a priority to schedule an appointment for a session at the makeup counter of your favorite department store. All of the major makeup manufacturers, such as Clinique, Lancôme, and others, will happily do a makeup session with you and explain every step of the process. If you already used the company's products, your only cost will be the price of any new products you purchase. Remember: you're not obligated to buy any of the products they use, but if you like how something looks on you, you should add it to your cadre of makeup. Either way, during this makeup demonstration, you will have learned about your skin tone, application techniques, and what products and colors work best on your skin.

# MAKE SURE YOUR EYES HAVE "IT"

Your eyes are one of your most important features. Because you're going to be the center of attention on your big day, it's important that you make sure your eyes look as good as they've ever looked. But having great-looking eyes is about more than just decorated lids or eyelashes.

Having well-arched eyebrows can really open your face. Before your wedding, have someone take a look at your brows. If you've got a unibrow—growth in between your two eyebrows—get rid of it. You can pluck your brows yourself or go to a salon to have them waxed. If you take the time to do your eyebrows, you'll see a huge difference in your face.

As for the eyes themselves, don't put thick eyeliner on your eyelids because it can make them look smaller. If you're addicted to eyeliner under the eyes, do a smudgy look instead. Maybe put black on the top lid and then a smoky gray on the bottom.

If you wear glasses, do yourself a favor and buy new frames for your wedding. Makeup artists recommend that you either go for "invisible" or pale pink frames. The idea is to find a frame that doesn't detract from but instead enhances your face.

## Hiring a Makeup Pro for Your Wedding Day

If you're not sure you want to tackle your wedding day makeup all on your own, there are some really good reasons for leaving this job to a pro. Here are four of them:

- A professional will have experience preparing people for photographs—something you'll be smiling a lot for on your big day.
- The pro will be able to take one look at your face and know what to accentuate and what to downplay.
- A makeup professional will know how to put on makeup so it stays in place and continues to look good, even when you're under stress.
- You can relax while someone else is doing your makeup.

Convinced? Here's how to find a makeup pro you'll love:

- Plan to book your makeup artist at least one to two months in advance during the off-season, perhaps as much as four months in advance during popular wedding times, such as the summer and fall.

- If a friend got married recently and you loved her makeup, have her refer you to her makeup artist.

- Visit your local department store's makeup counter and see if any of the makeup artists there do freelance work. Of course, sit down for a makeover at the counter first to see if you like what he or she does with your makeup. Then you can decide whether or not to hire the person for your wedding.

- When you find a makeup artist you'd like to consider, ask to see her *look book*, which will show you examples of past events she's worked on. "If you notice lots of blue eye shadow and ruby-red lips and you'd like a perfectly natural look, this makeup artist may not be for you," advises beauty expert Rachel Weingarten.

- Prepare to offer your makeup artist a 25 percent down payment. As with all of your vendors, put something in writing that outlines the day of your event, the time you need your makeup artist there, how long he or she will be working, if you've negotiated to have her do the hair and makeup for other women in your wedding party or for her to stick around for touch-ups, the colors you've agreed upon, and any other specifics you want to make sure that you both remember.

# MAKEUP AND HAIR IN A HURRY

Let's say the bride sleeps late on her wedding date and needs to do her hair and makeup in a hurry—and she hasn't hired a professional to help her out. If this happens to you, here are some quick "must dos" to help you look fabulous on your big day:

1. Start by covering up spots with concealer.

2. Turn to a three-in-one blush, eye shadow, and lipstick combination for your quick makeup needs. Whatever you do, don't forget to put on the blush so you don't look washed out with your white dress.

3. Remember your mascara, eyeliner, and lipstick, and do it in a hurry. The idea here is to get some color on your face because you're going to be wearing all white.

4.  Dust some powder on your face to get rid of shine.

5.  Go with casual hair that day. Either twist it back and hold it with little clips or figure on having a tousled look that day.

6.  Finally, smile and laugh about the fact that you slept late. It will make you feel a lot less stressed. No matter how your hair and makeup end up looking, your smile will make you a beautiful bride.

## Test-Driving Hair and Makeup Styles

Once you find the person who is going to do your wedding-day hair and makeup, you may think that you're set. Well, you're not. You can't wait until the day of to discuss how you want to do your hair or what kind of makeup you'd like to wear. Think about it this way: how many dresses did you try on before you found the right one? Probably at least a handful. You should approach your makeup styles and hairstyles the same way too.

Here's what I suggest: Once you narrow down your hair and makeup stylist to two or three choices, book a run-through with each. Allocate sufficient time for him or her to try out a few different hairstyles on you until you find the one you love. Once you do find the perfect hairstyle and makeup, capture it with a Polaroid or digital camera. That way on the big day, you can bring out that photo from the run-through and your hairdresser will immediately remember the look you're trying to achieve.

**note** Remember, in the weeks since that run-through, your hairdresser may have styled many other brides, and it's likely he or she isn't going to remember the exact hairstyle that you deemed your winner. That's why you want to have a photographic record of your favorite look—it will help jog the stylist's memory and get your hair done in a timely manner on your big day.

Expect to pay an extra fee for the hairstyling or makeup run-through session. You're booking the professional's time outside of your wedding, and there's a chance that you may not hire this person for the job—and therefore will not be paying him or her at a later date for the wedding job.

After the run-through, decide which person you liked working with best and who made you look terrific. Then book that person for your wedding.

# Taking Care of Last-Minute Necessities (and Niceties)

## To do list

- ❑ Schedule necessary doctor appointments
- ❑ Arrange for massage or spa day before the wedding

## You'll need list

- ❑ Health professionals' contact information
- ❑ Dates of previous exams
- ❑ Calendar or scheduling device

## Taking Care of His and Her Health

One of the ways I encourage you to take care of yourself and your future husband is to make sure that you don't leave any doctor's appointments or health checkups to the last minute. I've heard of too many brides and grooms who needed emergency surgery or a rushed root canal on their honeymoon because they hadn't been to the doctor or dentist in a long time.

Here's a basic list of what tests and self-checks men and women should do on a regular basis. If any of these seem odd or entirely unheard of, I strongly suggest that you schedule a full checkup with your primary care physician.

| Her Health | His Health |
| --- | --- |
| Blood pressure check | Blood pressure check |
| Dentist visit twice a year | Dentist visit twice a year |
| Breast self-exam at home once a month | Testicular self-exam at home once a month |
| Visit gynecologist once a year and have full exam, including Pap smear | A complete physical at least once every two to three years |
| A complete physical at least once every three to five years | |
| An annual mammogram for women after 40 | |

So you don't forget any of your upcoming pre-wedding doctor's visits, spend one lunch hour entering all of these appointments in your calendar or PDA. If you have an electronic calendar, set an alarm reminder for each appointment so that even if you forget to look at the calendars that day, it will automatically remind you when the alarm goes off.

## Making a Date to Pamper Yourself

In all the craziness of planning your wedding, you're probably not taking care of yourself. I'm guessing that you haven't slept through a full night in a long time, you're probably skipping meals, and your shoulders and back are filled with knots of tension. This is actually a topic I covered in one of my previous books, *The Balanced Bride* (see Appendix A, "References and Resources," for more information), and it's a topic worth repeating here.

Even though you're busy and feel as if you're time-starved, I want you to make a date to pamper yourself. You need time to kick back and relax, and you'll become a calmer, more focused bride-to-be once you've had an hour or two all to yourself. You can schedule a full body massage or just a manicure. I especially recommend a manicure, since your hands will likely garner a lot of attention at the wedding.

Also, while you're at it, schedule a massage or some other kind of pampering for the day before your wedding—if there's any day when you're going to be feeling the most stressed out, it's the day before the big event. Give yourself an hour of pampering so you can approach this exciting day a little more relaxed.

**note** And speaking of hands, way back in Chapter 1, "First Things First," I mentioned about the practice of Mehndi, which is when Hindu and Muslim brides decorate their hands and feet with henna tattoos. One of the main reasons for this ritual is it is forced relaxation for the bride-to-be. After her hands and feet are decorated, she isn't supposed to leave the house until her wedding. So not only does the act of having her hands and feet decorated soothe and calm her, but so does her period of rest at home. No last-minute running around is allowed for these brides.

**tip** When scheduling pre-wedding pampering sessions, do not go for a facial a few days before a big event, such as your bridal shower or the actual wedding. You don't know how your skin is going to react to a facial, given your stress level. I'd hate to have you look like a blotchy mess in front of your friends and family. Stick with safer pampering procedures, like massage, which won't leave you all broken out and icky.

# Q&A ON NAME CHANGE ISSUES

Q: Do I have to change my name after I get married?

A: There is no law that says a woman has to take her husband's name after they get married; doing so is merely a tradition that harkens back many years. Years ago wives were viewed as property and a way to represent the transfer of ownership of a woman from her parents to her husband was for her to take her husband's name.

Women aren't the only ones who might think about changing their name. Some men do, too. Some couples want to share the same last name but don't want to have one person feeling left out if his or her last name isn't the one they choose. These couples choose an entirely new name for their family, which could be a hyphenated version of their original names or a new name all together. Check with your state marriage license bureau to learn where on your marriage license or with which government agency you'll need to register your new name.

Keep in mind that it's perfectly okay to keep your maiden name after you get married. Your name will not be automatically changed without your consent, although you may have to get used to people assuming you're Mrs. (insert husband's last name), simply because that's the norm. Also, you may want to alert your officiant and the entertainer at your wedding not to introduce you as Mr. and Mrs. because you did not take his name.

Q: I've decided to take my husband's name after marriage. How do I make it official?

A: A name change is a top-down sort of process, meaning that once you start with your marriage license (which includes your new surname), you'll have to follow a certain sequence of notifications to make everything legal and legit with the government and companies that you deal with on a regular basis.

Once you have a copy of your marriage certificate, your next step would be to notify the Social Security Administration (SSA). Your marriage certificate will serve as proof of your name change, and you'll be required to apply for a new Social Security card. (Visit www.ssa.gov to find a Social Security Administration office near you or to request an application for a new card.) The SSA will issue you a new Social Security card with your married name on it but that also includes the same Social Security number that you had with your maiden name. This will help keep things consistent as far as your identity goes.

Once you have your new name matching your old Social Security number, the SSA should notify the Internal Revenue Service so that you won't have any problems the first time you file a tax return using your new identity. According to the IRS website, the SSA notifies the IRS of name changes in about 10 business days.

Next you should contact the Passport Agency so you can get an updated passport. At the same time apply for a new driver's license so that the names on all of your pieces of identification match.

After that you can begin notifying all the other companies that will need to know of your name change. These might include the following:

- Your employer
- Credit card companies
- Financial institutions
- Telephone and other public utility companies
- Voter registration

# Wedding-Day Checklist

On the day of your wedding, you're likely to feel excited, nervous, and rushed. The more prepared you are for the activities of the day, the more relaxed you'll feel. Toward that end, you can prepare a wedding-day checklist of items and tasks that you must remember to bring with you or perform on that day. Here are some of the items you should include in your wedding-day checklist:

- Your gown, headpiece, shoes, jewelry, and other accessories
- Extra pair of shoes, in case you want to change your footwear at the reception
- A going-away outfit you can change into after the reception, pajamas to wear that night, and, of course, a packed suitcase for your honeymoon
- Payments for any vendors that are still owed money
- Tickets for your honeymoon, passport, and any other travel documents you'll need
- Your wallet, cell phone, and anything else that you'll want to have in a purse with you on your honeymoon
- Keys to any cars that you may need to drive later or rental agreements for vehicles you need to return
- Personal toiletries, prescriptions, and touch-up items, such as lipstick, powder, and hair spray
- Something to eat on the way to the ceremony, if your stomach is too nervous to have breakfast. Choose something that you won't have to worry about getting stuck in your teeth, such as fruit or cheese

- Any last-minute gifts that you need to give to your attendants, spouse, parents, or other important people in your life

- A list of phone numbers of all of your vendors so you can reach someone, in case of an emergency

- A bride and bridesmaid "emergency kit" (see tip)

- Tissues in case you'll cry

> **tip**
>
> Make sure that you pack an emergency kit for yourself and your bridesmaids for the day of the wedding. You may also want to create an emergency kit for the women's bathroom of your ceremony and reception as well. What to put in an emergency kit? Here are some suggestions:
>
> - Lipstick for touch-ups
> - Mascara
> - Pressed powder
> - Tampons
> - Tylenol or Advil for headaches or cramps
> - Sewing kit
> - Safety pins
> - Clear nail polish for pantyhose runs
> - Extra pantyhose
> - Small bottle of hair spray
> - Bobby pins
> - Breath mints

# Summary

After all the planning you've done for the benefit of your wedding guests, finally you were able to spend time thinking about you, the bride.

In this chapter, we got you thinking about what kind of wedding gown you always imagined yourself wearing, and then helped you to find one in real life. I offered tips for making your shopping excursions efficient by focusing on dresses that would flatter your figure.

We also talked a bit about ordering a wedding gown versus buying a gown off the rack. I hope you determined which option works best for your needs, and that you are currently the proud owner of a gorgeous wedding gown. My accessories checklist also helped you organize the process of buying all the extras you'll need to wear with your gown.

Once we got the dress settled, we moved on to two other areas that have to do with how you're going to look on your big day—your hair and your makeup. I offered tips on how to make yourself look beautiful, all on your own, and what to do about last-minute hair and makeup should you sleep late the morning of your wedding. I also suggested ways to find a professional to take care of your hair and makeup on your wedding day—and why it may be one of the wisest investments you make in yourself for your wedding.

Speaking of investing in yourself, I also suggested that despite your crazy schedule, you take some time out of your wedding planning and go for a massage, manicure, or other kind of pampering. I find that brides who take care of themselves go on to be happier, healthier, and calmer people when they walk down the aisle. I want you to be that way, too, and I hope you've already booked yourself some time at a nearby spa.

We also talked about general health issues affecting the bride and groom, and why you shouldn't put off seeing your doctor or dentist for a checkup before your big day.

Finally, you learned about the benefits of creating and using a wedding-day check-list to make sure you don't forget any important items or tasks on your big day.

In Chapter 9, "Planning a Happy Honeymoon," we move on to a really fun part of your wedding plans, or should I say post-wedding plans, your honeymoon. I'll help you and your fiancé figure out exactly what kind of honeymoon you want to have and where you should go on your first vacation as husband and wife. I'll also help you sort out the details of all-inclusive resorts and other options and remind you why booking with a travel agent is still a smart move, especially for your honey-moon. Finally, I'll explain why you'll want to insure your honeymoon—especially if Mother Nature decides to throw your vacation a curve ball. It will be money well spent.

# Planning a Happy
# Honeymoon

# 9

Undoubtedly, your honeymoon is going to be a much-needed vacation after the excitement of your wedding and the planning that preceded it. I'm sure the two of you are looking forward to getting away together on your first trip as husband and wife.

In this chapter, you'll learn how to choose a honeymoon location you *both* can love. I'll help you choose and plan just the right honeymoon. You'll learn how to book a honeymoon location and how to plan ahead for activities you may want to pursue together while you're away. Of course, if all you two crave is a week of just sitting on the beach and reading a book, I'll show you how to make those arrangements as well. You'll also discover the advantages and disadvantages of all-inclusive packages, and how to locate and choose a travel agent who can help you make arrangements quickly and efficiently. Finally, you'll learn some of the basics about acquiring the passports, visas, and health information you'll need to enjoy that fabulous honeymoon abroad, and how travel insurance can help you handle unplanned-for emergencies while traveling.

With the advice and information you'll acquire in this chapter, you can count on your honeymoon being one of the best vacations that you'll take together.

## In this chapter:

* Deciding on a honeymoon location you both can love
* Working with a travel agent
* Getting necessary visas, passports, and medical information and obtaining travel insurance

## To do list

- ☐ Discuss your ideal honeymoon
- ☐ Consider how weather might affect your trip
- ☐ Consider benefits of an all-inclusive or an á la carte honeymoon

# Choosing a Honeymoon Location

There are a few factors that might affect how you decide where to have your honeymoon, including time of year and location of your wedding, your budget, and your expectations. Here's how they each might play out:

- **Time of year**—If all you've ever dreamed about doing is taking an Alaskan cruise for your honeymoon and you're getting married in the fall, you're going to have to plan an alternative honeymoon. Most cruise ships only sail to Alaska through the late summer, making it an ideal honeymoon option for a mid-summer's wedding. Beyond Alaskan cruises here's something else to consider: if either of you work in education and you're having your wedding during the school year, you may have to postpone your full-blown honeymoon to a time when you're on a school vacation and can devote more days to traveling.

- **Location**—A bride getting married on the East Coast may want to honeymoon in Hawaii, but she's going to have to take into consideration just how long it takes to fly from an eastern city to Hawaii and back. That's not to say that you can't honeymoon in Hawaii, but given that you'll likely be spending two days in transit, I would only recommend it as a honeymoon location for a couple with two weeks to travel. West Coast brides, though, will find getting to Hawaii a snap, but perhaps not so easy when traveling to Europe, a closer destination for East Coast brides.

- **Budget**—If you're having a winter wedding and you want to honeymoon in the Caribbean or another tropical location, you'll probably pay the highest prices for your vacation at this time of year. Winter is high season in warm-weather destinations—more people want to travel to these hot spots—and so you're less likely to find discounts and more likely to find fewer availabilities. So if you don't have a bottomless budget for your honeymoon or a flexible travel schedule, you'll have to reconsider where you're going to honeymoon.

- **Your expectations**—You may see your honeymoon as the ideal week for sitting by the pool and reading a book. Your new husband may be dreaming of waterskiing, playing golf, or hiking in the mountains. If the two of you have divergent expectations of your honeymoon, you're going to need to figure out one of two things—a location for your honeymoon that will allow each of you to pursue your ideal honeymoon activities, or a way for one of you to compromise your expectations of what you'll do on your honeymoon so you can plan the perfect trip together.

# You'll need list

- ❑  Time with your spouse-to-be
- ❑  Projected honeymoon budget
- ❑  Computer and Internet access

## A Quick Quiz to Determine Your Honeymoon Compatibility

If you're not sure where you should consider honeymooning, take this quick compatibility quiz, which should help you narrow down your options. Here's question 1:

1.  When you think about an ideal vacation, what does it include?

    (a)  Lying on the beach or beside the pool all day long

    (b)  Playing your favorite sport

    (c)  Investigating new destinations

    (d)  A vacation that combines all of the above

Now, let's look at your answers:

a.  If the two of you answered that lounging beachside or poolside is your idea of the perfect honeymoon, you should feel comfortable booking a vacation in a warm-weather destination with a pool or beach nearby. You could choose to travel to a Caribbean resort at any time of the year or you might even book a beach house at a shore town near you. Either will give you your ideal honeymoon.

b.  An active couple will definitely want to book a honeymoon that lets them pursue their favorite hobbies together. If you're having a winter wedding, you may want to take a ski vacation so you can spend your time together schussing down the slopes. Or if you favor playing golf or tennis together, you can travel to a warm-weather destination that offers ample opportunities to spend time on the links or on the tennis court. Maybe you want to book a truly active honeymoon, such as a biking, hiking, or walking through a picturesque destination. There are plenty of tour companies that offer these kinds of active itineraries.

c. If you like to investigate new destinations when traveling, I would think that a trip to a foreign land would be the perfect honeymoon for you. You can plan to travel through a number of different cities or countries abroad, where you can see the countryside, try new cuisine, and meet lots of interesting people. If foreign travel isn't your cup of tea, you could always explore North American cities that you haven't been to before for your honeymoon. Plenty of couples visit such chic cities as Chicago, New York, or San Francisco for their honeymoon, and maybe that's where you want to go, too.

d. For a honeymoon that combines a little bit of everything—lounging by the pool, pursuing activities together, and exploring new destinations—I think that you would both be very happy booking a cruise. There are many cruise ships available today that not only provide the lounging opportunities on board but also at private islands in the Caribbean or another tropical destination they sail to. In addition, most cruises are "active" now, with everything from rock climbing walls to spinning classes to basketball courts. Finally, the very nature of a cruise is to visit different destinations, so it will allow you to satisfy your urge to explore as well.

Now, for question 2:

2. How much time do you have to devote to your honeymoon and when do you have to be back at work?

   (a) We both have to be back at our jobs a week after our wedding.

   b) We've saved up our vacation days and will be taking two weeks or more off for our honeymoon.

   c) We only have a long weekend now but hope to take a longer trip together later this year.

   d) You mean we have to come back to our jobs? I was hoping we could travel for months on end.

And, we'll review your answers here:

a. For a honeymoon of a week or less, I think you would have a great honeymoon if you didn't have to travel too far away. I would stick with destinations in a nearby time zone so that you won't lose too much time traveling to and from your destination. So a couple being married in the Pacific time zone could choose a honeymoon in Hawaii, Mexico, or the Western Provinces of Canada without spending too much time in transit. Likewise, a wedding in mountain or central time could lend itself to a West Coast honeymoon or one in Central America. And the East Coast bride could stick relatively close to home by traveling to the Caribbean or somewhere on the East Coast for her honeymoon.

b.  If you've got two weeks or more to travel on your honeymoon, you can go wherever you'd like to. With that much time in your itinerary, you can afford to spend a day or two traveling to your ideal location, whether it's faraway Fiji or a romantic city in Europe. A two-week honeymoon also lends itself well to a combination honeymoon, such as a seven-day cruise followed by a few days spent at a resort on terra firma.

c.  When my husband and I got married in November, we could only afford to honeymoon for a long weekend—my husband works in academia, and we didn't time our wedding well for a honeymoon taken over a school break. So here's what we did—we took a weekend trip to a nearby inn immediately following our nuptials and spent the time together relaxing and sightseeing. Then seven months later, when school was out, we took our "real" honeymoon, which was a week spent golfing at a resort in St. Croix. I would recommend that time-crunched couples choose a similar two-part honeymoon, comprised of a quick trip after their actual wedding, and then a longer, more traditional honeymoon at a later date.

d.  If time is not of the essence in planning your honeymoon, you can really plan an amazing trip together. If you never had the chance to drive cross country or travel through Europe after graduating from college, now may be the time for you to take that trip—as long as you both agree that such a long-haul excursion sounds like the perfect way to spend your honeymoon. You also have another option—you could take a traditional length honeymoon of one or two weeks, and then spend the rest of your vacation time together at your new home, unpacking and setting up your new life together. There's no rule that says that if you've got three months off to travel you have to spend each and every day of that time on the road. You should spend your honeymoon doing exactly what you want to do—not what convention dictates. By doing so, you'll ensure that you have a great time together.

# HOW PROPER TIMING CAN EXPEDITE YOUR HONEYMOON PLANS

There are certain truths in travel—Thanksgiving week is one of the busiest and most expensive weeks to travel during the year, and if you travel to a family-friendly spot during school vacations, your resort is sure to be crawling with kids. But there are also times of the year when travel to certain destinations is less popular and you may be able to book a last-minute vacation that won't break your bank. Such times of the year include the week after New Year's, when most kids have already gone back to school yet weather in South Florida is still beautiful, or the first week of September, when, again, school is back in session. Talk to your travel agent about some of these options if you're looking to cut costs on your honeymoon. Of course, January could also be snowstorm time, and you might just hit a hurricane in September. So be sure to talk about your travel insurance options as well.

## Honeymoon Options for Cold-Weather Weddings

While the bulk of couples get married during June and September (the top two months for weddings), plenty of people tie the knot around Christmas, New Year's, or Valentine's Day—all cold-weather months. A Caribbean vacation at this time of year would seem the most obvious option. Plenty of cold-climate residents want to be in a warm-weather destination during the winter, so why should you be any different? Well, the popularity of the Caribbean during this high season means that you'll pay higher prices and may find less availability based on simple supply and demand.

With that in mind, remember: a Caribbean honeymoon is a wonderful trip to take but it isn't your only option for a cold-weather wedding. Here are some other locations to consider:

- Ski resorts in North America
- Florida
- Hawaii

**caution** Get the facts on potential honeymoon destinations before you plan your trip. "Most couples don't think about the honeymoon until they have already set their wedding date. Unfortunately, I have had couples marry in December and want to go to the Greek Islands, but that's not a good idea," says Maria Harner, a travel agent with Travel Duet, Inc., in Deerfield, Illinois. "Most people don't realize that it's cold in Greece in December, not the kind of weather folks want when they go to Greece."

- Mexico
- Australia (it's summer there when it's winter here)
- New Zealand
- Costa Rica

## Honeymoon Options for Warm-Weather Weddings

A warm-weather bride will definitely have more flexibility in choosing her honeymoon destination than her winter counterpart. That's because she won't have to travel very far to find warmer weather to enjoy her honeymoon. Here are some places to consider honeymooning:

- Hawaii
- Mexico (late spring)
- Caribbean (late spring)
- Tahiti
- Fiji
- Europe
- Greece

If you're planning a warm-weather honeymoon, here are some additional do's and don'ts to keep in mind as you make your travel plans:

- Don't plan a honeymoon in the Caribbean, Mexico, Central America, or on the eastern seaboard between August and October—that's when you'll find the greatest likelihood of hurricanes hitting.

- Do try to book your spring or early summer honeymoon before schools let out or in late August when many schools start back up for the year. That way your resort or cruise won't be overrun by children on summer vacation. Of course, if either of you is bringing children to your marriage—and that child will be honeymooning with you—you may want to plan for

**tip** Devote one weekend day to creating a packing list for your honeymoon. I know a packing list sounds like something your mother made you do way back when, before you went to camp, but Mom had a good thing going. In this crazy time before your wedding, you may start forgetting things. So if you don't take the time to write down exactly what you need to pack for your honeymoon, you may end up leaving out some very important things, such as birth control or passports. Here are some other items you might need:

- Film or memory sticks for camera
- Sunblock
- Motion-sickness medicine
- Daily medications or prescriptions
- Charger for cell phone and digital camera
- Travel insurance
- New luggage, if necessary

just the opposite. That is, plan to take your honeymoon at a time of year and in a place where there will be plenty of other children.

- Don't travel to Europe in August, no matter how great the bargains seem. There's a reason Europe is cheap in August—it's the month when most Europeans go on holiday, meaning that hotels, stores, and cafes shut down while their proprietors take time off. True, not all of Europe shuts down during this month, but you won't find as much to do during August as you would at other times of the year.

# CHECK WITH THE STATE DEPARTMENT

In our post-September 11th world, it is more important than ever that Americans only travel to safe locations around the world for their honeymoons. That's why I always advise that travelers check the United States State Department website of potentially dangerous places before booking travel. You may be surprised to learn that some seemingly innocuous locations are on the warning list.

So, before you get your heart set on a certain honeymoon destination, log on to http://travel.state.gov/travel/warnings.html to check out the latest warnings. This website will also give you overall travel and safety tips for visiting every country worldwide.

## All-Inclusive Versus Á La Carte Honeymoons

One of the places that your budget will affect your honeymoon is in deciding whether or not to go with an all-inclusive vacation. An all-inclusive is exactly what it sounds like—a trip where everything is included in one price, such as at Caribbean resorts like Sandals or Super Clubs. Cruises are usually quasi all-inclusive, in that your travel costs and dining room meals are included in one price, but you have to pay extra for alcohol, snacks, and shore excursions.

An á la carte vacation works just like an á la carte menu in a restaurant—you pick and choose (and pay for) only the items you're interested in. See which makes the most sense for you two based on your budget and your expectations.

If you're planning to take advantage of many on-site activities and off-site excursions—and all are included in the price you pay up front—then booking an all-inclusive would make a lot of sense. On the other hand, if you're not big eaters or drinkers or don't plan to do many extra activities, you can probably get away with paying for your trip with an á la carte plan.

# Working with a Travel Agent

## To do list

- ❑ Compile a list of reputable travel agents
- ❑ Screen potential agents
- ❑ Schedule meetings with agents

The American Society of Travel Agents (ASTA) motto says "Without a travel agent, you're on your own." This really applies to couples planning a honeymoon. If there's one vacation in your life when you don't want to go it alone, it's your honeymoon. That's why I strongly suggest that couples plan their honeymoon using a professional. Then if something goes wrong, you've got someone to turn to for help.

In fact, in my previous book, *The Complete Guide for the Anxious Bride* (see Appendix A, "References and Resources," for more information on this book), I interviewed a travel agent who really saved the day by being able to fix a problem a client was having on the other side of the world. In this instance a couple arrived at their honeymoon hotel in Italy and discovered that the hotel's front desk couldn't find their reservation. Because the couple had used a travel agent, they were able to call her even though it was 4:00 in the morning in the United States. The travel agent then made a few calls to all the right people at the hotel, and within an hour or so, she'd arranged for them to have the room she'd originally booked. Had the couple booked their honeymoon on their own and run into this problem, they might not have had such a speedy recourse.

## You'll need list

- ❑ Internet access and computer
- ❑ Recommendations from friends and associates

### Finding a Travel Agent

Want to find a reputable travel agent near you to help plan your honeymoon? Then ASTA can help. This trade association of travel agents has a consumer-oriented website chock full of travel tips as well as a searchable database of travel agents.

Log on to www.travelsense.org and plug in your ZIP code to find a travel agent near you. Also, take a look around the website to find other important information about traveling, such as how to deal with airport security. There's even a section on planning honeymoons.

And don't forget the value of personal recommendations. Ask people you know and respect if they've used a fabulous travel agent to plan a recent vacation, and then follow up on promising leads. You can save a lot of time screening travel agents with this kind of personal recommendation.

## Choosing the Right Travel Agent

Your approach to finding the perfect travel agent to plan your honeymoon is a lot like how you approached hiring the other professionals you've used to plan your wedding:

- Meet with a couple of travel agents to see if you like them and if you feel their expertise meshes well with the honeymoon you hope to take.
- Discuss with the travel agent whether your planned budget will work for your honeymoon expectations. If not, ask him or her for suggestions on how you can alter your plans to fit your budget without cutting quality.
- Make sure that your travel agent is affiliated with a well-known organization that prides itself on providing reputable travel experiences. Two such names to look for are ASTA and Virtuoso, a renowned network of luxury travel specialists.

# Preparing for a Safe and Secure Trip

## To do list

- ☐ Find out about visas, vaccinations, travel advisories, and other necessities of travel to your chosen destination
- ☐ Plan to get your passport for international travel
- ☐ Research travel insurance options

If you're traveling to a foreign locale for your honeymoon—and even the Caribbean is considered to be a foreign location—you may have to secure certain paperwork and immunizations before you leave.

The Center for Disease Control maintains a traveler's health website that lists everything you need to know to remain healthy while on the road.

Log on to http://www.cdc.gov/travel/ to find out all you need to know about vaccinations, virus outbreaks, and other health-related news that could potentially affect your honeymoon.

While you're surfing the Web, go to the U.S. Department of State's travel section at http://www.state.gov/travel/ to get the basics on passports and any visas you may need when traveling to certain countries.

# WHAT TO PACK?

If you're unsure what you should pack for your honeymoon, turn to the Internet for some help with that task, too. You can use your favorite search engine to look for packing tips for your destination (try searching with "packing tips" in quotes and a mention of where you're traveling to). Or you can check out one of these websites, which will help you get your clothes folded and suitcases zipped up in a flash:

- Rick Steves is a television host and travel expert. His website offers destination-specific packing tips along with suggestions for both sexes.
www.ricksteves.com

- This consumer site of ASTA offers a good overview of what you should keep in mind as you pack for a trip here or abroad.
www.travelsense.org

- The Transportation Security Administration (TSA) is the government arm that regulates security at airports. It's wise to surf this site ahead of time so you can make sure you don't pack anything that could raise a red flag and get you hung up on your way to your honeymoon.
www.tsa.dot.gov

## Passport Primer

Here's the reason you need a passport when traveling to a foreign land—a passport is recognized worldwide as a document of nationality and identity. If you're traveling outside the country, you need to have a passport.

Ordinarily it takes the U.S. State Department, which issues passports, six weeks minimum to get your passport to you. If you want expedited service (you know, speeded up), you can pay $60 extra plus two-way overnight delivery charges (which vary by carrier), and then you can expect to receive your passport in only two weeks. What this all means is this: if you need to renew your passport or are applying for one for the first time, definitely don't leave it to the last minute. Give yourself a minimum of three months before your honeymoon so that should you hit any snafus, you'll still have plenty of time to go on your trip.

Other important issues to keep in mind when applying for a passport include:

- Photos. The Passport Services Office has specific criteria for photographs they'll accept for your passport. First, the photograph must have a white or light background. Second, it has to be of your head and shoulders only. Third, you need to submit two identical photos. Fourth, the photos must be two inches by two inches.

  There are other specific criteria for a passport photo, which you can find at http://travel.state.gov/passport/get_first_apply.html. Make sure you read through this information carefully before you apply for a passport. I've heard stories of travelers who submitted insufficient photos for their passport and had to postpone a trip because they couldn't get their passport done in time.

- Identification. Yes, your passport will serve as your international ID document but in order to get one you first have to prove that you're a U.S. citizen. Again, visit the State Department's website for specifics of what you'll need to bring with you, but for starters it would be a good idea to locate your birth certificate. Keep in mind that a Social Security card is not considered to be a valid form of identification, as far as passports are concerned.

- Scheduling an appointment. If you are applying for your first passport, you're going to need to do so in person. (Only renewals can be done via the mail.) You can find the nearest passport facility by visiting the www.travel.state.gov.

## Thinking About Travel Insurance

One of the best reasons for you to look into buying a travel insurance policy for your honeymoon is so you have peace of mind should anything go wrong on your trip. There are a number of different kinds of travel insurance policies, and the two of you need to decide which ones are right for your trip.

You can buy travel insurance through your travel agent or from an independent insurance agent. Here's a brief rundown of the kinds of policies you may want to consider:

- Trip cancellation. Literally what it sounds like—a policy to protect you should you have to cancel your trip. Different carriers have different ideas of what qualifies as a legit reason for canceling, so make sure you find out ahead of time what's covered and what isn't.

- Trip interruption. This policy will reimburse your expenses if your trip is altered after it's already underway. Of course, again you need to see what's covered (usually illness) and what's not (usually war or terrorism).

- Emergency travel medical insurance. You may want to purchase this additional insurance if your day-to-day health insurance policy won't cover you, should you fall ill while traveling.

- Medical evacuation. This kind of policy covers your care and transportation should you be seriously injured while traveling. Truthfully, this policy can be quite expensive and may only be worth thinking about if you're planning on taking an "extreme" honeymoon, where injuries will be par for the course.

A number of companies offer travel insurance, and their websites are a great place to educate yourself. Two worth checking out are:

> www.accessamerica.com
> www.travelguard.com

In addition, some consumer sites also provide a good overview on travel insurance. I recommend you click over to the Practical Nomad's website, which you'll find here:

> www.hasbrouck.org/articles/insurance.html

# WHY YOU DON'T WANT TO TRAVEL WITHOUT TRAVEL INSURANCE

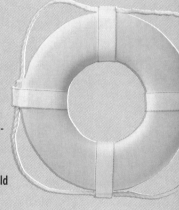

I hope that I've convinced you to insure your wedding—weddings cost as much as if not more than a car these days, and you wouldn't drive your car around without insuring it, right? You need to think the same way about your honeymoon—it's a vacation well worth insuring. In fact, you should always insure any trip you take because you just never know what could happen while you're away that could affect your ability to enjoy your vacation.

Case in point: Last summer my husband and I took a cruise to Canada. The week before we left, I was diagnosed with gallbladder disease. While surgery wasn't imminent, I knew there was a chance that I might have an attack during our trip that could potentially lead to a trip to a hospital. So we bought travel insurance for a couple hundred bucks, which not only bought us protection but also peace of mind. I ended up feeling just fine during the entire trip but I knew that the travel insurance had been money well spent.

Then one day away from our first stop in Nova Scotia, one of the cruise ship passengers had to be taken off the boat by helicopter to a hospital on the mainland—he'd suffered a heart attack and the ship's doctor wasn't equipped to treat him on board. I found out later that this passenger had purchased a specific travel insurance policy before embarkation that allowed all of his medical expenses to be covered. Also, because he had purchased trip interruption insurance, he received a partial refund for the remainder of the cruise he was unable to take.

# Summary

It may be hard to imagine but your wedding day is getting closer and closer, and soon enough you and your new husband are going to be off on your honeymoon, your first vacation together as a married couple.

In this chapter, I outlined certain ways that the two of you can figure out the perfect honeymoon for you to take together. I had you take a quick quiz on your vacation likes and dislikes, which should have helped you to narrow down your trip possibilities. I also talked a lot about how weather can affect your honeymoon decision—from the time of year of your wedding and good places to visit to how a hurricane or snowstorm could really throw a monkey wrench into your travel plans. That's why I followed up the weather discussions with a discussion about why you don't want to skimp on travel insurance to cover your honeymoon. Like I said, not only will it buy you financial protection for your very first vacation as husband and wife, but also it will buy you peace of mind.

Another way to buy yourself peace of mind is to work with a travel agent when booking your honeymoon. He or she will be able to help you figure out the best places for you to travel, and when to go. Also, he or she will be there to fix things, should something go wrong with your travels. Of course, I only recommend working with a known entity, such as a travel agent that friends or family members have had a positive experience dealing with and which is affiliated with a reputable association like the American Society of Travel Agents (ASTA). With all this good advice in mind, you're sure to have a fabulous honeymoon.

In the next part of the book, we're going to tacklet all of the things you'll need to deal with after the big day. These include organizing your gifts--and writing thank-you notes for all of them--along with getting your wedding photos in order and putting together any wedding mementoes that you hope to cherish from this day forward.

# Part III

## After the Big Day

# 10

# Organizing Your Gifts

If you're like most couples, your family and friends generously showered you with gifts at your wedding. But before you dive in and start ripping open all of the packages or tearing apart all of the money envelopes, stop! You must remember that you're going to have to write thank-you notes down the line, which means you'll need to know who gave you what.

In this chapter, I'm going to help you approach opening your gifts in an organized fashion. Remember that guest list database you created way back in Chapter 1, "First Things First"? That is going to come in handy now as it will be a resource for finding everyone's address for your thank-you notes. It will also be a place for writing down who gave you what and keeping track of the thank-you notes you've already written and sent.

Keeping track of your gifts will make your thank-you note writing easier. It will also ensure that you don't lose any gifts between your wedding night (when you're probably going to be opening everything) and when you get back from your honeymoon (when you'll begin to absorb just how much stuff and/or money you now have, thanks to all of those gifts).

In addition, I'll help you figure out how to put all of these new gifts to good use. You may also need to return or exchange some of the gifts you received, so we'll talk a bit about how to avoid becoming overwhelmed by this task. It's likely that most of your guests bought your gifts at the stores where you registered, which should make returns a snap. In case they didn't, I'll help you figure out how to handle that scenario as well.

## To do list

❑ Record gifts and their givers in your guest list database
❑ Order pictures from the wedding to enclose with thank-you notes
❑ Begin writing thank-you notes
❑ Deposit gift checks and organize gifts to check for duplicates
❑ Return duplicate or unwanted gifts

## You'll need list

❑ Guest list database (see Chapter 1)
❑ Thank-you cards
❑ Postage stamps

## Keeping Track of Who Gave You What

As you might recall back in Chapter 1, you created your guest list. At the same time, I also suggested that you create a database of your guests' addresses and other pertinent information that would come in handy down the line. Now it's "down the line," and it is time to take that database out again.

You're going to use that database to write down each of the gifts that your guests gave you. This includes gifts you received at the wedding, gifts that were sent to you or your parents' home when someone couldn't attend, or unsolicited gifts you received from well-wishers who were not invited. (You can add in this extra gift information at the bottom of your database. Just be sure you save the return address label from the package so you'll have an address to send your thank-you note to.)

Here's how you can approach your gifts in an organized fashion that will help you remember who gave you what—and later on you can transfer gift information to your database.

The easiest way to keep track of your wedding gifts is to record them in your guest list database. The easiest way to accomplish this is to wait until after you've returned from your honeymoon to open your gifts. Then you can take your time unwrapping everything and marking down gifts received in your guest list database.

Many couples can't stand the suspense of waiting to open gifts and don't have a laptop computer nearby, so they can't immediately record gift and gift-giver information into their guest list database. Here's another simple way to record every gift you receive: Because nearly every gift comes with a card, on the inside of each card, write down what the person gave you—whether it was towels from your registry or a check for $100. On gifts that came without cards, record the gift-giver's name and the gift she gave you on a sheet of paper. Then, when you return from your honeymoon, you can transfer all of this information into your guest list database and start tackling your thank-you notes.

# RETURNING TO YOUR GUEST LIST DATABASE

To refresh your memory, here's what that database should include:

* Entry for guests (in alphabetical order) including name, address, phone number, and email address
* Date engagement announcement sent (if you decide to send them out)
* Engagement gift received (if any)/Date thank-you note sent
* Shower gift received (if any)/Date thank-you note sent
* Date wedding invitation sent
* Number of people you've invited with this person
* Date RSVP received and answered (yes or no)
* Number RSVPing yes
* Date called to follow up, if no RSVP received
* Gift received
* Date thank-you note sent

You can keep some of the lines at the end of the database blank for additional gifts received from unexpected sources.

# Writing and Sending Your Thank-You Notes on Time

Because you have a guest-list database, you won't have to scramble to find your guests' addresses for your thank-you notes—you have all of that information right there in front of you. That's the good news. The bad news is this: depending on the size of your wedding, you may have hundreds of thank-you notes to write in the next few weeks. The information in this section of the chapter will help you accomplish that task quickly and (relatively) painlessly.

## The Six-Week Rule

Here's one of the most important reasons I'd like to see you get right to writing your thank-you notes: proper etiquette says that the bride and groom have six weeks to send thank-you notes out after receiving a gift. So you really don't want to put things off for too long. Between your wedding and your honeymoon, you may return home to find you have less than a month to write all your thank-you notes. Also, I hope that after your engagement party and your bridal shower you were timely in thanking your guests for their generosity.

## How to Write a Heartfelt Thank-You Note Fast

One of the reasons that so many people become paralyzed when it comes to writing thank-you notes is this: no one ever taught them a way to write a meaningful thank-you note in no time. It's actually a lot easier than you may realize. That's why I've outlined the following steps to thank-you note writing, regardless of the occasion, so that you can get all of yours done fast:

1. Start with your salutation: "Dear Sally," or whomever it is that you're writing the note to.

2. Thank the gift-giver for his or her gift: "Thank you so much for the generous check to commemorate our wedding" or "Thank you so much for the three place settings of our china."

3. Next, tell briefly how you plan to use the gift: "I can't wait to use our new china the next time we have a dinner party." If it feels too awkward telling someone how you're going to use the gift of money, you can add something generic: "It was awfully nice of you to give us such a thoughtful gift."

4. Thank the gift-giver one more time: "Thanks again for the wonderful gift" or "Thanks again for joining us at our wedding."

5. Sign your name, and you're done.

Keep in mind that there are two things you should always do with thank-you notes: hand write them (no emailing allowed), and proofread each note before sending it.

## Creative Ways to Thank Your Guests

There's no rule that says that you can't have some fun with your thank-you notes. Here are some creative thank-you note ideas for you to consider:

- Send travel postcards as thank-you notes. I'm not suggesting that you mail any old postcard but rather find fun postcards from your honeymoon location that you can use to send salutations to your friends and family and to thank them for their wedding gifts (if you have your gift list with you).

- Use photos as thank-you notes. If you've already received proofs from your photographer and don't have to return them, why not turn those photos into postcard thank-you notes? If you're lucky enough to have a picture of you and your new husband with each person on your guest list, you can use a photo of all of you for your thank-you note.

I mentioned earlier that the bride and groom have six weeks to write thank-you notes for wedding gifts they've received. Well, your guests have up to a year to send you a gift to celebrate your wedding. (Many couples mix up the six-week thank-you note rule and the one-year gift rule, which can lead to many annoyed guests. Please don't make that mistake.)

In reality, this means gifts could be arriving on your doorstep for up to a year after your actual wedding. That's why I suggest that you keep a stash of thank-you notes and postage stamps on hand at all times. That way when a gift arrives unexpectedly, you can dash off a quick thank-you note and get it into the next day's mail without breaking a sweat.

**tip** *Using Your Lunch Hour*

Freaked out that you'll never get your thank-you notes written and mailed in time? Use your lunch hour to dedicate time to writing your notes. Bring your guest list database to the office with you, along with an ample supply of thank-you cards and postage stamps. Then figure out how many thank-you notes you need to write in the next week or so to get your list done. In no time you'll have thanked everyone for his or her gift.

**tip** Most couples like to enclose a wallet-sized photo from their wedding in their thank-you cards. Why not make the lives of your guests easier? If your guests are anything like my friends and family, those wedding photos always end up on the refrigerator. So wouldn't it be great if you could create a magnetized photo to send? That way your guests can just slap that wedding photo up on the refrigerator or on a filing cabinet in their office.

# Making Use of Your New Things

Now that you've unwrapped all the gifts and written your thank-you notes, you've got to figure out how to put all your new gifts to good use. Here is an organized fashion for approaching that task, step-by-step:

> **note** If you've changed your name but you've received checks made out to your maiden name, you can endorse the checks using all three names—first, maiden, and new surname. That way the bank will recognize the signature and the endorsement. Truth is, this approach works equally well for women who didn't change their name but who receive checks made out to their supposedly new surname. By endorsing the checks with all three names, you shouldn't have any problem making a deposit. Of course, if you're not sure this will work, check with your branch manager first.

1. Deposit any checks you've received into your bank account. Hopefully by now you've changed over everything to your new name, if you've taken your husband's name, so you can make deposits in a timely manner. There's nothing more frustrating to a check writer than to have a check remain outstanding for months on end.

2. If you received any gift cards or gift certificates as gifts, create a gift wallet. You should take an empty wallet that you're not using for any other purpose, and place all of your gift cards and gift certificates in it. Then whenever you go shopping, take that gift wallet with you. You never know when you might end up at a store where you have a gift card or a gift certificate, and this way you'll ensure that you have ample opportunities to use up any gift cards or gift certificates that your friends and family so generously gave to you.

3. Organize your gifts based on rooms in the house. That way you can take inventory of what you've received and you can either start putting it to good use or, if you discover that you've received duplicates, you can plan a trip to the stores to make returns or exchanges.

## Taking Inventory of Gifts

A systematic way to take inventory of your gifts is to create a chart based on rooms in your house. Then you can go through your gifts box-by-box and write down what you've received. Once you have all your gifts organized by room, you'll have a better sense of where to put things or whether you need to make any returns to the store.

Here's how I suggest organizing your chart:

| Rooms in the Home | Gifts Received |
|---|---|
| Kitchen | |
| Living room | |
| Dining room | |
| Bedroom | |
| Bath | |
| Garage/basement | |
| Backyard/patio | |

Another way to take inventory is to tap into your gift registries at the stores where you registered. Most stores keep this information online, so devote one weekend morning to logging on to all the store websites and printing out your registries. This allows you to see all the gifts that guests purchased—and what remains outstanding.

If you can't access all your registries via the Web, spend another weekend morning visiting all the brick-and-mortar locations of the stores where you registered and getting printouts of your current registry list there.

## Returning Unwanted or Duplicate Gifts

With both your gift inventory list and your registry lists in hand, you should have a clear sense by now of which items you want to keep—and how you're going to use them around the house—and which items you need to return.

To save time when making returns, I suggest one more organizational project: Create a list of all the gifts on your return list and put it together based on stores where you registered.

Here's what your chart might look like if you registered at Target, Crate and Barrel, and Bed Bath & Beyond:

| Store | Items to Return |
|---|---|
| Target | Duplicate Michael Graves toaster |
| Crate and Barrel | Only needed 12 place settings of everyday dishes—need to return four extra sets |
| Bed Bath & Beyond | Didn't receive enough hand towels to make a full set—want to return the three I got for a store credit |

# HOW TO RETURN A GIFT OF UNKNOWN ORIGIN

Sometimes you receive a wedding gift that you need to return, but you aren't sure from what store it was purchased. Some of these "odd" gifts may even be items from your registry but have arrived in duplicate.

The first thing you can do with any duplicate gifts that appear on your registry is to attempt to return them to the store where you registered—even if you suspect they were purchased somewhere else. See if they'll take them back for a store credit. It's unlikely but it's worth a try.

Next, if the stores won't take back items that weren't purchased there (which is a reasonable expectation), try to determine the store where your guest purchased the gift. Unfortunately, the only likely clue to this mystery will be a price tag on the gift, a store name on the box, or a gift receipt tucked inside—items you probably would have noticed.

If you can't return a duplicate registry gift or can't figure out what to do with a one-of-a-kind gift of unknown origin, you could consider recycling it in the future. Every home should have a gift closet where you stockpile presents so that, should you find yourself in a last minute gift-giving situation, you don't have to run to the store and frantically search for a gift. With a gift closet on the premises—and one stocked with wedding gifts that you couldn't use or return—you'll be set the next time you need a gift for a bridal shower or a wedding. You can also consider donating the gift to charity.

## Summary

I'm confident that all of your wedding guests were gracious in giving you great gifts, and now you've got a new home filled to the brim with good tidings. In this chapter, we talked about organizing your gifts and writing your thank-you notes.

I suggested that you revisit the notion of your guest list database, which is an excellent place to record which guest gave you what gift—and to write down when you wrote that person a thank-you note. And you are writing thank-you notes in a timely manner, right? Although your well-wishers have up to a year to send you a gift to celebrate your wedding, you do not have a year to reply with a thank-you note. All your thank-you notes should be written and mailed no later than six weeks after you received a gift. As long as you stay organized and on top of the gifts coming in, this shouldn't be a difficult task to complete.

I also suggested that you create a chart so that you can go gift-by-gift, room-by-room, and figure out a place for everything that your wedding guests so graciously gave you. In addition, I suggested that you use a chart to organize any returns you need to make for duplicate or unwanted gifts. Doing both tasks in a timely manner will help cut down on any wedding gift clutter that could accumulate around your house.

By this time, after you've returned from your honeymoon and taken care of your gifts and thank-you notes, you should be hearing from your photographer and videographer about the photographic memories he or she captured at your wedding. In Chapter 11, "Photographic Memories," I'll discuss everything related to your wedding photographs and video. This includes what to do with your proofs, when to get any outstanding rolls of film developed, and how to put together your wedding album in no time.

# Photographic Memories

**Y**ou've spent all this money on a wedding photographer and videographer, and you want to be sure you reap the benefits of their hard work. Now that you're back from your honeymoon, you should contact your photographer and videographer and find out when you can expect to see proofs from your wedding. He or she may have told you beforehand how long it will take to get proofs or a rough cut of your video, but it doesn't hurt to give them a reminder call or send an email.

Once you have your photos and video, what are you going to do with them? I hope you don't put them in a box at the bottom of your coat closet, never to be seen again. In this chapter, I'll offer suggestions for putting your wedding photographs and video to good use. I'll provide ways to get everything organized, and tips for creating a photo album and choosing wedding pictures to frame and place around your home. In addition, I'll help ensure that you get any single-use cameras developed that your guests used at your reception.

## To do list

- ☐ Touch base with photographer and videographer
- ☐ Develop film from any single-use cameras
- ☐ Review wedding photo proofs
- ☐ Watch rough cut of wedding video
- ☐ Organize your wedding album
- ☐ Frame favorite wedding photos

# Viewing Your Photo Proofs and Video Rough Cut

It has likely been at least two weeks since your wedding day—amazing how times flies, isn't it? Your wedding photographer and videographer should be well on their way towards getting you proofs of your pictures and putting together a rough cut of your wedding video. Just in case they aren't, I suggest that you call or email each just to check in. Sometimes a subtle reminder like this will get you those proofs and the rough cut faster.

Exactly how long does it take for a wedding videographer and photographer to have something to show for your wedding? The following sections help you estimate a turnaround timeline for each.

## Estimating the Photographer's Turnaround Timeline

The film format your photographer uses will determine how quickly he or she can turn around images from your wedding. A photographer who shoots digitally should be able to upload pictures within days of the event. (She may even have a secure section on a website where you can view the pictures from home.) A photographer who shoots on traditional film will need to send that film out to a lab for developing. Unless you want to pay a markup price to expedite the order, you should expect that it will take at least five to seven business days for the photographer to get the film back, if not more, especially during the busy wedding seasons when labs are likely to be overwhelmed with orders.

Once your photographer has *proofs* (the name used to describe the first set of prints a photographer gets), he may insist on putting them in a proof album. This helps to protect the photos. If you're in a hurry, you may be able to convince him to let you look at the photos as-is, right away. Be prepared to look through a lot of images— the average wedding photographer shoots 300 or more pictures at a four-hour affair.

If you're feeling overwhelmed with viewing photographs from your wedding, set aside a lunch hour to get the task done. Either bring your proof album with you to work or plan to spend an hour viewing your photographs at the photographer's website. Keep a list of the images you like for your album, your parents' album, or for enlargements that you'll eventually frame. Suggest that your husband also spend one of his lunch hours going over the pictures. Then when you get home at night, you can compare your notes, make your final photo decisions, and call your photographer with the information. In no time you'll have chosen all of your photos.

Once you've decided on the photographs you like, you can place the order for your album and your parents' albums as well. You should budget between three and six months for receiving these albums.

## Estimating the Videographer's Turnaround Timeline

It may take a few weeks for the videographer to put together a *rough-cut* of your video (a first draft, if you will, of the movie that documents your wedding day), especially if you've asked her to include images from your honeymoon in the video. Obviously, you won't be able to deliver anything from your honeymoon, such as post-cards and snapshots, until after you've returned. And those kinds of last-minute additions can lengthen the turnaround time. In addition, the amount of extras you've asked for in your video, such as montages or slow-motion sequences, can also add time to the production process. Repeatedly asking the videographer for different images to be added to the final video will also delay production. So have a fairly clear idea upfront of what you'd definitely like to see in your video, such as certain groupings of people, how much dance floor time you want captured, and other special moments from your wedding. Then, after viewing the rough cut a month or so later—and suggesting any final additions, changes, or deletions—you should expect to see the final version of your video two to three months after that.

> **tip**
>
> Encourage your wedding videographer to put your video on both VHS and DVD. That way you'll be able to play a copy of your wedding video whenever you visit a home with either a VCR or DVD player.

# DEVELOPING SINGLE-USE CAMERA PHOTOS

Many brides and grooms choose to place single-use cameras on their reception tables. This gives their guests a chance to capture the wedding from their individual perspectives. It's also a great backup plan should anything go awry with the professional photographer. Chances are your photos turned out fine and now you've got a shopping bag filled with these single-use cameras. They've probably been lying around since you returned from your honeymoon, and I'm sure you're just dying to see what's on each roll of film.

Dedicate one weekend day to bringing these single-use cameras to your local drugstore, supermarket, photo lab, or whichever company you use to have your film developed. There's no reason to pay for expedited developing—I know that many of the places I use to get film developed can turn the job around in 24 to 48 hours without charging extra, and that's plenty fast enough. What you may want to consider paying extra for is getting your photos placed on CD or sent to your email address. That way you can share some of these images with your family and friends electronically. I hope that you'll end up discovering some really fun, creative, and touching photos in the batches you've had developed. I'm sure at least one guest got a great, unexpected shot from your wedding day.

## Making Your Album in a Minimum Amount of Time

Don't fret over how to put together a wedding album. Your photographer should provide some guidance in this respect, and as long as you approach the task in an organized fashion, it should be a breeze.

First things first, the easiest way to have an album come to life is to arrange it chronologically so it starts with your ceremony and ends with the last dance at your reception. And, before you can organize your album, you also have to remember to order the album—along with any mini-albums you want to give to family and special friends. The following sections explain each of these tasks in more detail.

## Organizing Your Album

Given that, as I said earlier, a photographer could take hundreds of photographs at the average wedding, how do you figure out which of these chronological images will work best in your album? Well, you guided your photographer in capturing your wedding by providing him or her with a shot list. I would suggest that you use a similar tactic in putting together your album—it will save you time in the long run.

Here is a rough outline of a shot list, so to speak, of pictures to look for in your proofs that will help you put together the perfect wedding album. You should try to find the following images:

- The wedding party entering the ceremony
- The parents of both the bride and groom entering the ceremony
- The officiant (if you choose)
- The bride
- The groom
- Any special moments at the ceremony, such as lighting the unity candle, jumping the broom, or stepping on the glass
- The recessional
- The wedding party, bride, and groom posing together
- The bride and groom with each of their respective family members, alone and together; these might include siblings, parents, and grandparents
- Significant moments at the reception—first dance, cake cutting, or bouquet toss
- Details of the reception, if you've asked for them, such as an overview of the packed dance floor
- Candids of guests at the reception
- Bride and groom leaving the reception

If you don't want a strictly chronological record of your wedding, you may want to start your album with group shots of the *dramatis personae*, including the two of you alone and with your

**note** If you hired a candid or photojournalistic photographer to capture your wedding, you may not find a traditional clustering of typical wedding photos to go by when putting together your album. But you can still create a quasi-chronological view of your wedding day, which may begin with details of your wedding dress or a candid photo of you having your makeup done. Because you hired a nontraditional photographer you will end up having a nontraditional photo album. And that's just fine, as long as you realize that the photos you're going to be reviewing will be outside the norm that I've outlined families and wedding party. Then you can move onto a more quasi-chronological order of pictures from your wedding, starting with your ceremony and ending with your reception.

## Ordering Your Album

Most traditional wedding photographers include making a leather-bound or similar kind of formal album for the bride and groom as part of their package. Understand that this added element of the photographer's package is anything but your run-of-the-mill photo album. These custom-designed albums often feature oversized photographs, gilded page edges, and other special design elements that you simply can't get at the photo lab around the corner.

When placing the order for yourself, don't forget to order mini-albums for the important people in your life and your wedding as well. These people could include

- Your respective parents
- Your grandparents
- Your maid of honor and best man

Remember, it may take your photographer three to six months to deliver the finished albums, so don't call about an album for your grandmother as her Christmas gift in November—the photographer probably won't be able to make that kind of deadline.

# Getting the Most out of Your Wedding Photographs

After ordering your wedding album and your wedding video, you may think that there isn't anything else that you can do with your wedding images, but you would be wrong. There are plenty of ways to work your wedding pictures into your everyday life, including decorating your house or creating gifts to give family members for upcoming birthdays or holidays. Read on for how to get the most out of the wedding photographs that you spent so much time planning for and probably spent a decent amount of money to secure.

## Framing Photos

When I got married some years ago, there was one gift that I received repeatedly for my bridal shower and wedding—picture frames. At first I thought I would never have enough photos to fill all of these frames. Then my photographer delivered the proofs from my wedding, and suddenly I had more photos than I knew what to do with. Luckily I had tons of picture frames to use. If you find yourself in the same situation—overrun with both frames and great photos from your wedding—here's what I suggest you do:

1. Take inventory of all of your favorite wedding pictures. These could be images from your photographer, part of the batch of pictures that you got when you had the single-use cameras developed, or photos that friends and relatives took at your wedding and sent to you for your own enjoyment.

2. Make a pile of all the pictures you'd like to frame.

3. Next, take inventory of all the picture frames you have. While it's likely that most pictures from your wedding will be 4×6 inches, not all of your frames will be.

4. Separate all of the 4×6 frames so you can put pictures in them immediately.

5. Compare different size frames with all of the remaining pictures. With the larger frames you've received—5×7, 8×10, or even larger—determine which photographs you should have enlarged to place in these frames. With the smaller frames, figure out which pictures you could crop to fit in frames that would work well on a desktop, bedside table, or tiny mantle.

6. Set aside the photos you want to have enlarged and visit the photo lab the next day to place your order. Or, if your photographer has control of your negatives and is going to be handling any reprint requests, contact him or her to accomplish the same.

7. If you end up with any leftover frames or photographs, see if you can't put them together as gifts for special people in your life.

> **tip**
> If you're stumped for a gift to give someone in the year after your wedding, a framed picture of you and your new husband from your wedding day will always be a cherished gift. So stock up on frames when you see them on sale at your favorite retailer—that is, if you don't have any left over from bridal gifts—and you'll always have them on hand when you need to put together a quick gift.

## Traditional Wedding Photos in Nontraditional Places

Framing your wedding pictures is a great idea for making the most of your wedding photos, but it isn't your only option. Here are some creative ways to give new life to your photos:

• Use your scanner to turn them into a t-shirt transfer and iron the photo onto a shirt or sweatshirt for a his-and-her memento from your wedding that you and your new husband can enjoy. You can do the same for your wedding party.

- You can turn your wedding photo into a screensaver on your computer.

- You can put your wedding photo on the mouse pad you use with your computer in your office or at home.

- Make note cards that feature your wedding photo on the front cover. You can create these on your own, using your personal computer, or order them from a company that specializes in this kind of digital reproduction.

# CREATING YOUR OWN ALBUMS AND PHOTO DISPLAYS

If you're a DIY bride who is looking forward to creating customized photo albums or photo-related gifts for your friends and family members, you can do just that using your computer—as long as you visit a website that specializes in helping people create these kinds of photo-centric items.

Kodak's Ofoto.com website is a place to store your wedding photos online and to order things like photo calendars, photo cards, and even a traditional album to put all of your wedding photos in—that is, if your photographer isn't supplying one for you.

Another great online resource is Exposures at www.exposuresonline.com, where you can order unique photo albums, keepsakes, and even custom greeting cards that feature images from your wedding.

# Summary

Before the memories of your wedding day fade away, you should have heard from the very people who captured those memories for you—namely, your wedding photographer and videographer. If you've already been back from your honeymoon for a little while and haven't received an update on your photo or video order, it's perfectly fine to call or email either vendor to find out what's up.

In this chapter, we talked about all things related to your wedding photographs and video. This included how long you should expect your photographer to take to create proofs of your pictures and then a completed album. Similarly, we discussed the timeline for your videographer to go from rough cut to final cut of your wedding video. All in all I hope that neither vendor makes you wait too long.

A wedding photographer might take 300 pictures or more at the average wedding. If you're currently looking at a huge pile of proofs, that reality has surely hit home. But you don't have to be overwhelmed by reviewing your photos or thinking about how you want to organize your album. In this chapter, I provided simple ways you can accomplish all your photography-related tasks in a timely manner. I even offered suggestions on how you can turn ho-hum wedding pictures into cool items, such as mouse pads and note cards.

In Chapter 12, "Keeping Keepsakes," we're going to talk a bit more about keepsakes, but those that go beyond wedding photographs. If you want to hand down your wedding gown one day, you'll definitely want to find a conservation cleaner who will know the right way to treat a wedding gown. We'll also discuss ways you can preserve your flowers and ensure that the piece of wedding cake you've saved from your reception will still taste yummy on your first anniversary.

# 12

# Keeping Keepsakes

You're sure to have many keepsakes of your wedding day, thanks to the photographer and videographer that you hired to capture the event. You will also have your own memories, based on your first-hand experience walking down the aisle (although it may seem like a bit of a blur at this point, given how busy that day probably was).

But there are other mementos that you may want to keep as vivid as your memories of your wedding that go beyond photographs or fond remembrances. These include your wedding gown and the flowers you carried with you as you walked down the aisle. There are ways to preserve both so that years from now, when you're feeling nostalgic for your wedding day, you will be able to see both preserved in perfect form. This chapter delves into the remaining keepsakes that you may want to create or preserve to remember your wedding day by.

## To do list

- ☐ Find a conservation cleaner for your wedding gown
- ☐ Ask the right questions to make sure you have the right cleaner
- ☐ Figure out how and where you're going to store your gown

# Cleaning and Storing Your Wedding Gown

A wedding gown is unlike any other article of clothing you own, or will ever own, because it represents one of the most important days in your life. As such, you should treat the cleaning of your wedding dress with the requisite importance it deserves. After your wedding you shouldn't just toss your wedding gown in a laundry basket and forget about it. You definitely shouldn't throw it in the washing machine either. Nor should you just drop it off at the dry cleaner around the corner, who may have little experience handling wedding gowns. Instead, you need to get it cleaned immediately, and done so by a cleaner who specializes in wedding gowns and other delicate articles of clothing.

## You'll need list

- ☐ List of wedding-gown cleaners in your area
- ☐ Computer/Internet access
- ☐ Camera and film for photographing gown before cleaning
- ☐ Storage location for gown

## Finding the Right Cleaner

Many dry cleaners that you see in strip malls and other shopping centers will be decorated with bridal gowns in dry cleaning bags, hanging from their rafters. If you see this at a dry cleaner near you, run, do not walk, away from that business.

Anyone in the bridal gown preservation business (a step up from traditional dry cleaners) knows that the worst thing you can do with a wedding gown is clean it like it was an ordinary garment (it isn't), hang it out in the open (it should be kept in a cool dry place), and put it in a plastic bag (plastic causes mildew; an acid-free box is the best place for a bridal gown).

There is tough competition among cleaners who specialize in wedding gowns vying for the lucrative bridal business. On one side of the spectrum are the nearly 500 dry cleaners in the United States that are members of the Association of Wedding Gown Specialists, an organization that promotes the proper cleaning and storing of delicate items like wedding gowns. Use the association's website at www.weddinggownspecialists.com to find a cleaner near you, but keep in mind that membership in this association is by fee-only. That is, dry cleaners' credentials aren't vetted before they're allowed to join, so *caveat emptor* (buyer beware).

On the other end of the spectrum are conservation cleaners that do not dry clean gowns but rather wet clean them by hand, which is how museums take care of tapestries and other costumes that they have in their collections. One of these companies is Imperial Gown Cleaning in Fairfax, Virginia (www.gown.com), and another is J. Scheer Wedding Gown Preservation in New York City (www.jscheer.com). Both work long distance with thousands of brides each year—they cover the shipping and insuring of your gown to and from their headquarters—and have the testimonials to back up their services.

> **caution** Of course, you should give your wedding dress a careful once over before you take it in for cleaning. I might even suggest taking a Polaroid or digital picture of the dress so you'll have something to compare it to after the dress has been cleaned. You want to be certain that your dress is returned to you from the cleaner in sound shape. You should be aware of all visible stains, rips, or other damage your gown might have received during your wedding celebration, discuss the stains with the cleaner, and ask that your cleaner repair damage (within the cleaner's capabilities, of course).

## Questions to Ask Your Gown Cleaner

There are also many reputable cleaners that aren't a part of an association that will know how to treat your wedding gown. Here's a little Q&A that will help you know you've found the right cleaner to handle your wedding gown:

- **Question**: Where do you clean wedding gowns?
- **Answer you want to hear**: On site. A cleaner is going to act more responsible and be held more accountable for the safe and careful handling of your wedding dress if she cleans it on the premises. Some cleaners will send gowns out to a consolidated cleaner that supposedly specializes in cleaning gowns, but this doesn't ensure that your gown will receive the individual attention it deserves. If you find out that a cleaner outsources wedding-gown cleaning, find another cleaner to take care of your wedding dress.

- **Question**: How do you clean wedding gowns?
- **Answer you want to hear**: One at a time and with caution. A smart gown specialist will always clean one dress at a time, and will be sure to inspect a gown first and take any precautions against ruining delicate fabrics or intricate beading. If he is unsure of how the fabric will withstand cleaning, he should offer to test it first—and let you know ahead of time that he will be doing this. In addition, the cleaner should tell you that it will be cleaned by hand—the best way to handle the most delicate of items. Finally, don't freak if your cleaner talks about wet cleaning (as opposed to dry cleaning) your gown. "Ninety-five out of 100 gowns should be wet cleaned," says Steven Saidman, president and third-generation owner of Imperial Gown Cleaning in Fairfax, Virginia. "Dry cleaning can't get out visible stains, like perspiration and champagne, but wet cleaning can."
- **Question**: What do you do to remove dirt that can evolve into a latent stain (these are stains that are invisible to the eye today but will look terrible 5 or 10 years from now)?
- **Answer you want to hear**: Find them first. Some cleaners will use a hand-held black light to uncover stains that are invisible to the eye but which will turn ugly down the road. Once the cleaner can identify the stains, he can treat the dress preventatively. You may not realize this but when you get sugar or salt on fabric, it looks clear and you may not even realize that there's a stain forming. The cleaner should explain how he treats the dress first against latent stains. "Keep in mind that stains can only come out the way they went into the fabric," adds Saidman. "That is, a wet stain like wine can only come out by making the fabric wet. A dry stain like makeup will come out with dry cleaning." So find out ahead of time how the cleaner will treat both "wet" and "dry" stains on your dress.
- **Question**: Will you stand behind your cleaning services after I've picked up my gown?
- **Answer you want to hear**: Yes, absolutely. I've heard too many stories of brides who've had their wedding gown dry cleaned and placed in a box for storage, only to open the box years later and discover that the box did not contain her actual wedding gown. But because the cleaner offered no warranty against mix-ups, there was nothing the bride could do to reclaim her original gown. Also, some cleaners tell you that once your gown is sealed after cleaning, you shouldn't open it up to inspect it—and if you do so, you'll void any warranty against its preservation. "Nonsense," says Saidman, who believes that such break-the-seal warranties are just subterfuges that cleaners use so brides can't inspect their gown to make sure that it hasn't been

damaged in any way (see the previous Caution for more information on this point). "You should have the right to look at your gown at any time after your wedding and feel confident that it was cleaned properly."

- **Question**: How do you store gowns after cleaning?

- **Answer you want to hear**: In a box made of acid-free paper. Not only should the cleaner tell you that he uses a box made of acid-free paper, but if his staff is going to stuff your gown with tissue paper to keep its shape or line the box with paper, you want to hear that those papers are going to be acid free as well. Why acid free? Like invisible stains that brown over time, the acid in paper will, over time, seep into your dress and slowly eat away at your fabric (like so many moths in a closet full of wool sweaters) or slowly burn the fabric so that, decades from now, it will look as if someone took a lighted cigarette to your beloved wedding gown.

In addition, make sure that your cleaner puts no plastic whatsoever near your dress. Like I mentioned earlier, plastic encourages mildew growth, and if you've gone through all of this trouble to have your dress properly cleaned, you'll negate all of this hard work and care if you store your dress in a plastic bag.

Finally, if your cleaner likes to store wedding gowns in a box with a window, ask about that window. You want to hear that it is made from an acid-free material, not plastic, which, as you know by now, is *verboten* when it comes to wedding gowns.

**caution** Find out ahead of time what kind of warranty your cleaner will offer against damage done to your dress. Some cleaners offer a lifetime guarantee with a full refund, should you find any damage, but the refund is usually only for the cleaning costs, not the cost of the gown. The kind of warranty you want to look for in your cleaner is one that allows you to take the dress back at any time in the relatively near future if you find stains or damage. Also, you want a cleaner that, if it can't fix your dress, will pay for the replacement of the garment, not just a refund of cleaning services. Though you're unlikely to wear the gown again, you might someday have handed it down to a loved one for her wedding. And, in any event, if you spent $4,000 on a gown that has been ruined, you'll feel better having that $4,000 compensation in your pocket.

**caution** Cats and their claws seem to be attracted to wedding gowns stored in boxes underneath a bed. If you have a feline living with you and your wedding gown is stored under your bed, you may want to ban the cat from the bedroom. Otherwise, find another, non-cat-accessible place to store the dress.

Been putting off getting your gown cleaned? Not sure which cleaner you want to use? Use your lunch hour to search the Web for cleaners in your area and look for those that specialize in wedding gown cleaning. Then, take the list of questions provided and either email or call a handful of cleaners to see how they answer them. When you find a cleaner that gives you all the right answers, find out her hours and then take the gown in for cleaning as soon as you can.

# FINDING SAFE STORAGE FOR YOUR GOWN

If you thought your wedding dress was huge when you took it home from the bridal gown shop on the day before your wedding, just wait until it comes back from the cleaner in its acid-free box: as one bride described it, it's a honking big package. So where are you going to put your dress for safekeeping? Well, first things first: you want to store the dress laid down flat and in a place that's temperature- and humidity-controlled. So the attic is out as are the rafters of your garage. Your finished basement might be a good place, except you have to take caution that you haven't placed the dress near any pipes that could eventually burst and ruin your dress. Believe it or not, one of the best places to store a wedding gown is underneath a bed. Think about it this way—your bedroom is kept at the proper temperature and humidity for people to live comfortably in it, so it's an ideal place for your gown, too. The only caveat would be if you don't have air conditioning in your bedroom or if you have a platform or waterbed with no storage space underneath. If your bedroom falls into any of these categories, then see if friends or family members might be able to help you out with the storage of your gown. Whatever you do, don't store the gown standing straight up in a closet. Like cereal that settles to the bottom of the box, your dress will settle to the bottom of the box and, over time, will become misshapen.

# Creating Keepsakes

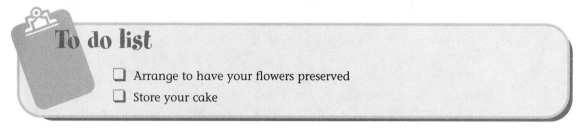

## To do list

- ☐ Arrange to have your flowers preserved
- ☐ Store your cake

I hope that many of the mementos from your wedding will bring you happy memories for years to come. Now that you've cleaned and stored your wedding gown, you can focus on creating other keepsakes from your wedding, namely with your bouquet and your wedding cake.

## Preserving Your Flowers

I'll bet that your wedding bouquet looked gorgeous on your special day, and I'm sure you'd like to keep those flowers alive forever so you can enjoy them day after day. Unless you live in a time warp, though, that's not going to happen and your flowers will eventually fade and die. But they don't have to shrivel up and turn brown.

There are a couple of ways that you can turn your bouquet or any other flowers from your wedding and reception into a lifelong keepsake. These include:

- **Freeze-drying your flowers**—This is a process that's sort of like cryogenics for flowers—it preserves something by removing the water and freezing it. It isn't ice-frozen but rather, by taking out the moisture from the flowers and the plants, it prevents them from getting old.

  You can turn to a specialist to preserve your flowers like this, such as a florist that offers freeze-dried flowers. The International Freeze-Dry Floral Association (www.ifdfa.com) is a good place to start, not only for finding a freeze-dry florist near you but also to answer basic questions on freeze drying flowers.

- **Drying your bouquet**—You can turn to your local craft store for instructions on how to make a cluster of live flowers into a pretty collection of dried flowers after your wedding. You'll probably have to invest in something called silica gel, which preserves the flowers, and it may take a week or more for the drying to be complete.

> "I took all of the wedding cards I received and decoupaged them onto three hat boxes of varying sizes. I then used those hat boxes as a place to put all of my wedding keepsakes."
>
> Liz, Michigan

## DIY Keepsakes

If you'd like to learn more about do-it-yourself keepsakes, why not sign up for a class in this very topic at a local craft store? Many of the national chains offer craft classes every night of the week, and during wedding season you may find appropriate class offerings to help you in your quest to complete DIY wedding keepsakes or even skills to learn that will help with your overall wedding plans.

You can learn more about the different classes that certain retailers offer by visiting their websites. These three national stores are a good place to start and, best of all, if you're too busy to attend a class at a store, you can learn craft techniques from step-by-step instructions listed on their respective websites.

- A.C. Moore (www.acmoore.com). This store, with 70 locations nationwide, really is art and crafts and more. It offers craft classes in a variety of topics for all aspects of your wedding, including the fine art of decoupage.

- Joann Fabrics and Crafts (www.joann.com). You may think of this retailer as just a place to go for sewing supplies, but the more than 900 locations nationwide offer a variety of craft classes. Recent class offerings that are perfect for the bride include the art of calligraphy (in case you want to address your wedding envelopes yourself) and how to make a wedding scrapbook.

- Michaels—The Arts and Crafts Store (www.michaels.com). This haven for hobbyists and do-it-yourselfers devotes an entire section of its website to wedding-related crafts, such as handmade favor boxes or place-card holders. You can also get information on the various classes it offers in the more than 800 stores it has in 48 states and Canada.

**tip** If you've got your heart set on having your wedding cake on your first anniversary but aren't convinced that the cake you've saved will last for a year in the freezer, consider using a stand-in cake instead. Take pictures from your wedding of your cake and bring it to a local baker. Ask him or her to make a mini version of that cake, and then you can enjoy the fresh (albeit impostor) version of your cake on your first anniversary instead.

# KEEPING YOUR WEDDING CAKE FOR YOUR FIRST ANNIVERSARY

One of the most endearing traditions for a bride and groom is to enjoy a slice of their wedding cake on their first anniversary. Problem is, any food experts you talk to will tell you that most foods only stay good in the freezer for three to six months. But if you pack it right, you should be able to have your cake—and enjoy it too—on your first anniversary.

Start by placing a slice of your wedding cake in an air-tight plastic container as soon as possible after the reception. (The longer the cake stays out, the staler it will be when you put it away in the freezer.)

Next, push down the container's cover slowly yet firmly to remove all the extraneous air.

Finally, put the container of cake in the far back of your freezer, where the temperature will stay the coldest.

Hopefully, by the time your first anniversary rolls around, your cake will still taste pretty good.

## Summary

This last chapter of the book discussed all of the keepsakes that you may have decided to keep from your wedding but weren't sure how to handle. These include the special care, cleaning, and storing of your wedding gown, which, if done properly, will allow you to hand down your gown for generations to come.

We also talked about other kinds of keepsakes that would be wonderful to keep around after your wedding, such as the flowers from your bouquet or a piece of your wedding cake, which you can enjoy on your first anniversary.

If you turn a few pages more you'll find an appendix that lists contact information for all the companies and websites worth surfing that I've mentioned in the book.

# Part IV

## Appendices

# References and Resources

This appendix will provide contact information for all of the companies, services, and publications mentioned in the book that will help you plan your wedding in no time.

## Stores

You're going to be doing a lot of shopping while planning your wedding, and there are a number of both brick-and-mortar and online stores where you can find many of the items you'll need for your wedding. Of course, this list is hardly exhaustive—if you know a store near you that will work well for your needs, by all means do your wedding-planning shopping there.

**A.C. Moore**, craft-store chain, local numbers only, www.acmoore.com

**David's Bridal**, bridal and attendant attire in a range of sizes, www.davidsbridal.com, 1-888-480-BRIDE

**Exposures** at www.exposuresonline.com, where you can order unique photo albums, keepsakes, and even custom greeting cards that feature images from your wedding

**Joann Fabrics and Crafts**, 1-888-739-4120, www.joann.com

**Michaels—The Arts and Crafts Store**, 1-800-642-4235, www.michaels.com

**Paper Direct**, online catalog of paper products for do-it-yourself invitations, place cards, and more, 1-800-A-PAPERS, www.paperdirect.com

**Staples**, stocks paper goods and other tools that you can use to make your own invitations, programs, and more for your wedding, www.staples.com

# Government Organizations and Trade Associations

There is a handful of government and trade groups that can provide advice or information that will help you make smart decisions about your wedding. See below for more information on each.

**American Society of Travel Agents (ASTA)**, www.travelsense.org

**Association of Bridal Consultants**, www.bridalassn.com

**Association of Wedding Gown Specialists**, www.weddinggownspecialists.com

**Caribbean Tourism Organization**, www.doitcaribbean.com

**The Center for Disease Control National Center for Infectious Diseases Travelers Health** website, http://www.cdc.gov/travel/. It offers tips on staying healthy while traveling.

**International Special Events Society**, www.ises.com

**Meeting Planners International**, www.mpiweb.org

**The National Association of Mobile Entertainers**, www.djkj.com

**Social Security Administration (SSA)**, www.ssa.gov

**U.S. Department of State** provides the basics on getting passports and visas for travel, http://www.state.gov/travel

**U.S. Department of State's** travel website, http://travel.state.gov/travel/ warnings.html, lists travel warnings worldwide

**U.S. Postal Service Online Store**, www.usps.gov

# Businesses and Professionals for Hire

You may be interested in hiring some of the businesses or professionals that specialize in weddings for your big day. To make that easier I've included contact information for those folks.

**Lorraine Altamura**, makeup artist, 914-969-6007

**Ann Hamilton Wedding Photography**, www.annhamilton.com, 415-346-5595

**Joyce Scardina Becker**, Wedding Planner, Events of Distinction, www.eventsofdistinction.com, 415-751-0211 or 1-866-99-EVENT

**Chicago City Centre Hotel**, full-service hotel and event location in downtown Chicago, www.chicc.com, 312-787-6100

**Dan Harris Wedding Photography**, www.danharrisphotoart.com, 904-398-7668

**Imperial Gown Cleaning** in Fairfax, Virginia, wedding gown cleaning and restoration, www.gown.com, 1-800-WED-GOWN

**McCory James Wedding Photography**, www.mccory.com, 720-205-4830

**Kodak's Ofoto.com**, online resources for photos and photo-related keepsakes, www.ofoto.com

**Nationwide Insurance** provides insurance policies to protect valuables, including engagement rings, 1-800-882-2822, www.nationwide.com

**Novell Design Studio Wedding Rings**, custom wedding jewelry available nationwide, 888-916-6835, www.novelldesignstudio.com

**Renaissance Jamaica Grande Resort**, property that offers destination weddings, www.renaissancejamaica.com, 1-800-421-8188

**A Papier**, www.apapier.com, 323-465-0084, a Los Angeles-based company that creates custom-tailored invitations, announcements, and stationery.

**J. Scheer Wedding Gown Preservation** in New York state, www.jscheer.com, 1-800-448-7291

**Tanya Tucka Wedding Photography**, www.tanyatuckaphotography.com, 733-271-7118

**Travel Duet**, honeymoon-planning services, www.travelduet.com, 1-800-201-6525

# Useful Websites

Use your computer to check out some of these websites that can provide good background information for your various wedding plans.

**www.airkisses.com**, online beauty and fashion information

**Bank Rate**, www.bankrate.com, financial information on paying for a wedding

**Benevolink**, www.benevolink.com

**California Cut Flower Commission** (CCFC), www.ccfc.org

**Fair Credit Billing Act**, www.ftc.gov

**I Do Foundation**, www.idofoundation.org

**Lending Tree**, www.lendingtree.com

**MapQuest**, www.mapquest.com

**Married for Good**, www.marriedforgood.com

**Parishes Online**, www.parishesonline.com. This site provides a compilation of Roman Catholic Churches across the United States.

**Switchboard Online Phone Book**, www.switchboard.com

**Virtuoso**, www.virtuoso.com, specialists in the art of travel

**Wed Safe Wedding Insurance**, www.wedsafe.com

**Wedding Ink by Leah Ingram,** www.weddingink.com

**Wells Fargo Consumer Credit Group**, www.wellsfargo.com

**Worship Here**, www.worshiphere.org. This website lets you search for houses of worship, in most denominations, via ZIP code.

## Credit Report Resources

Before applying for a loan to help pay for your wedding, you should get a good sense of how banks see you as far as being a credit asset or liability. The following three organizations supply credit reports to consumers like you:

- Experian.com
- Equifax.com
- Transunion.com

## Interfaith Wedding Resources

If you're planning a wedding that will include more than one religion, you may want to turn to one of these online venues for help and ideas for your special day:

- www.dovetailinstitute.org
- www.interfaithfamily.com
- www.multifaithweddings.com
- www.rcrconline.org
- www.weddinggoddess.com

# Books

*The Balanced Bride: Preparing Your Mind, Body and Spirit for Your Wedding and Beyond*, Leah Ingram, Contemporary Books, 2002

*The Complete Guide for the Anxious Bride: How to Avoid Everything That Could Go Wrong On Your Big Day*, Leah Ingram, New Pages Books, 2004

# Planning Charts and Aids

T his appendix gathers some of the planning charts that appeared throughout the book into one easy-to-access group. These aids can help you make the process of planning your wedding fast, efficient, and (relatively) trouble free. Each form is listed at the end of the appendix for you to be able to print them off.

## Guest List Database

One of the documents that you will refer to time and time again during your plans is your guest list database, the basics of which I explained in Chapter 1, "First Things First." You can create this database on paper or on your computer, and include any columns of information that work best for you (see Chart B.1 on page 234).

## Registry Planning Chart

In Chapter 1, I suggested you use a chart to help organize your thoughts for all the gifts you may want to register for by looking at what you already own, what you'd like to own in the future, and what you definitely don't need. Here is that chart for you to use again (see Chart B.2 on page 236).

B

## Gift Registry Haves, Wants, and Don't Needs

| What We Have | What We Want | What We Don't Need |
|---|---|---|
| | | |
| | | |
| | | |

# Gown-Shopping Organizer

In Chapter 4, "Planning for Attendants and Family Participants," I provided a chart that you can use to track your dress shopping expeditions with your attendants. You can also use this chart to track the progress of the wedding gown you order. Here it is again for your reference (see Chart B.3 on page 237):

| Attire | Style Number/ Designer | Store Info | Price | Payment Details | Order Date | Pickup Date | Notes |
|---|---|---|---|---|---|---|---|
| Dress | | | | | | | |
| Accessories | | | | | | | |
| Shoes | | | | | | | |
| Notes | | | | | | | |

# Sample Vendor Contract

In Chapter 3, "Planning for 'I Do' Expediently," I offered the outline of a sample contract that you should use when hiring a vendor. You can tweak this contract to fit the needs of the specific vendor, but always get something in writing. Here are the basics to include in any contract you draw up with a wedding-related vendor:

- Name, address, phone number, fax number, and email of person/place providing services
- Date of agreed-upon services
- Location of agreed-upon services (if different from address)
- Brief description of agreed-upon services (for example, if you were booking a ceremony site, you might write down the setup for the ceremony, the number of chairs they are to provide, what decorations will be on hand, and so on)
- Vendor-specific details that might not be covered above, such as if you've requested a vegetarian menu up front or have agreed upon a buffet dinner with 10 different stations
- Time frame, if any, for agreed-upon service, such as when the vendor should show up, how many breaks he or she should take (and for how long each time), and when he or she is done
- Fee to be paid and, if necessary, schedule of payment (for example, one third of the fee up front, one third of the fee one week before the wedding, and one third of the fee on the day of the wedding)
- Attire, if applicable (basically, what kind of clothing you want the officiant or other service provider to wear)
- Cancellation agreement (figure out what kind of refund or other compensation you would want if the officiant, vendor, or venue cancels on you)
- Don't forget to date and sign the contract with both you and your fiancé's signatures along with the signature of the person you are hiring

# Planning Chart

Some couples take more than a year to plan a wedding. Others can pull together their nuptials in less than a month. Regardless of how much time you have to plan your celebration, you need to tackle certain items on your wedding to-do list in a specific order. The following chart lists the tasks you'll need to accomplish, in the order you'll want to tackle them. The chart also provides a time budget in a perfect world (time is on your side) and in a crunch (you need to plan your wedding fast):

| Tasks to do, in relative order | Time budget, in a perfect world | Time budget, in a crunch |
| --- | --- | --- |
| 1. Formulate your guest list | One year before your wedding | Six weeks ahead of time |
| 2. Register for gifts | One year before your wedding | Two weeks before your first pre-wedding celebration |
| 3. Set your budget | One year before your wedding | Day before you set your wedding date |
| 4. Look at ceremony sites/interview officiants | One year before your wedding | Four to six months ahead of time |
| 5. Book ceremony officiant and set wedding date | Eight to 12 months before your wedding | Four months ahead of time |
| 6. Look at/book reception side | Eight to 12 months before your wedding | Four months ahead of time |
| 7. Send "Save the Date" cards | As soon as you book your wedding date, if travel is involved, or you've planned your wedding on a holiday weekend | Don't bother |
| 8. Choose attendants | As soon as you book your wedding day or at least nine months in advance | The month before |
| 9. Choose wedding colors | As soon as you book your wedding date and base it on time of year and/or location of ceremony and reception | Not a priority |
| 10. Start shopping for wedding gown/order it | Nine to 12 months in advance so you can budget time for multiple dress fittings | Buy it off the rack the week before |
| 11. Book entertainment for ceremony and reception | Six to nine months in advance | If music doesn't matter, two to three months ahead of time |
| 12. Book photographer and videographer | Six to nine months in advance | If photography isn't part of your big picture, give yourself two or three months |

| Tasks to do, in relative order | Time budget, in a perfect world | Time budget, in a crunch |
|---|---|---|
| 13. Book florist for ceremony flowers, bouquet, and centerpieces for reception | Six to nine months or more, especially if you want flowers that match your wedding colors | One month ahead of time if you don't mind taking whatever blooms are available or making centerpieces yourself |
| 14. Meet with travel agent to talk about and book honeymoon | Six months in advance | Book it last minute on Priceline.com |
| 15. Book hotel rooms for out-of-town guests | Six months in advance | Let them do it themselves using Priceline.com or any online travel service |
| 16. Order invitations | Six months in advance | Make them yourself about eight weeks ahead of time |
| 17. Check out and book hair and makeup pros | Three months ahead of time | One month beforehand or do it yourself |
| 18. Send invitations | Two months in advance | Two months in advance; in a real pinch, just call everyone |
| 19. Order programs, place cards, and other printed materials | As soon as RSVPs are in or about three weeks beforehand | Do it on the desktop the week before |
| 20. Do seating arrangements | As soon as RSVPs are in or about three weeks beforehand | Do it as soon as you know who is coming and who is staying home |
| 21. Buy favors | About three weeks ahead of time | Make a donation to charity instead so you can save yourself shopping time |
| 22. Confirm with all vendors | Two weeks ahead of time, then one week, and then the week of the wedding | Confirm at least once and at least one week ahead, if you have that much time to spare |

## Chart B.1 Guest List Database

| Contact Information: Name, Address, Phone #, Email | Date Engagement Announcement Sent | Engagement Gift Received/ Date Thank-you Note Sent | Shower Gift Received/ Date Thank-you Note Sent |
|---|---|---|---|
| | | | |
| | | | |
| | | | |
| | | | |
| | | | |
| | | | |
| | | | |
| | | | |
| | | | |
| | | | |
| | | | |
| | | | |
| | | | |

| | Date Wedding Invitation Sent | Number of People Invited to Wedding | Date RSVP Received and Yes or No | Number RSVP Yes, if Any | Date Called to Follow Up if No RSVP Received | Gift Received/ Date Thank-you Note Sent |
|---|---|---|---|---|---|---|
| | | | | | | |
| | | | | | | |
| | | | | | | |
| | | | | | | |
| | | | | | | |
| | | | | | | |
| | | | | | | |
| | | | | | | |
| | | | | | | |
| | | | | | | |
| | | | | | | |
| | | | | | | |
| | | | | | | |
| | | | | | | |
| | | | | | | |

# Chart B.2 Gift Registry Haves, Wants, and Don't Needs

| What We Have | What We Want | What We Don't Need |
|---|---|---|
| | | |

# B.3 Gown-Shopping Organizer

| Attire | Style Number/ Designer | Store Info | Price | Payment Details | Order Date | Pickup Date | Notes |
|---|---|---|---|---|---|---|---|
| Maid of Honor Dress | | | | | | | |
| Accessories | | | | | | | |
| Shoes | | | | | | | |
| Notes | | | | | | | |
| Bridesmaids Dresses | | | | | | | |
| Accessories | | | | | | | |
| Shoes | | | | | | | |
| Notes | | | | | | | |
| Flower Girl Dress | | | | | | | |
| Accessories | | | | | | | |
| Shoes | | | | | | | |
| Notes | | | | | | | |

# Index

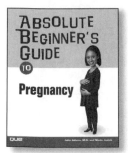
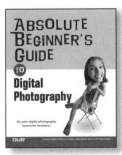

# Do Even More
## ...In No Time

**G**et ready to cross off those items on your to-do list! In No Time helps you tackle the projects that you don't think you have time to finish. With shopping lists and step-by-step instructions, these books get you working toward accomplishing your goals.

## Check out these other *In No Time* books, coming soon!

**Start Your Own Home Business In No Time**
ISBN: **0-7897-3224-6**
**$16.95**
September 2004

**Plan a Fabulous Party In No Time**
ISBN: **0-7897-3221-1**
**$16.95**
November 2004

**Speak Basic Spanish In No Time**
ISBN: **0-7897-3223-8**
**$16.95**
September 2004

**Organize Your Garage In No Time**
ISBN: **0-7897-3219-X**
**$16.95**
February 2005

**Quick Family Meals In No Time**
ISBN: **0-7897-3299-8**
**$16.95**
October 2004

**Organize Your Family's Schedule In No Time**
ISBN: **0-7897-3220-3**
**$16.95**
October 2004